"The true story of how two pilots' passion for flying and lifelong friendship grew stronger through their shared exploits. A remarkable book dedicated to the finest qualities of the human spirit: courage, dedication to family and country, and the thrill of exploring the frontiers of flight."

—Doug Champlin, Curator Emeritus, Champlin Fighter Collection

"The fascinating experiences of two citizen-soldiers both as military pilots and successful entrepreneurs. To anyone thrilled by the magic of flight, this book will touch your heart."

—Curtis G. Williams, Brigadier General, USAF (Ret.), past Chairman of the American Hotel & Lodging Association.

Jack —
I reiss talized with you yesterday, It was so
very good for me!" That's really
anything more to say!
We hope you enjoy reading this as
much as we did in trying to remember
everything! Peter H. Wurts
12/20/06

WINGMEN

Two Friends, Four Wars,

Flying and Fighting

Through the 20th Century

Peter J. Wurts & William R. Yoakley

A great friendship
has no bounds —

Bill Yoakley

ISBN 1-4196-4932-9

Library of Congress Control Number: 2006908496
Published in 2006 by BookSurge, LLC
North Charleston, South Carolina

Visit the authors' web site at www.wingmentwofriends.com
Visit the publisher's website at www.booksurgepublishing.com
Developmental writing by: Jay Wurts, www.jaywurts.com
Book and jacket designed by: Andrew Fox, www.foxarts.com
Imaging by: www.peggitys.com

CONTENTS

EDITOR'S NOTE

Friendship is a remarkable thing. It's one of the few human institutions celebrated in myth (Castor and Pollux, Ajax and Achilles), entertainment (Martin and Lewis, Hope and Crosby), history (Lewis and Clark, Churchill and Roosevelt), business (Sears and Roebuck, Ben and Jerry), and recreation (Smith & Wesson, Martini & Rossi) that the rest of us can experience each day. Cicero thought friendship was the perfect relationship, "that union of all things human and divine"—and he was probably right. Husbands and wives may populate the earth, but not all spouses are friends. And friendlessness is worse than loneliness: it's a tunnel with no light at the end.

Best friends have a category all their own. Acquaintances are friends when they're around, but *best* friends are with us all the time—no matter how far we're separated, no matter how long it's been since our last reunion. A friendship needs cultivation; but *best* friends cultivate each other. They are two flowers on a single branch, two roots of the same mighty tree.

For about nine months—the gestation period of a baby or the length of an air combat tour in Korea—I was privileged to peek inside a friendship that has lasted over sixty years and shows no sign of fading. It's a fellowship of flying, but it's also something more. Pete Wurts and Bill Yoakley—one a father who became a great friend, the other a friend who became like a second father—took the joys and challenges of flying and made them an integral part of their lives. Through four wars—World War II, Korea, the Cold War, and the Vietnam era—they manned our country's ramparts as citizen-soldiers in aircraft of every type: some jet-powered, top secret, and experimental; others dusted-off, propeller-driven relics of a bygone age. Out of the cockpit, their collaboration went beyond the usual bonds of foxhole buddies. While Bill helped North American Aviation (later, Rockwell International) test the planes that made America great, Pete (continuing until retirement as an Air Guard pilot) helped create the world's largest lodging chain: *Best Western International*. After retiring from their careers—which included several joint business ventures—both continued to serve their community: Bill as Director of the Champlin Air Museum at Falcon Field; Pete as a volunteer Deputy Sheriff for Yavapai County. Time may have dampened their ability to do the things they love, but it hasn't quenched their spirit. Theirs is the story of how the seeds of friendship sown in war came to fruition in peace: for good wingmen put comradeship and service first, helping the community and each other—especially when the going gets tough.

Although a book like this is a labor of love, the authors tackled it with the same gusto and persistence they showed in their flying adventures. First, they organized their thoughts by creating a time-line of their long association, then recorded their joint and separate recollections—adding details and stories as faded photos, dog-eared letters, newspaper clippings, military documents, and my occasionally nagging questions jogged old memories. We met for several days in March 2006, in Scottsdale and Mesa, Arizona, shortly before Bill returned to Florida, to fit those memories together like a jigsaw puzzle from which an amazing picture emerged: the portrait of two lives lived literally above "the surly bonds of earth."

We continued to communicate by letter, telephone, and e-mail as the manuscript containing their stories came together: the authors patiently correcting, amplifying, and modulating my sometimes over-zealous or off-the-beam re-telling of their remarkable adventures. A person rarely gets to see the past through a parent's eyes, or the perspective of a lifelong friend, but I was lucky enough to do both. I found the experience not just enlightening, but fun. Whatever value or pleasure you find in these pages you owe not to the scribe but to the quality of two lives well-lived. I thank the authors for their willingness to share the thoughts and feelings that flowed from their experience, and for allowing friends, relatives, aviation fans, historians, and generations yet unborn to become, for at least awhile, their honorary wingmen.

Jay Wurts
Pacific Grove, California
2006

AUTHORS' PREFACE

We've done a lot in our lives, separately and together, but until now authoring a book wasn't one of them. Hang around long enough and you'll see everything.

The idea began in 2005 when we read a book written by several ex-Air Guard pilots about their adventures flying F-86s stateside in the 1950s. The same thought occurred to us both: Heck, our flying stories are as good as these—in fact, the exciting ones are more exciting and the funny ones are funnier—although that may just be one set of fighter pilots getting competitive with another, something you'll see a lot of in these pages. Pete sent the book to his son, Jay—a former pilot who works in publishing—and he agreed. "Why don't you guys write your own story?" he asked. "Get it down on tape and I'll put it on paper and we'll see where it goes from there."

Where it went is here: the book you hold in your hands. Putting it together was an adventure unto itself, and we learned a lot about ourselves and each other along the way. Almost at once we saw that, unlike many books rooted in aviation, the real story was as much about our lifelong friendship as about the planes we flew and the people we knew, though the love of flying is what drew us together and has kept us close ever since. When life takes people in different directions, as it often does, most friendships get strained or pulled apart. Ours endured, in spirit if not always in the same geographic location. Of course, it was a journey we didn't make alone...

PJW: Preparing a book like this makes you think about things that usually slip by unnoticed. Time makes once-familiar faces hazy and can blur the names that go with them; though those original faces stay vivid in the mind and those names still evoke warm memories. I can't list everyone who meant something to me—helped me when I needed it or taught me how life and friendships worked—but I can list a few and hope that those not mentioned realize their omission was caused by the veil of time and the limits of the printed page, and not a lack of appreciation and affection.

This book begins about the time of World War II, so that's where I find the longest list of unsung heroes. To a long succession of fellow Instructor Pilots and gifted (and some not-so-gifted, but hard-working) student flyers, I give my thanks for showing me how aircraft and human beings work. I'm especially grateful to the crew of the B-24 Liberator we *almost* got into combat. For a brief time we were truly brothers.

After the war, I experienced another kind of brotherhood with various partners in the Phoenix Police Department—virtually all of whom went on to notable careers, retiring as lieutenants, captains, assistant police chiefs, and even chief of police in such exotic towns as Tempe, Yuma, and Nogales, which are all better places because of them. My special thanks go to one of my first partners, Fred Green, and one of my last, Clarence Meyers (who, as you'll see, helped me and Bill get started in commercial aviation in Florida); and to the deputies of the Yavapai County Sheriff's Department for showing an old cop some new tricks.

After Korea, I made many friends in the Arizona Air Guard—many pilots, of course, but also fine men in different crew stations of the C-97, people I would never have met if we'd stayed in fighters, such as flight engineers Terry Kidd and Tim Wheeler, who knew that big machine better than Mr. Boeing. First and foremost, though, I should salute the commanding officers whose patience I tested and ulcers I inflamed from the day I joined the 197th: Roy Jacobson, Don Morris, Tom Barnard, and Cliff Gipson. Thanks for being great guys as well as great C.O.s, and accommodating enough of us "loose cannons" over the years to form a squadron of our own. Among these excellent (if not always humble and obedient) fighter pilots I include Ted Crane, Bill Kemp, and Bob Kanaga, whose friendship and fellowship I've always treasured, even when it didn't get us into trouble. My gratitude, too, goes to our intelligence officer, Curt Williams, a "ground pounder" who became a general like so many of my other friends (what's wrong with this picture?), despite the fact that Curt bested me in every department, from his Chairmanship of the prestigious American Hotel Association to that fine Porsche he drove in Germany while the rest of us bought Volkswagens. Curt, I forgive you your enormous talent and the wonderful things you did with it.

Some of the best friendships, of course, come from people you meet in unexpected ways. Around 1960, a group of horsemen in the Valley formed the Scottsdale Polo Club, where I met and became long-time friends with such fine players and gentlemen as Bill Dent and Jim Cowan (both ex-military flyers) and Bob Dwyer, former polo coach at Judson School; not to mention Bob Cowie, another ex-AAF pilot, who carried the excitement of his combat bailout from a P-38 into every hair-raising chukkar, ski trip, and scuba dive we shared over the past forty years. His biggest disappointment in life has been his failure to kill me in these adventures, though Lord knows he tried often enough. Thanks, Bob, for the memories—and your enthusiastic zest for life.

From my long association with Best Western, I recall with special fondness my perennial partner and "hit man," Daniel ("Danko") Gurovich—one tough businessman who, although sometimes exasperating, always came through in a pinch; as well as Dr. Chuck Collopy, who introduced us: a fine physician, friend, and long-time investor. I also take special satisfaction in having known Peggy Bainbridge, now Peggy Wurts, who married my son Jay and helped him and his family in countless ways; Ken Hickel, who became a most valued and trusted ally in turning Best Western around and making it the international icon it is today; and Marguerite Harris (nee Baldwin), who designed the interiors of my first motels and went on to become a dear friend with whom Mary Lou and I have toured the world. She made that world a more beautiful place just by being in it.

Finally, I save my biggest hug for my wife, frequent copilot, and partner in business, adventure, and crime: Mary Lou, without whose encouragement and care my life would've been far less remarkable, enjoyable, and productive. Thanks, Mary Lou, for all the magic.

✪ ✪ ✪

WRY: Even a single life is populated by a cast of thousands. I can't recall every player on the broad stage of my career, but more than a few had starring roles and deserve better acknowledgment than I can give them here. Many more people provided friendship and support when I needed them—often under less than ideal circumstances—so if I've failed to mention a familiar name, it's not from lack of gratitude. Chalk it up to a life that's been filled with more than its fair share of wonderful people.

I have to say that whatever positive traits I acquired on the road to adulthood, I owe mostly to my sister and my Dad. "Sis" Hilda was my buddy and my judge; and although I teased the heck out of her, we never really quarreled. She made me feel important and worthwhile even when I veered from the straight and narrow and never gave up on me. She was wise beyond her years and her counsel meant a lot. My Dad, too, was more than a caring father: he was a great companion and mentor. A super guy, I loved him deeply not just for who he was, but what he taught me: hunting, fishing, camping, shooting—how to be generous, how to be responsible, how to find the silver lining around any cloud; how to be a man both respectful and worthy of respect.

Another "father figure" I didn't meet until much later in life was Charles Lindbergh. Though I knew him only briefly, his effect on me was enormous and began at an early age. My Dad and Stepmom took me out to the airport, introduced me to some local pilots, and the excitement of Lucky Lindy's 1927 accomplishment filled the hangars and our living room with an enthusiasm you could cut with a propeller. His positive attitude and quiet determination buoys me up to this day.

I thank my Dad, too, for encouraging me to join the Air Corps after Pearl Harbor—though he would've had a fight on his hands if he'd tried to hold me back. It's always nice to know the "old man" is behind you on a major life decision. It was in cadets when I met Pete and where the story you are about to read began. It seems obvious to thank a father and a mother for giving you life, but I sure thank mine for the special life I had.

After WWII, I met Warren Spratt, a flight instructor at a sea plane school called Skytel in Jacksonville. Warren's friendship and ambition led to our purchase of the school and my reunion with Pete, and our subsequent membership in the

Florida Air Guard—another life-changing decision I might not have made on my own. I treasure my time performing with the *Florida Rockets,* the Guard's all-jet precision flying team, and especially the chance to get to know and fly with fine pilots like Jack Nunnally—not all of whom made it back from the war that was about to descend on us. I'm grateful every day for the honor of having known these fine fellows and for the chance to share their lives.

In a later chapter, you'll read about some of the great guys I knew in Korea, but I'd feel remiss if I didn't mention one of them now: Lt. William "Willie" Wall. Willie was my element leader on many missions and flew my wing the day I bailed out over Wonsan harbor. He pressed his fuel and his luck to stick with me until he knew that I had a good chute and the Navy boys were on their way to my rescue. Willie was shot down and killed before I got back, so I never got a chance to thank him—until now. *Thanks, Willie, for being there. Your guts and your friendship did more to keep that shattered old bird in the air than my shaky hands and all of Mr. Lockheed's half-busted rivets...*

After Korea, I spent most of my working life in the air wearing a North American Aviation flight suit. During the course of that long flight-test career, I rubbed shoulders with—and got to know—some pretty remarkable people whose lives, style, and attitude undoubtedly left their mark on me. Leading any parade— right up there with Lindbergh, in my view—is Bob Hoover, a real southern gentleman and one of history's great flyers. I'm proud to have called him *friend* for over half a century. For his leadership skills, I have to rank General Jimmy Doolittle high as a personal role model. I never got to serve under him, but I'm jealous of the guys who did. For sheer professionalism and brainpower that extends right down to their toes: NASA's Scott Crossfield, Joe Engle, and Neil Armstrong stand at the top of a very tall ladder—I feel privileged to have known and learned from them all. For lessons in how to have fun flying while keeping your eye on the prize, I recommend Roscoe Turner: a true "golden boy" from aviation's Golden Age, a heck of a guy and a real treat to know. I'm grateful, too, to writer Warren Thompson for working hard to preserve so many documents and photos from a rapidly vanishing era of America's aviation history; and Arv Shultz, publisher of *Arizona Airways,* who introduced me to that great group of veteran pilots, the *Quiet Birdmen,* who have done so much to keep the fellowship of flying alive and well.

Others whose paths at NAA crossed mine and in whose footsteps I both consciously and unconsciously walked, I affectionately recall: Bob Rushworth, whom I checked out in F-86Ds at Tyndall and who later became C.O. of Edwards Air Force Base; Corwin "Corky" Meyer, Chief Pilot then CEO of Grumman and now a near-neighbor of mine in Florida; Craig Isbel, a close friend of "Slim" Lindbergh and who almost became a centenarian; Rick Cotton, a test pilot for Ryan before switching his flight gear to a locker at NAA; Frank Smith, who was one of my '86D students at Perrin, AFB, and who later became a QA pilot for NAA and after that, Sabreliner's super-salesman in government marketing; Harry Hoch and George Smith, company test pilots par excellence; Charles "Chuck" Livergood, the man behind NAA's publications and a fine pilot who often helped out in the right seat of our "green" Sabreliners; Chuck Sell, a former Marine pilot and my colleague in customer relations, and his wife Joan, also an NAA alumna; Al White and Gage Mace, two of the company's great engineering test pilots; Henry "Hank" West, our B-70 military attaché and an old boating buddy; Evan Meyers, my Assistant Chief Test Pilot at Sabreliner and a fine flyer; Silky Morris, one of our engineering test pilots in LA and his wife, Shirley, whose faithful service as my secretary brightened every day at the office; Bert Bantle, NAA corporate pilot, whose devilish check rides kept us all on our toes; Val Yarborough, a most accomplished woman, who ran the Los Angeles Division's Quality Engineering department; and Dan McKinnon, whose Navy helicopter plucked me out of the soup near Catalina Island after my second bailout. Dan was a great guy and a fine pilot, and I have nothing against the Navy—but guys, we've got to stop meeting like this!

Life after NAA (or Rockwell International, as it became known) took me in many directions, but a few people shone like beacons in what might easily have become a long period adrift. Good friends Ralph Bufano and Dave Goss come to mind, as does my Mesa neighbor, Vietnam helicopter vet Jim Trupe, who helped me in countless ways. Of course, I can't forget Doug Champlin, who gave me an excuse to rekindle an old love affair with lots of fine flying machines at the Champlin Air Museum. If I transmitted at least part of that love to a few young Americans during those years at Falcon, it was well worth all the effort. My thanks, too, go to FAA veteran and former Alaskan, Mel Derry, a docent who helped save at least one rare bird from extinction; and Betty Jo Reed, a former WASP (and still one heck-of-a pilot) who recruited many WASPs for our corps of docents and helped create one of the few exhibits commemorating that group's great contributions to WWII.

Finally, what dad can "sign off" without a big hug and proud pat on the back to the next generation of Yoakleys: Bill Jr., Ann, Don, Trisa, and David. Gang, you made it all worthwhile. More than that, you did good.

1

THE MAKING OF TWO AIRMEN

Our fathers were born at a time when the battleship Maine was the last word in military technology. When it blew up in 1898 in Havana harbor under suspicious circumstances, sparking the Spanish-American War, it set the stage for much of our families' and our nation's history over the next hundred years—at least that part of it we'd see from the cockpits of various warplanes, or read about in newspapers, or hear about on the radio, or see on TV. Even the technology for getting news, good or bad, and staying in touch with friends and family changed enormously during that century, though most of it seems now to have gone by in a flash. As we recall this history, and the way it shaped our lives and friendship, terrorists are still blowing things up: attacking a culture and technology they envy and can scarcely understand. They say 1900 to 2001 was "America's Century." We guess they're right and we were there to see a lot of it.

PJW: My father, Burkhardt Wurts, was a cowboy from Connecticut. His father, my grandfather, was Dean of the Yale Law School, but a life behind a desk surrounded by musty books just didn't appeal to my father—or "Sir," as my two brothers, sister, and I always called him. Although there was a streak of adventurer in him a mile wide and he always thought for himself, a few bits of received wisdom stuck with him all of his life. One was that older folks—and especially your parents—deserved respect; if not for their accomplishments, then for the simple fact that they'd been around longer than you. Another star that guided him was the idea that life was what you made it. There was nothing wrong with asking for, or giving, help when it was needed; what mattered most was taking care of yourself and your loved ones.

If you botched an opportunity, you didn't cry about it, you just learned from it and moved on.

Now, having said that, I have to admit that my Dad was a bit of a buccaneer—or at least a gypsy—a characteristic that became something of a family trait. Born in Jacksonville, Florida—a place I would revisit after World War II—he ran away from home as a teenager, wanting more than anything to become a cowboy in the American west. The quickest way to get there, in those days, was by sea, so he signed on as a deck hand on a freighter until it reached Houston, where he jumped ship. I guess the west in the early 1900s wasn't all that he expected, so he sought new frontiers and a wider horizon by going on to Canada. You see, after 1917, something called the "progressive income tax" had kicked in and what originally passed Congress as a temporary way to fund the Spanish-American war—taking a little money from the top one or two percent of America's wealthiest people—had turned into a permanent way of taking more and more money from everyone else. It became a feature on the American economic landscape that my Dad didn't like it one bit. To him, it meant we were going the way of every other big empire in history, especially the Europeans, and he didn't want any part of it. He renounced his U.S. citizenship and made what he thought was a permanent move to the province of Alberta, Canada, where he'd start a fresh life as a homesteader.

Life was tough in the frozen north, particularly on the land he'd staked out, which was a long way from the city and its amenities. This harsh life was made a little sweeter when he met the daughter of a British schoolmaster, recently emigrated from Surrey, England, named Muriel Reddish. She was Clara Bow to his Tom Mix—an outgoing "it girl" with a ready wit and love for people that rivaled his own longing for wide plains, big mountains, and western sunsets. Where he was taciturn, self-reliant, and a little grumpy, she was quick to laugh, sociable and, I think, had a gentle way of easing him down from his occasional high horse. If it wasn't a match made in heaven, then it was one that worked well on earth. They got married, moved back to the U.S., and he regained his citizenship through the naturalization process—a practical if humbling experience—though Muriel, his wife who'd started it all, never did "convert" and remained a British subject to the day she died.

I came along on September 7, 1920. Maybe in honor of their Canadian courtship, they christened me Pierre: a name I hated and never responded to, so everyone called me Pete. I didn't have anything against the French—even in those days they made good punch lines for a lot of jokes—but I never thought of myself as "Pierre" and my first official act after turning 18 was to change my legal name to Peter. I guess my father had taught me to think for myself.

WRY: I was born on October 10, 1921, in Tampa, Florida, making me one year younger than Pete. I won't say that alone made me the handsomer devil of the two, but it probably explains why it takes him just a little longer to figure things out—like how to scissor away from a P-51 or F-80 that's glued to your tail, or why commanding officers sometimes had to say things twice, or shout, to get him to do things their way instead of his.

Fifteen days after I was born, a killer hurricane swamped Tampa—the worst storm to hit that fair city since 1848. The 10-1/2 foot storm surge sent half the population packing, but my family hung around and toughed things out, probably because moving a newborn was even riskier than braving the storm. At any rate, I came into this world amid a lot of hubbub and confusion: a portent, perhaps, of an exciting life to come.

I was given my father's name of William Reginald Yoakley, making me a "junior" for the rest of my life. Frankly, I couldn't think of a finer man to subordinate myself to, and he was *senior* in character to most of the men I would eventually meet. He and my mom were both from Tennessee and we'd trek there from time to time to keep family ties alive. A chemical engineer by trade, he was whiz with mechanical equipment—a trait yours truly seems to have inherited, at least in part. After relocating to Tampa, he joined with a Mr. Ballanger to develop a new paving material. Mr. McDonald of the William P. McDonald Construction Company (a big outfit with contracts all over North America) funded this research into a marvelous new surfacing material that had great potential for highways, city streets, and parking lots—all in high demand during the Roaring Twenties and 1930's, when the WPA rebuilt America. He gave his invention a catchy name, "McAsphalt," after the fellow who provided the funding. Only the last part of that name stuck to the sticky product; and since he who pays the piper keeps the patent, the Yoakley family got a nice bonus but no royalties. My Dad still had to get up and go to work every morning, as did my kid brother and I when our turn came.

I wish I could say that was the worst thing that happened to me as a kid, but one of the real low points of my life happened early. My mother, Anne Saylor, passed away when I was four. That's a bad time to lose what for most of us at that age is our most important parent and I took it pretty hard. My younger sister, Hilda, and I were cared for by our grandmother in Tampa while my Dad traveled the country to supervise his projects. He remarried a few years later to a "damned Yankee" from New Jersey. My step-mom, also named Hilda, was a fine woman but I didn't think so at the time. As a little kid, I was used to sleeping with my Dad when he came home between assignments—a real treat, like camping out with an older brother—and we always had a ball. I guess that's why I resented Hilda for "taking my place"—a childish gripe that turned into a grudge when she started asking me to call her "Mom" even though she wasn't my real mother. Actually, she was one of the kindest, most understanding people I ever knew—strict but fair, like any good parent—but you sure couldn't convince me of that at the time.

So I became, as they say, a "problem child" which persisted through my teenage years. I wasn't a juvenile delinquent or anything like that, but if there was a way to cause my stepmother grief and throw a monkey wrench into family plans, I'd find a way to do it. At last, when I turned 18 and we were living in Flushing Meadows, New York, I decided enough was enough and ran away from home.

I waited until everyone was asleep one night, then threw some belongings into a cardboard box and climbed out through our attic window. I tossed the box down first, which was a mistake because it woke my sister up. She stared at me through the window but I knew from her expression she wouldn't turn me in. We had always been close—especially after our mother died—and although I hadn't told her about my plan, she knew my situation and understood. I ran to the subway and took it to the Washington Bridge, where I got out and crossed on foot. About halfway across I stopped, put the box down, and stared at the glittering lights on each side. It was getting pretty dang cold and the world now looked pretty big. I knew I was "crossing my Rubicon" and never doubted for a minute that I was doing

RIGHT: Bill and "sis" Hilda in Tampa. They remained close all their lives.

LEFT: Bill's mother, Ann Saylor. She died when Bill was four, leaving a big hole in a young life.

RIGHT: Bill's brother, Dave (L) and their Dad, William Senior.

the right thing. I picked up the box and hurried off toward New Jersey and the rest of my life.

I hitch-hiked to Tennessee where we had lots of relatives. Nobody there was too surprised to see me. My Dad had probably tipped them off; but even if he hadn't, they all understood completely if one of their own just couldn't take it any more in the "Yankee nawth." I had a nice visit, worked at a couple of odd jobs, then saw an ad that would change my life. The George A. Fuller Company was hiring young men for a massive construction project in Newfoundland—at a good wage and with all expenses paid. For a kid who was born almost in the eye of a hurricane, it was an offer—and an adventure—I couldn't refuse.

*A*s school kids, the 1920s didn't "roar"much for us and the Great Depression went by like a speed bump because both our fathers were self-employed and pretty careful about their business. Pete's Dad built a chain of gas stations along the east coast under a Sinclair Oil franchise, and his family divided its time between New Jersey, where Pete was born, and West Palm Beach, Florida—a winter retreat for the well-to-do. Bill's father got a lot of construction contracts through "Old Mr. McDonald," who became something of a family friend, so the Yoakley kids, growing up, never wanted for much—at least those things that money could buy. Neither family was what you'd call upper crust, but we were upper middle class and that mutual experience, world view, and the self-confidence born of parental encouragement undoubtedly drew us together—particularly in the melting pot of the U.S. Army on the eve of World War II.

PJW: My Dad and Mom's "little Pierre" was joined eighteen months later by another son, my brother Burke (named after our Dad—although I never called my brother Sir!), and our sister, Muriel, named after our mother, three years after that. My brother Richard, called Dick, was six years younger than me and, like Bill's half-brother, Dave, I always thought of him as "that funny little kid" who got to climb trees and play in the yard while the rest of us had to behave and dress up for dinner in stiff collars and itchy jackets. Dick was smart as a whip, though, an intellect cultivated by spending a lot of time on his own. But I was the oldest, and my parents expected me to set an example—which I did, whenever I got trapped into

RIGHT: From L to R: Pete, Burke, Muriel, and Richard in Atherton, CA

LEFT: Pete's father, Burkhardt. His children called him by his first name: "Sir."

RIGHT: Pete's mother, Muriel. She was a fun-loving "It girl" to his father's stoic "Tom Mix."

doing it. But I was really more like my Mom than my Dad and usually put having fun ahead of keeping my nose to the grindstone. Burke and I were probably closest, as we were nearest in age and he was always getting into trouble then turning to me to get him out of it. Muriel was playful, too, but she had her serious side, like Dick and our Dad, and often found socializing a chore. Later in life, they both became somewhat reclusive, which was a shame since I admired Dick's intellect and always loved spending time with my sister.

One of my earliest memories was of watching waterbugs—those amazing little insects that can fly, walk on water, then dive below the surface. To me that was the greatest thing in the world: to see life from the air, go for a swim, then explore the murky depths. I really envied those little creatures and vowed—as only five or six year olds can do, with complete and utter sincerity—that I would one day do the same. Oddly enough, between flying and scuba diving—passions for most of my adult life—that's exactly what I did.

My interest in aviation started with all the hoopla over "Lucky Lindy"— Charles Lindbergh and his earth-shrinking solo flight across the Atlantic. Like every other kid in America, I wanted to be famous and heroic like Lindy, but somehow just the idea of flying, of soaring effortlessly in these beautiful, mysterious machines, was even more appealing than fame.

As it turned out, I would meet my hero during one of our annual visits to West Palm Beach—and under very unusual circumstances. We were staying in a Victorian-style hotel near the ocean when management warned the guests of an approaching hurricane. They didn't have weather satellites in those days, so big storms could sneak up on you fast. The hotel had a lot of vacancies and we had no place to go inland, so my brother Burke and I watched in fascination as the staff hurriedly nailed plywood boards over all the windows. As we kids shuttled from floor to floor, "supervising" the emergency preparations, the elevator operator winked and said, "Hey boys, do you want to meet the famous Charles Lindbergh?"

We said "Sure!" and he told us to stay in the elevator, since he'd been told by the front desk that Lucky Lindy would be coming down soon. Well, I don't know the manager's definition of "soon," but we rode that little elevator for what seemed like an hour until the famous man—so familiar from newspaper and magazine pictures—suddenly stepped through the cage door. We were awestruck, especially me, and couldn't think of a thing to say. Aside from staring, I vaguely remember the famous aviator patting me on the head like a kindly uncle—though it may have been the elevator man, amused at how quickly we two noisy boys shut up.

My biggest adventure as a teenager came in 1938 when I graduated from high school—a place called Montezuma Ranch in the Santa Cruz mountains south of San Francisco, a well-known boarding school in its day. We didn't do any flying, but did a lot of other things I liked: riding, roping, swimming, and shooting, along with our junior high and high school studies. At first, I resented going there, since our family had moved to California and had a big house in Atherton about thirty miles away. I guess my Dad still hadn't worked the cowboy bug out of his system and felt a few years in a ranch environment would build my character. If nothing else, living around livestock, day in and day out, and pitching in on chores teaches you confidence, cooperation, self-reliance, and a bit of humility—cornerstones of my Dad's philosophy which quickly became my own. As a reward, he told me shortly before I graduated that he and I would be going to Africa, visiting several major European cities along the way.

I thought that was a great graduation present—it was not uncommon for fathers who could afford it to send their college-age sons for a "summer abroad"—and what red-blooded 18-year old guy could resist an African safari? But I soon learned he had ulterior motives. His defection to Canada years earlier had done nothing to change U.S. tax policy, and F.D.R.'s New Deal had moved the country even further away from his idea of a rough-and-tumble, free-enterprise society. His new dream was to immigrate to South Africa, which was supposed to be like the American west, but this time he wanted to check things out before starting over. It proved to be a wise precaution, as well as a heck of a trip.

In September 1938, we began our epic journey. We crossed to Europe on a steamship, then (after touring England, France, Germany, and Switzerland by train) took a plane from Egypt down the length of Africa. In those days, there were no navigation aids, so airliners flew only in daylight at low altitude, putting their passengers up for the night at posh hotels until the trip was complete, which sometimes took over a week. We went on safari and bagged a few trophies (this was back when you shot bullets, not film, at big game) but I could see the fire in my Dad's eyes fade as the trip neared its end. He was no longer that adventurous teenaged runaway, but a sober man with lots of responsibilities—and, new frontier or not, South Africa wasn't Montana. Suddenly, the American way didn't seem quite so bad, and having just seen where Europe was headed in 1938, it was probably worth defending. When we got back to the U.S. and I started college in Arizona, I discovered that part of that responsibility would fall on me.

WRY: In 1940, I was on my way to Argentia, Newfoundland, to help the Fuller Company construct a massive new naval air station on Placentia Bay. The war in Europe had been blazing for a couple of years while America buried its head in the sand, hoping that somehow Hitler and Mussolini would just go away. Winston Churchill—half American—was the new Prime Minister of Britain and President Franklin Roosevelt had been elected to an unprecedented third term. Although our government made a big deal of America's supposed neutrality, programs like Lend-Lease (in which the U.S. supplied warships and other equipment to England at low or no cost) and big, Anglo-American defense projects, like the naval installation at Placentia Bay, went ahead full-steam. We weren't officially in the war yet, but we all knew that day was coming. I was just glad I had a job that was contributing to our being ready.

The crew I was assigned to left New York on the S.S. *Amherst,* an old steamer that had seen better days and was confined to making passenger and cargo runs in coastal waters—not that those waters were any safer than the high seas. The company was concerned about German U-boats, which now operated with impunity off American shores, and any ship bound for Britain or a Commonwealth country was considered fair game. As a teenager, I liked to tinker with radios and brought one with me on the ship. At night, some of the guys would gather around my bunk as I tuned in the big bands and quiz shows that were so popular in those days. Unfortunately, one of the U.S. Naval officers escorting us heard about it and immediately confiscated my equipment.

"Maybe you don't know it, son, but there's a war on!" he snapped. "Those

Jerry subs can use that radio to find us!"

I didn't completely understand his reasoning—could their sonar hear the music through our hull? But I didn't argue and the officer was nice enough to return my home-made radio when we docked at Argentia. His concerns, however, were justified. We learned later that the *Amherst* had been sunk by a German submarine on the voyage home.

My first assignment, appropriately enough, was at an asphalt plant. My job was to mix aggregate with the liquid asphalt and meter (which meant dump) it into trucks as they passed under our facility on their way to build the runway. It paid well but was boring as hell, so I began looking for a second job. We were paid by the hour, not a fixed salary, so the more you worked the more you made. I got checked out on a bulldozer and later drove a utility truck; so with three jobs going simultaneously and a willingness to jump whenever they whistled, I built up my bank account about as fast as they built the airport.

Work rules required we take a day off from time to time, so a bunch of us would hitch-hike or walk to the town of Placentia, or take a taxi or train into St. John: a port city where most of the convoys heading out over the North Atlantic were made up.

This last place was a real eye-opener for me. Cargo ships and warships from all over Canada, the U.S., and Britain pulled in at all hours of the day and night, like Grand Central Station. Many showed signs of battle damage from a previous crossing: torpedo holes in the hull, missing masts, broken funnels, and other parts of the structure shot away by enemy surface or aerial attacks. Up to then, "the war" had been something you just read about in the paper or listened to on the radio. Now here it was, big as life—or death—spread out in front of us like a Hollywood epic.

Known by my buddies, now, as a guy with more enthusiasm than good sense, I bought a cheap little brownie camera and went down to the docks. I wanted to snap a few souvenir pictures of all this grandeur and hired a small motorboat to take me around the bay. I suspected the Navy wouldn't like me taking pictures of their ships, so I kept my camera in the bag it came in, tearing a little hole for the

TOP: Young Yoakley was a bull-dozing man: Argentia, Newfoundland

BOTTOM: St. Johns Harbor, Newfoundland, 1941: A catapult-launched Hurricane fighter on the bow of a cargo ship bound for England. Bill got in trouble for taking this classified photo.

lens. My guide was a good one and we covered a lot of territory, even going out to the anti-submarine nets to get some panoramic shots. I got some great pictures of one freighter with a catapult-launched, RAF Hurricane fighter mounted on the bow—a last-ditch defense against U-boats attacking a convoy when there were no friendly aircraft or destroyers around. We hadn't heard about that from the press, but the brave pilots who flew them, if launched, knew they were likely on a one-way trip. To be recovered, they had to make a belly landing in the water and hope to be picked up—never a sure thing in the stormy North Atlantic. I'd always had an interest in aviation, starting with Lindbergh when I was a kid, but that was the first time I ever imagined what it would be like to sit in a cockpit and fight for my life. It was an intriguing and exciting idea.

Anyway, we got back to the dock and, at the top of the ladder, I was greeted by three men wearing very serious suits.

"Hello there," one of them said pleasantly. "You been out taking some pictures?"

"Yes, sir," I saw no point in lying, since the sack I carried obviously wasn't my lunch.

"Mind if we see your camera?" another asked.

I handed it over.

"Thank you. Now if you'll kindly come with us."

"What for?" I yammered. "I work for Fuller in Placentia. I've got to get back to my job!"

"That may be a problem," one of them gently but firmly took my elbow. "You're under arrest for espionage."

To make a long story short, they were St. John's police detectives who regularly patrolled the docks looking for Nazi spies or, in my case, idiots who might unknowingly compromise security. They hauled me downtown for questioning. Fortunately, we workers had been given a "brass number"—a 24-hour telephone line to the company's local, senior manager—in case we ever had a run-in with the authorities, which in St. John could be anyone from the local constabulary or Naval Intelligence to Her Majesty's Secret Service. Fortunately, the Canadian police were very reasonable and let me go as soon as they confirmed my physical description and employment with Fuller—although they kept my camera and film. I knew I had gotten off easy, but I really missed having those great, one-of-a-kind pictures, so after the war, when I was living in Florida, I wrote a letter to the Chief of Police in St. John, asking if they still had my film. Thank goodness for English courtesy and fastidious bureaucrats. The chief not only wrote back, but returned my camera and a complete set of 8 x 10 glossies of every picture I took.

As my job with Fuller wound down, the war in Europe stepped up. The Germans invaded Greece, then Russia, but they lost the pride of their fleet—the giant battleship *Bismark*—in a dramatic battle at sea. By the end of the summer, America was at war in reality, if not on paper, as F.D.R. authorized U.S. forces to open fire on any German or Italian vessels sighted in American waters. As it turned out, political pretense and wartime reality were about to bump heads, and I'd have a ring-side seat.

On August 9th, 1941, while a bunch of us were eating lunch on the headlands overlooking Placentia Bay, two of the biggest warships we'd ever seen steamed into the harbor and dropped anchor. One, we found out, was the *H.M.S. Prince of Wales*—Britain's biggest battleship. The other was the American heavy cruiser, the *U.S.S. Augusta.* A flotilla of destroyers and other escort ships surrounded both vessels, so we knew something big was going on. Within an hour of their arrival, a launch was dropped from the *Prince of Wales* and motored over to the *Augusta,* to be received with pomp and ceremony: crackling semaphores, bosun's whistles piping dignitaries aboard, an honor guard of Marines in dress uniform lining the deck, a brass band playing "God Save the Queen"—the whole nine yards. It wasn't long before rumor passed that the man in the launch was none other than Winston Churchill, and his host aboard the cruiser was the President of the United States. If so, it was the first face-to-face meeting of these two already-legendary figures and a landmark in Anglo-American relations; indeed, in world history, for the purpose of their meeting, the newspapers shortly revealed, was to hammer out eight articles, or principles, that would become the famous Atlantic Charter: the basis for American participation in WWII and the beginning of an alliance that would eventually turn into NATO.

That was on a Saturday. The next day, we watched spellbound as F.D.R. returned the visit, boarding the British battleship to participate in church services. This time a British band played the "Star-Spangled Banner" but the rest of the pageantry was the same. Today, too, we had a lot more company on our vantage point. Half the town and most of the workers turned out to watch history being made, and we sure weren't disappointed. For the next few days, the leaders or their delegates made numerous trips between the vessels until suddenly, on August 12th, both ships weighed anchor and the flotillas were gone. We found out later that Churchill had sailed to Iceland, then returned to England, while F.D.R. went straight back to the U.S.

It wasn't long until the Atlantic Charter was put to the test. On December 7th, another lazy Sunday afternoon, we were lounging around the workers' dormitory when we heard over my home-made radio that the Japanese had bombed Pearl Harbor. Nobody knew exactly how bad the attack had been, and most of us were hard pressed to find Hawaii on a map, though we all knew what it meant. America was now at war. The next day, we learned that Britain, too, had been attacked by the Japanese and their possessions in Malaya and Siam were being overrun. Parliament, like Congress, declared war on Japan—the Atlantic Charter had kicked in. The following day, word came over the radio that the majestic British battleship, the *H.M.S. Prince of Wales*—the vessel we had so admired in Placentia Bay just four months earlier—was now at the bottom of the Pacific, a victim of Japanese torpedo bombers. It was a world at war, all right, but somehow that made it personal.

M*any of our friends considered Pearl Harbor the defining moment of their lives, in retrospect, if not at the time. We can't speak for them, but for us it was a lens that focused the energy of our active but otherwise undirected young lives. Like most Americans, we felt a strong urge to strike back—to contribute to the war effort any way we could. For men our age, that meant joining the armed forces. Looking back, the Japanese sneak attack was also the catalyst that eventually brought us together and began a friendship that would last the rest of our lives.*

✪ ✪ ✪

PJW: I spent most of 1939 through 1941 in school. My Dad always wished he'd known more about accounting, since so much of business success depends upon interpreting financial statements, so he gently persuaded me to enroll in a private accounting school when we got back from Africa. That wasn't nearly as exciting as riding and roping and hunting big game, so I gave it one semester then broke the news to him that what I really wanted to do was fly. Trouble was brewing around the world (Britain and Germany were already at war) and America surely wouldn't be left out of it. If I was going to see action, I wanted it to be from the air. Unfortunately, the Army Air Corps required all pilots to be officers and to become an officer, you had to have at least two years of college. Fortunately from my parents' perspective, that became a good argument for my staying in school. Fortunately, too, we had a winter house outside of Mesa, Arizona, close to the Arizona State Teacher's College in Tempe and about halfway between Falcon Field (a small airport that trained student pilots for the RAF) and Sky Harbor Airport in Phoenix, where the U.S. government had started something called the Civilian Pilot Training (CPT) program a few years earlier. I would wind up spending a lot of time at both airfields, dropping in on my classes at Arizona State just long enough to sign the roll sheet, sleep through a few lectures, and get my homework assignments.

The CPT program represented one of those rare moments when defense planners looked into their crystal ball and clearly saw the future: one in which the U.S., drawn into a world-wide conflict, would be woefully short of pilots. You don't create skilled flyers overnight, let alone those that can survive aerial combat and perform the duties of an Army officer, so they sought to shorten that cycle by building a cadre of flight-qualified civilians who could enter cadet training immediately in case of a national emergency. It was a good idea—especially for flight-minded guys like me—but it didn't work exactly as planned. You could become a private pilot fairly quickly, with just a month or two of training in a light plane, but military flying, which included "boot camp" that turned you into a soldier, meant you had to master considerably bigger, faster, and more complex aircraft and not every CPT graduate was up to it.

So I split my time during '40 and '41 shuttling between college classes, which I hated, and the CPT flight program at Sky Harbor (with occasional visits

Pete in a WACO during his Secondary Civilian Pilot Training (CPT) days, 1940.

to Falcon), which I loved. CPT in Phoenix was run by a private contractor, a local fixed-base operator (FBO), on contract to the federal government. In addition to building the 40 hours of flight time needed for a private pilot's license, I took courses in weather, navigation, and powerplants. My group contained about 30 students, including two women. In fact, my first instructor was a woman, Ruth Chalmers (later marrying and becoming Ruth Reinhold) who served in the '50s and '60s as Senator (and U.S. Presidential candidate) Barry Goldwater's personal pilot. For that matter, many CPT women students went on to play important wartime roles as Women Auxiliary Service Pilots, or WASPs, mostly as production flight test and ferry pilots, delivering every kind of warplane from U.S. factories to embarkation points for every theater of operations.

Most of my primary CPT training was in a Taylor Craft, or "T-Craft," a high-wing, single-engine monoplane whose enclosed cabin and automobile-like control wheel made it look and feel a bit like driving a car. Later, in secondary CPT which led to a commercial pilot's license, I flew the WACO UPF-7, a classic, open-cockpit biplane that looked and flew like a WWI fighter. My last CPT instructor was a great guy named Al Storrs whom I would meet again after joining the Army. Because I was committed to two years at the Arizona State college, I continued training and flying both types of planes until I obtained a commercial license. This put me ahead of many CPT graduates, who quit after getting their private license. It also made me feel like a hotshot, which went with my age—I was now about twenty and thought that, in addition to being the world's greatest aviator, I was also indestructible. On one occasion, that overconfidence almost got me killed.

I decided one day to take the T-Craft on a surprise visit to some friends in Scottsdale, Arizona, at a place called Judson School—a ranch-type boarding school that had a polo field. Normally, this 900 by 300 foot patch of ground would be adequate for landing a bug-smasher like the Taylor Craft, especially if you landed lengthwise. Unfortunately, the field was oriented north to south, and the wind that day was from the west, so I decided to land in that direction, across the polo field's width—after all, that's what they teach you in flight school, right? Always land into the wind? Well, that 300 feet of oiled dirt just wasn't enough to get me stopped, especially since I floated half that distance trying to impress my friends with a three-point landing. I saw I was landing long but couldn't go around because of the school buildings and telephone lines beside the field, so I jammed on the brakes almost as soon as I touched down, sending the airplane onto its nose. I didn't get hurt—except my pride—but I broke the prop and Falcon had to send a maintenance man and an instructor to fix the plane and fly it out. It was my first close call in flying and taught me an important lesson: the most critical safety device in any airplane is the pilot.

By the summer of '41, I was getting restless and tired of the Arizona heat, so my brother Burke and I took a driving trip to California. Passing through the beach cities around LA, we liked the balmy weather and decided to get summer jobs. We both landed positions with the Douglas Aircraft plant at Santa Monica. Burke worked on the production line but with CPT and some college under my belt, I wangled a job as a sheet metal inspector—a quality control assignment that put a star on my badge and gave me run of the plant. That meant I could visit other departments whenever I liked, which made the job less boring and gave me an opportunity to goof off if I felt like it. Burke quit after a few weeks and went back to Arizona, saying the work was too tough and the pay was too low, and I can't say that I blamed him. The downside to my job was the hours. I drew the swing shift, from 4 PM to midnight, which I was stuck with the whole time I was there. However, this, too, soon worked to my advantage.

In the summer of 1941, the Battle of Britain was raging. It was the height of the "blitz"—the Luftwaffe was bombing London, factories, and airfields all over England—and the RAF was desperate for pilots. Because the CPT program had been active for a couple of years, the United States was seen as a fertile recruiting ground for new flyers and Britain's agent was the Royal Canadian Air Force, or RCAF, who offered free, military-style primary flight training to any American CPT graduate who cared to sign up for their program.

Well, this sounded too good to be true, so I met with an RAF Wing Commander—a soft-spoken, gentlemanly "bloke" with an office in Hollywood, of all places. His pitch was convincing—those poor British were really in trouble—so I signed up. Because I hadn't turned 21 and this was definitely a combat assignment,

I needed my parents' permission, which they gave—assuming, I suppose, that I was determined to fly for the military eventually and if it had to be now, it might as well be defending my mother's native soil. She was, after all, a British subject.

Anyway, since their training facility was in Anaheim (about an hour from the coast—there were no freeways in those days) and I had a car, I figured I could commute from my efficiency apartment in Santa Monica, fly an hour or two in Anaheim, then make it back to the Douglas plant in time for my shift. That's exactly how it worked, too, although spending that much time on the road was kind of a grind. One thing all that driving *did* do was give me plenty of time to think about what I was getting into and if I really wanted to do it. My mother was English, true, but my father's ancestors came from Germany—and America was still a neutral country. I began to wonder if this was really my fight, especially since the life expectancy of a new Spitfire pilot, they said, was measured in hours, not even days or weeks.

So after the 10 flight-hour screening program, which I passed with ease, I was called back to the Wing Commander's office to complete my paperwork and prepare for the move to Canada, where I would receive an RCAF uniform and a month's worth of "advanced" flight training before shipping off to Jolly Olde England and a Spitfire of my own.

I must admit, the RAF chap was quite candid about the perils I would face. He was equally understanding when I explained that, on second thought, I was just too young to die in somebody else's war. He stood up from behind his desk, shook my hand, and thanked me (and I believe, sincerely) for considering their program and told me he thought it wouldn't be long before we'd be fighting together against the Bosch. We wished each other luck and parted amicably. I couldn't help thinking, though, that he would need it more than me.

Summer ended and with it my job at Douglas. I returned to Arizona and found work at Falcon Field—doing odd jobs for my old CPT instructor, Al Storrs, who was now chief pilot in charge of training British airmen on contract to the U.S. government. Not long after I started, a Hollywood film crew arrived at Falcon to shoot a movie called *Thunder Birds*—coincidentally about American civilians training British flyers on contract to the U.S. government. It starred John Sutton, Preston Foster, and a glamorous actress named Gene Tierney—one of the most popular leading ladies of the day. Since my job involved hanging around the base anyway—taking planes up on maintenance hops, working as radio dispatcher, helping RAF student pilots practice for flight checks, and so on—I was called upon by the movie's director (along with a hundred other young airmen and cadets, including my brother Burke) to put on an RAF uniform and appear as an extra in the film.

The movie involved a lot of stunt flying, as you'd expect, so they hired an expert pilot named Paul Mantz—a flier who became a legend in the business. We aviation-minded extras got a real kick out of talking to him whenever we could, and learned that—sometimes—a lot more goes into a scene than you see on the screen.

For example, in an early part of the picture, Mantz (doubling for Preston Foster) was told to fly over an open-topped water tower where Gene Tierney's character was supposedly taking a bath. The stunt called for him to roll inverted and drop her a flight suit. Gene would catch it, get dressed, and climb down from the tank. Well, on the day they filmed it, almost nothing went right. Paul had no problem flying upside down, close to the ground, but he just couldn't hit that tank. After the third or forth try, he landed and the director said they'd just assemble the sequence using shots of the flight suit dropping away from the plane, then Gene catching it in a studio close up.

Landing after the last attempt, Paul was white as a sheet. "Boy," he said, shaking his head, "That's the closest I've ever come to buying it on a shoot!"

"What happened?" one of us asked.

It seems that on the last take, as he rolled inverted and tried to drop the suit, it got tangled over his face and he couldn't pull it off. That's a bad time and place to be flying blind and if the director hadn't canceled further attempts, Mantz said he would've made that decision for him. Tragically, despite dozens of pictures where Paul made the most dangerous stunts look easy, he was killed making a simple

RIGHT: The Wurts ranch near Falcon Field. The former "dude ranch" was home to Gene Tierney and Oleg Casini during the filming of the 1941 movie, *Thunder Birds*.

TOP: *Thunder Birds* crew filming on the Wurts ranch near Mesa. That's Gene Tierney (back to the camera) in the checkered blouse.

RIGHT: Movie poster for *Thunder Birds*.

flyover in the 1966 James Stewart classic, *Flight of the Phoenix,* when his specially built aircraft—a plane supposedly assembled from bits and pieces of a crashed C-119 cargo plane—broke up in mid air.

Because Falcon Field was fairly remote—near Superstition Mountain east of Phoenix—the stars lodged at the only decent hotel in the area, a place called the Maricopa Inn in downtown Mesa. Each day, a line of buses picked up the cast and crew and drove them to the day's location on or around the field. Of course, for the cast, movie making is mostly about waiting for the crew to set up and the technicians to prepare the camera, props, lighting, and so on. As a result, the actors had a lot of time to kill between scenes. None of them liked waiting in trailers and it took too long to drive back to Mesa, so they searched for a closer, comfortable place to stay while they waited to be called on set. As it turned out, my family's house—a former dude ranch—had plenty of amenities to keep visitors entertained: guest rooms where they could sleep, a big living room and dining room for relaxing or eating meals, plus a tennis court, pool, and stables. The director was so taken with it, in fact, that he used the ranch as a location for the RAF cadets' festive "graduation party" sequence.

Gene Tierney and her husband, Oleg ("Olie") Casini—the famous fashion designer—spent a lot of time at the ranch and became good friends with our family, particularly my mother, who remained Gene's lifelong friend. Burke and I took Gene and Olie riding and rabbit hunting, and she repaid us with private singing recitals at our family's piano. This surprised us because, although she was a conservatory trained singer with a beautiful voice, she never sang in her movies. She was an appealing actress but not exactly what you'd call beautiful—at least when compared to her contemporaries like Olivia de Haviland and Vivien Leigh. Instead she exuded an aura of very genuine "niceness" that made everyone want to like her, a quality reflected on the screen.

Unfortunately, like so many in that business, she had a lot of problems, both health-wise and emotionally, and spend her last years in a sanitarium. For the rest of her life, however, she continued to correspond with my mother and talk with her on the phone, always asking about our family. She even invited me, when I was a B-24 pilot at March Field in California near the end of the war, to bring my crew to visit her on the set of a movie, *A Bell for Adano,* she was making in Los Angeles with John Hodiak, another star of the day. I got a weekend pass with four buddies and took her up on the offer. I think they thought I was kidding when I said she was friends with my family—that is, until we arrived on the set and she walked over, gave me a hug, and said, "Pete, it's great to see you!" We drove back to the base that same night, though I probably could've flown without an airplane.

By the end of the year, the Japanese attack on Pearl Harbor brought us all back to earth. The war was no longer a plot for a movie, or clips from a newsreel, or some other country's problem—it was now banging on America's door. As a CPT graduate, I was committed to enlisting in the Army and applying for pilot training—so with a hundred thousand other guys, that's exactly what I did. The problem was, the military pipeline wasn't ready yet to handle so many cadets—either in boot camp, called "pre-flight" training, or for flight school—so we were given a number and told to cool our heels until we got called for service, which might take several months.

A lot of guys got impatient and enlisted immediately in another branch of the service, like the Navy or Marines. My brother Burke, who felt no particular affinity for ships or planes, enlisted in the Coast Guard—mostly because he had heard they didn't wear ties, but also because he figured, "Hey, I'm guarding the coast—how far from America can they send me?" He found out when he manned an anti-aircraft gun on a troop transport in the South Pacific.

Personally, I used the delay to date a perky young coed from Mesa named Maxine Stone. She was a year ahead of me in college and so was a lot more certain about her domestic future than I was. Her Dad, Charlie, was a local barber and a heck of a nice guy. Her mother, Addie Lee, was from a small town in Tennessee and barely out of grade school when she and Charlie eloped. You couldn't find two families more different than hers and mine, but somehow that didn't matter. She was indifferent to flying but understood what it meant to me, so there were no problems on that score. We were married shortly before I was ordered to report for

Pete and Maxine on their wedding day in 1942.

pre-flight training at Santa Ana, California.

WRY: Everybody knew that Pearl Harbor changed everything. Top management at the Fuller Company told every American on the job at Placentia Bay that they could break their contract and return to the U.S. if they wanted to enlist in the armed forces. I was one of the guys who raised his hand and said, "Let's go."

They put us on a coastal freighter like the *Amherst* for the voyage home, though this one had better luck—just barely. We hit a terrible storm out of Nova Scotia and everyone on board got sick. The only people who seemed to enjoy the ride were the crew, who told us that they prayed for bad weather like this, since it meant the U-boats couldn't surface to run their "fish"—the torpedoes that sank so many ships. I admit, that comforting thought made a horrible passage a little less miserable. I still felt like I wanted to die, but at least I knew now I probably wouldn't.

From Halifax, I took a train to New York where I visited my stepmother, brother, and sister. I hadn't seen any of them since my abrupt departure, but they all acted like they were glad to see me. Given all that had happened in the last year or so and the uncertain future that lay ahead, it was a time to let bygones be bygones. The world had suddenly become a more dangerous place, but there was always room for hope. The best place for that hope to begin, we agreed, was at home.

From there I continued by train to Brooksville, Florida, where my father superintended a construction crew for Mr. McDonald. We too had a nice reunion; he seemed to understand where I was coming from and where I was headed, which I hoped was the Army Air Corps. We hung out for a few days, getting reacquainted as men, then I headed for the local Army recruiter. Unfortunately, I lacked the prerequisite two years of college for flight training and a commission. Fortunately, Uncle Sam provided an alternative for the truly motivated. The recruiter said I could take a lengthy aptitude and equivalency test which, if it's not immodest to say so, I aced on the first try. I was given a waiting number for pre-flight training and told to expect a call—sooner or later. After Pearl Harbor, the system was jammed with aviation candidates and the Axis powers would have to wait a few extra months to experience the full wrath of the Yoakleys. As it turned out, my waiting time would be just under a year.

In the meantime, I took a job with McDonald working in the main quarry at Brooksville. It was hard work, but not mentally demanding, so it gave me some time to think about what the future may hold. Dad and I called home a couple of times a week during this period; so often, in fact, that the female long-distance operator (there was no direct dial in those days) began to recognize our voices.

"Mr. Yoakley again, eh?" she'd say. "Junior or senior?"

"Which one do you think?" I'd joke.

"Well, you're the one who sounds like a movie star, you tell me!"

We'd flirt like that for a minute or so then our call would go through, though I have to say, I began to look forward to our twice- or thrice-weekly calls just for the pleasure of hearing her voice. After awhile, we'd chat about different things; the course of the war (always bad news at this point, so we didn't dwell on that), the beginning of war rationing, the latest movies in theaters (Disney's *Bambi* and Bogart's *Casablanca* were big), and Glenn Miller's latest hit, which I think was "Chattanooga Choo Choo." I finally worked up the courage to ask to her out, and to my surprise she said yes, so I said I'd pick her up when she got off work.

"So, what kind of car do you drive?" she asked in a coy little tone.

Oddly enough, that threw me a bit. It's the kind of question you get from a gold-digger, not a gold nugget. "I dunno," I stammered, "My Dad's Oldsmobile, I guess. Why do you ask?"

"Silly! How will I know it's you in the parking lot?"

Good point, and it eased my mind while I silently kicked myself in the pants. Her name was Marian Shepherd—as beautiful and sweet in person as she was on the phone—and we hit it off immediately. I picked her up and drove her home and we began dating regularly—a relationship initially as innocent as an Andy Hardy film and later as intense as the million other wartime romances that were blossoming all over the country. By October of 1942, just after I turned 21, we agreed to get married. Breaking the news to my Dad was a lot harder than getting his approval to enlist in the Army.

"This is a big decision, you know," he said glumly, "especially since you're going to war."

"I know, Dad, but she's *real* pretty—you know, like Mom." I didn't say which mom.

He only shrugged and shook his head. I had a track record in the family of running off half-cocked and he wasn't sure that I'd thought through this particular decision.

"You know, if you get married," he said, "I won't attend the wedding. I just can't. I think you're making a big mistake."

"I know, Dad. But I hope you change your mind."

He didn't, and later that same month we were married. It was a modest affair and we didn't have the cash or inclination to take a big honeymoon—that wasn't the point. At long last, in a world that seemed to be coming unraveled, my life was finally coming together.

In December, about a year after Pearl Harbor, I received my call to active duty. Within a week, I was on a train to Santa Ana, California, and my appointment with the wild, blue yonder.

2

WORLD WAR II: TRAINING AMERICANS TO FLY AND FIGHT

*I*n February 1943, we arrived separately at Santa Ana, California—a huge Army Air Corps pre-flight training installation receiving recruits from all over the country. Its purpose was to begin the process of turning energetic, eager young men like ourselves into sober, disciplined aerial warriors. At least that was the theory.

The fact was, America pretty much improvised the first year or two of the war. As a country, we had to play catch-up—fast—but the Army was still the Army. Before you even thought about going near an airplane, you had to become a soldier, and before you could be a soldier, you had to stop being a civilian. Thus our first six weeks in uniform, spent in the same BMT (Basic Military Training) squadron but in different barracks, had a lot more to do with Bill Mauldin's "Willy and Joe" than "Terry and the Pirates"—a popular cartoon strip based loosely on the Flying Tigers. We wore khaki uniforms, carried duffle bags stuffed with baggy underwear, woolen socks, and brown shoe polish, and spent a lot of time standing in line or in formation. We didn't meet each other until four months later, after we'd finished Pre-flight and Primary Flight Training—and then only because our names came at the end of the alphabet and that's how the Army kept track of you; either that or by your serial number, and ours ended within three digits of each other. So when we filed into the barracks at Gardner Field in Taft, California, and were ordered to stop in ranks by the unmade beds, it was pretty clear that the guys on either side of us would become pretty close for the next few months, whether we liked them or not. In our case, we became the best of friends—a friendship we owe entirely to the convenience of the Army and an organizational habit that for all we knew went back to Valley Forge.

✪ ✪ ✪

PJW: I originally got orders to report for Pre-flight training in class 43E. (Classes were named for their scheduled graduation sequence, so "class 43E" was the fifth class to be commissioned and get its wings in 1943). I said farewell to my new wife and family and packed my bags and showed up along with a few hundred other guys from around the country at Santa Ana. Induction to "the system" was pretty depressing, as every new solider knows, so when word came down after a week that there had been a mix-up in our orders and that our assigned class was actually 43J, we were given the choice of either staying put or going home, to report back later at the proper time. Since I had just been married and pre-flight training so far seemed like misery on a stick, I decided to put if off for as long as I could. I went to the Post Exchange—the military "department store" on every big Army facility—and bought a better tailored shirt so I would at least look more like an officer and a gentlemen when I returned to my family which, if I had anything to say about it, would be on the next train out of town.

While I waited in Arizona, I got a job as a bus driver for the Sun Valley Lines in Phoenix, a franchise of All American Bus Lines—the nation's third largest carrier. I liked the idea of handling big equipment and the routes weren't too long: my longest leg was from Phoenix to El Paso. Along with the passengers, drivers got free meals and lodging in nice hotels, so I even got to see some pretty scenery. What was there not to like?

Well, I found out. Late one summer day on the way from Williams Field (even farther out than Falcon) to Chandler, Arizona, I had a mishap that for once wasn't my fault. The passengers were mostly GI's, but also quite a few elderly people and women with kids. The bus was really jammed and people were standing or kneeling in the aisle, talking and smoking. We were headed into the setting sun toward a patch of highway under repair. The work crew had raised a big cloud of dust so the cars ahead of me began to slow—their brake lights flaring just before they went into the "fog." I was always conscientious about keeping a safe distance from the vehicle ahead of me, so I let up on the gas well before the concrete ended and the dirt began. The bus slowed, but not enough, so I tapped the brakes. Nothing happened. I hit them again and the pedal went to the floor. Still nothing, and those tail lights loomed bigger than ever. I glanced to the right. A steep embankment kept

Pete drove a bus for Sun Valley Lines while awaiting his call to active duty in 1942.

me from pulling off on the shoulder—we'd surely roll over and that would be it for all those people in the aisle. So when we were almost on top of the car ahead, I swerved to the left into the oncoming lane. I prayed there would be a hole in the eastbound traffic—now hidden by dust—big enough, literally, to drive a bus through. As it turned out, there was, though the drivers we passed undoubtedly thought I was crazy.

We rumbled harmlessly around the line of slowed cars then pulled back onto the finished highway where I geared down until we coasted to a stop. I got up and told my passengers that, due to a technical problem, they'd be a little late getting to Chandler. Because of loyalty to the company, I left out the part about total brake failure. Because of a desire to not get punched in the nose, I also didn't mention the fact that I had risked a head-on collision to avoid a fatal rollover. Like my crackup on the Judson polo field, I learned once more that when big machines get moving, they don't always stop when and where you want them to, so you'd better think ahead.

WRY: As I said, I got my shot at flight training by passing the Army's equivalency exam rather than investing two years in college. This was dandy except for one little problem: a nagging sense of insecurity. I didn't lack self-confidence—when we finally got in the air, I took to flying like the proverbial duck to water—but there was a lot more to aviation, particularly military aviation, than just manipulating the wires and tires. Classes included the theory of flight, navigation, systems and powerplants, and a ton of regulations, most of which didn't make much sense but we had to know them anyway. None of it was particularly hard. I was always a good student and did as well in ground school as I did in the cockpit. But because of that niggling insecurity, I never quite got over the biggest fear most of us had: the terror of "washing out," of being eliminated for any of a dozen reasons. Some of these reasons made sense—like chronic airsickness or lack of physical coordination— you just couldn't get around those and if they were bad enough, they got you killed. Others seemed more arbitrary, like military bearing, attitude, and of course, scholastics. We all knew the program was designed to weed people out, not help them get through (though some instructors went the extra mile to help struggling students) so I worked my tail off—probably harder than I had to—in every phase of training. The least it did was make me a better pilot; and while I respect anyone who's good with a slide rule or can name the kings of England or elements on the Periodic Table, I saw more than a few sharp college kids wash out due to a lack of respect for the task at hand. I decided right then that I'd take this flying game seriously and get as good at it as I could.

At Santa Ana, we had between three- and five-thousand enlisted troops, all of whom wanted to be pilots. The first six weeks of the program were devoted to basic military training—the same "boot camp" every civilian gets as indoctrination to military life. Each squadron had its own barracks of forty to sixty guys. We had our own guidon, or unit flag, that we carried while we marched, just like soldiers back in the Civil War. And the drill sergeants still yelled at us and we had to keep the barracks spic and span and pass white-glove inspections: the more some things change, the more others stay the same.

During this Pre-Flight phase, we took a bunch of tests to classify us for further training. The top of the pecking order, of course, was pilot; but other aircrew positions involved getting different kinds of wings as well as a commission. Some guys scoring low on pilot aptitude but high in everything else went directly to navigator or bombardier school. Guys who really stubbed their toe and were no longer eligible for a commission, might serve as aerial gunners or flight engineers. Beyond that, there wasn't much left for them but the infantry. A few people thought that since they had volunteered to be pilots, but didn't make the grade, they'd be discharged to civilian life. Un-uh. Once Uncle Sam had you, you were in for the duration, so you went where you were told, even if it meant wearing a "steel pot" and carrying a rifle. Most of us could only hope we'd get good scores and agree with the Army's decision.

All this drilling and saluting and whatnot got pretty old, pretty quick. Although I wouldn't meet Pete until we'd finished Pre-flight and Primary Flight Training a few months later, I think our mutual dislike of military Mickey Mouse, not to mention a big preference for flying instead of marching, made us kindred

TOP: Temporary housing for Air Corps recruits during pre-flight training, Santa Ana, 1942.

BOTTOM: Inside the barracks during Pre-flight Training, Santa Ana, 1942.

Sure, he's smiling *now*...Pete seems happy with his decision
to join the Army.

spirits. Our backgrounds were similar enough for us to share the same values and sense of humor, but our personalities and life experiences were different enough to keep things interesting—even a little competitive.

After three months of Primary Flight School at Cal-Aero in Ontario, an excellent civilian-run school teaching novice cadets the rudiments of flight in Stearman biplanes, we were assigned to Gardner Field at Taft, California for Basic Flight Training in the BT-13: a fixed-gear, single-engine trainer with a "greenhouse" canopy that at least looked like a modern warplane. Pete and I had bunks next to each other and made friends pretty quick—and for several practical reasons. One was our extreme dislike of reveille—that blast of a bugle on the loudspeaker that told everyone the sun was up. We had five minutes to jump out of our bunks, make our beds (the Army way, of course, with hospital corners, blankets tight enough to bounce a quarter on, the whole bit), put on our uniforms, and fall-in for roll call outside the barracks. That sounds like a lot to do in five minutes, but believe me, it didn't take long to master (particularly if you did things cooperatively) so we habitually found ourselves in position ahead of the other guys. Well, nuts to that. If they got more time to shave and tuck in their shirttails, so would we. Since the hardest part of getting up was putting that first toe out of bed, Pete and I rigged a shaving mirror by the window outside the barracks so we could see the parade ground from our bunks. That way, when reveille sounded, we had a few extra minutes to lounge in the sack while everyone else ran around like chickens. When the squadron was almost in place, we'd pile out and race through our "two minute drill," falling in just as roll call began. Of course, having names that began with Y and W was a help, but we tried not to depend on that too much.

On the other hand, when things slowed down, life at Gardner could get pretty boring. One weekend about sundown while we were lounging on our bunks, we noticed two earth-movers parked outside the barracks. Construction went on constantly around the base, so when the whistle blew on Friday, the crews just parked their machines and took off. Anyway, Pete and I were anxious to start rat-racing in P-47s or P-38s or whatever other first-line fighters we knew we'd get after graduation, so we thought we'd get a jump on all that by having a dogfight of our own with those two vehicles.

Since it was sundown on a Sunday and most guys (especially those in authority) were somewhere else, we ran out and jumped in our respective "fighters." Pete had been a bus-driver before going on active duty, and I'd driven my share of bulldozers in Newfoundland and Florida, so we started our engines and the fight was on. I had a Caterpillar road grader while Pete "flew" a diesel asphalt roller. We spent the next half hour or so zooming back and forth in spine-tingling head-on passes and crushing "high G" turns trying to get on each other's tail. Finally, Pete lost control of his machine and clipped the edge of the barracks, making a terrible noise and alerting us to the possibility that between the roaring engines, grinding gears, and now the sound of splintering wood, somebody (beyond the few bored cadets cheering us on) might get curious and investigate. We shut off the engines and left the vehicles where they stood. We returned to our bunks (though not right away) and the machines were still there the next morning. Nobody said anything, but when we returned to the barracks later that day, the equipment had been moved. Pete still doesn't like to talk about it, but it was the first rat-race he lost to me. It wouldn't be the last.

PJW: From mid-April through mid-June of '43, we flew PT-17 biplanes in Primary Flight Training at Cal Aero in Ontario, California. I'd flown the two-place, open-cockpit Stearman a number of times at Falcon after receiving my "Secondary" (commercial) CPT training in the WACO, a similar biplane, so it was like meeting an old friend. The required flight maneuvers were similar to those used for commercial pilot training and ground handling (including takeoffs and landings, which can be tricky in conventional-gear aircraft—"tail draggers" with two main landing gear and a tail wheel) can be tough for beginners, so I was ahead in that department, too. All in all, I was pretty optimistic about this phase of the program—though that fear of washing out and the stigma attached to it always tugged at the back of my mind. But Cal Aero had some good instructors and I worked hard to keep up with them. They respected my skills, and I got pretty friendly with several IPs. On one

Pete climbs into the AAF's primary flight trainer, a PT-17 Stearman.

occasion, though, that friendly relation backfired.

The instructor was seated in front, as usual, and was about to demonstrate a loop. I'd flown with him several times and we got along well—so well, in fact, that I thought I'd play a little trick on him. The seats in the Stearman were raised or lowered with a bungee cord: basically a thick elastic band that could be stretched over one of several hooks. The cord was accessible from the side of each seat, but the bungee on the front seat could also be reached from the rear cockpit by leaning under the instrument panel. So I waited until he reached the top of the loop and we were upside down, then I leaned forward and snapped his bungee. It whipped against his metal seat with a resounding *twang* and I swear he almost jumped out of the plane.

"What the hell was *that*?" he yelled into the gosport tube—the one-way communication device used by the IP to talk to the student. I had no way of answering, so I kept quiet. He rolled wings level and looked to the right and left. Some Stearmans had been having structural problems and I guess he thought the upper wing spar may have cracked. He immediately reduced power and began a gradual descent in the direction of the field.

"I don't know if she'll hold together," he said, voice quivering, "I'll put her down as quick and gently as I can. If you hear another crack or see a wing start to fold, don't wait for my command—just bail out if we have enough altitude!"

It now occurred to me that my little joke had probably gone too far and (especially if I wound up explaining it in a plowed field or on a dirt road instead of back at Ontario) not nearly as funny as I thought. We made it back and landed safely and before he could write up the airplane as needing a major structural inspection, I explained as delicately and deferentially as I could what actually happened. I said I didn't mean to scare him; it was just an old joke we used to play on front-seat passengers. He said he understood and hoped I would continue to think it was funny as I marched around the base perimeter wearing full flight gear (including boots, heavy jacket, and parachute—which was a seat-pack and banged your legs when you walked) until sundown. I ended the day with some bruised thighs and

blisters but a better appreciation of military discipline.

Not all of my prior flying experience was put to such frivolous uses. Once, it even saved some lives.

There is an old tradition in aviation, both civil and military, called "hangar flying." That's when pilots sit around, maybe over a Coke or a beer, and swap war stories about their experiences, close calls, tricks of the trade, and share tips about how to fly better and more safely. During one of these bull sessions, probably in the barracks, I was shooting the breeze with a few students in our class. Somebody said how amazing it was that stunt pilots could fly under telephone wires and power lines: low flying of the most hazardous sort. I replied there was no real trick to it, provided you did it the right way. The key was to forget about the wires and just keep watching the ground. Assuming they were strung at the usual height—about 30 to 40 feet in the air—you had plenty of clearance for the tail as long as your landing gear or propeller cleared any obstacles. After all, I said, you fly near the ground all the time when you takeoff and land. You don't have any problems then because you're watching the runway, not the sky above you. Just do the same thing when you fly under wires.

Well, this didn't start a rash of utility pole diving in our squadron, but I could see the idea stuck with a couple of pilots. One of them was a guy named Ortho Zacon, a hairdresser (of all things) from the Bronx, but a very motivated flyer. He wasn't ace material, though, and later washed out during advanced flight training at Luke Field in Arizona. He was assigned to troop-carrying gliders (they figured he'd do better without an engine to worry about) and participated in the D-Day invasion. His job was to fly in formation with two other gliders as they were pulled aloft, then released, by a C-47 transport. Their goal was to make a safe landing on a pasture or plowed field behind enemy lines, then disgorge their passengers—troops who were armed and ready for battle. Since the troops on each glider had to join up as soon as they landed, glider pilots were taught to follow the leader as closely as possible all the way to the ground.

Well, that's exactly what Ortho did. His three-ship glider formation came down in French hedgerow country, where the Germans had ignited flare-pots filled

with white phosphorous to obscure the landing site with heavy smoke. They had just about reached the ground when the flight leader spotted some power lines right on their glide path. Instinctively, he pulled up and tried to go over them, but without engine power, the heavy glider just stalled and nosed over—as did the second ship on his wing—killing everybody on board. Ortho, however, remembered what I'd said about flying under wires. Instead of pulling up, he pushed the yoke forward, picked up speed, then leveled off just above the ground. His glider zoomed under the wires without mishap, then made a standard assault landing, which was little more than a controlled crackup, but everyone walked away. I know all this because I got a letter from Ortho towards the end of 1944, well after the invasion, describing the whole thing. I'm sure that over the years, after I became an IP myself, the tips and tricks I offered my students proved useful on various occasions, but it felt especially good that my off-hand remark, made on a lazy afternoon about a usually pointless maneuver, wound up saving so many lives.

*I*n late June, after completing Primary Flight Training at Cal-Aero, we went on to *Gardner Field in Taft, California, for Basic Flight Training in the BT-13. Near the end of August, we were transferred to Luke Field, just west of Phoenix, Arizona, for three months of Advanced Flight Training, where we would remain until graduation, winning our pilot's wings and the gold bars of a second lieutenant on November 3, 1943.*

The standard advanced trainer of the day was the North American AT-6 "Harvard," a low-wing monoplane with a long "greenhouse" canopy like the BT-13, but with retractable landing gear and a more powerful radial engine. The only problem was, by this time we had been classified as "standard pilots" rather than "fighter pilots," which was our first choice. There were a few reasons for this, none of which had to do with our test scores or flying abilities. The air war in Europe was now primarily a bombing campaign (the Luftwaffe was still a threat, but the allies had air superiority over the whole theater); and in the Pacific, Naval air power—both carrier and land-based—was handling most of the air-to-air action, although demand for medium and heavy AAF bombers, as well as cargo planes, remained high. This was disappointing, particularly since those anointed few selected for fighter training went directly into the P-40, a now-obsolete but still admirable

TOP: Cadets wives' club for class of 43J. That's Maxine (seated) on the far left; Marian (standing) on the far right.

BOTTOM: They got their wings! Bill and Marian (L), celebrate with Max and Pete (R), 1943.

war bird made famous by Chennault's Flying Tigers, whose distinctive shark's teeth painted on the nose had been adopted by several other combat squadrons and was already an icon of the war.

Still, a plane is a plane and we both got a kick out of the old AT-6, though we wound up spending a lot more time in it than we planned. After we got our wings and commission, we were assigned to Randolph Field to become Instructor Pilots ourselves.

WRY: Pete and I both felt cheated out of combat by that first IP assignment. We joined to fight the Axis, not to be professors with parachutes, but that was the assignment we drew so we just saluted and went where we were told. For prospective instructors, that was Randolph Field in Texas, where new IP's received additional training in dealing with students and honed our skills flying required maneuvers *the Army way.* Through some mix-up in his orders, though, Pete didn't stay long and went back to Marana Field in Arizona, where he got a "crash course" in flight instruction—though that's not the phrase they used.

Once I got assigned to a training squadron, though, my attitude improved real fast. I got a kick out of watching my students progress, though some IPs worried less about building skills than exposing weaknesses. They approached fight instruction like drill sergeants, and intimidated anyone who climbed into the cockpit. They thought the added pressure would help eliminate weak sisters—those students who might crack under the strain of combat. Maybe they had a point, but that definitely wasn't my style. My way was to start by establishing trust between student and instructor. They knew I was there to help them meet Uncle Sam's criteria, not shoot them out of the sky. I wanted them to feel that flying could be enjoyable as well as hard work. Most of my "studs" responded to that. I took it as a badge of honor that during the whole time I taught cadets, I only washed out one student while other IP's eliminated dozens. Even then, I'd spent lots of extra time with the fellow—in the air and on the ground—trying to talk him through his problems, figuring out just *why* he couldn't master a certain maneuver or understand a certain principle, because his failure felt like mine. Still, you can only hold somebody's hand so long then they've got to stand on their own. Like every other IP, I didn't want to send a guy up for a flight check before he was ready, or "pencil whip" him through the program with phoney scores only to have him screw up later when the chips were down in more complex or less forgiving aircraft, in combat, or in bad weather.

PJW: I admit, I was not pleased when I learned that my reward for investing all that time in CPT, then later as a commercial pilot at Falcon, and even my brief stint in the RCAF Spitfire qualification program—not to mention those months at Ontario, Gardner, and Luke—was to simply shift my parachute from one cockpit to the other. I wanted to get in the war and knew I'd make a good combat pilot. This was now America's fight and I was better prepared than most. After all, I'd waxed Yoakley good in our dogfight with those earth-movers back at Gardner, maneuvering him into a wall, though to this day he still doesn't remember it that way. But that's not where Uncle Sam thought I'd make my best contribution and, of course, while the boss may not always be right, he's still the boss.

Most IP's went through flight instructor school at Randolph before being assigned to a training squadron. I started out that way, too, and with my orders in my pocket, set out with Maxine on a bus to Texas. Somewhere enroute, though, I got a telegram from her father, Charlie Stone, saying that new orders had come to the house re-assigning me immediately to Marana. Well, the Army was pretty strict in those days about troops in transit and not overstaying your leave, so we jumped on the next westbound bus and I reported by the skin of my teeth. The personnel guy at Marana just laughed.

"You should've gone on to Randolph like your original orders said," he told me. "That way, the government would've paid for your transportation back. Now, that trip to Texas was just a vacation. Hope you had a good time."

That was not the best way to start an assignment I already disliked, but at least it taught me something useful about the system. The reason they reassigned me was that Marana was terribly short on instrument instructors and needed somebody who could start right away. I got a few quick lessons on working with students—mostly how to fill out the required forms—then hopped in the front seat of a BT-13 with a new student in back and went to work.

My approach to instruction was pretty much based on the kind of flight instructors I'd had myself—imitating the good ones and avoiding the mistakes of the bad. I tailored my style to the needs of the particular student. If a young man was timid, I'd go slow and explain things thoroughly, giving him plenty of encouragement even for the tiniest accomplishment. On the other hand, if a kid was too cocky or dangerously aggressive, I'd have to rein him in, mostly by impressing him with the consequences of careless mistakes—something I knew about personally. All in all, I was a serious instructor, but not a harsh one. We had some hard-nosed IP's who would discipline students by "whipping" them with the control stick: saying "I have the airplane," which was supposed to be accompanied by a quick waggle of the stick to show that the instructor was now flying the airplane. Only in this case, instead of the quick waggle, the instructor would bang the stick from side to side as hard as he could, hitting the student on the knees. This didn't really hurt, but it sure got their attention. As far as I was concerned, such tactics said more about the shortcomings of the teacher rather than the student.

Of course, when a student was conscientious and keeping up with the program, we'd find little ways of having fun. One "extra-curricular" maneuver I sometimes added to the night-flying syllabus was to drop down to a railroad trestle and fly just above the rails as a locomotive approached. Remember, this was in the dead of night during wartime, so unless the moon was out, the surrounding area was pitch-black. Anyway, we'd steady the plane just above the tracks, turn off the position lights, and as soon as we saw the locomotive coming in the opposite direction, snap on the landing light, making us look like another train headed straight for him. This obviously woke up a few drowsy engineers—our contribution to railway safety—and we always pulled up well before he could slam on the brakes or do anything drastic. Nobody ever reported us for doing this, but I was ready with my story. "Just doing a little low-level navigation training, sir. Sorry if we upset anybody at the Union Pacific!"

✪ ✪ ✪

*E*arly in 1944, Bill left Randolph for a basic training squadron at Gardner Field, instructing in BT-13s. At Marana, Pete got "promoted" to the AT-6, but still as an instrument instructor. The war raged on, but we only knew what we read in the papers, heard on the radio, or learned from the occasional combat pilot rotating back to the states. The hours were long and the work was repetitive. Although we got satisfaction from watching our students succeed, we couldn't help thinking the world, and the war, was passing us by.

That summer, Pete and Maxine's first child—a daughter named Barbara Lynn— was born, and shortly after that, Bill and Marian had their first baby, William Preston.

WRY: The summer of '44 was a real roller coaster for me. Pete and Max had their first baby, a girl, which tickled us pink and made us even sorrier we didn't live close enough for regular visits. I guess family was especially on my mind at that time, since my Dad had just passed away and I wanted to spend some time with my sister Hilda and half-brother Dave, but the training schedule just wouldn't allow it. Instead, I asked the squadron commander if I could borrow a BT-13 for a quick overnight cross-country to Marana, promising to get back in time for the next day's flying. He agreed, and I spent one long, cold night in that little cockpit going from California's Central Valley to Arizona and back. I arrived at Pete's about two in the morning and we had a nice visit for an hour or so, then I got back in the plane. I reported for duty the next day, as promised, and was a little bleary eyed for the first hour or two, then I got my second wind. Oh, to be 22 again!

PJW: The June visit from Bill to welcome our daughter into the world was a big surprise and really boosted my morale. Basic flight training was never particularly exciting, especially the instrument phase, and now it was getting to be drudgery. All of us instructors wanted to be fighter pilots, so when combat slots were posted, everyone flooded our commander's office with requests for transfer. After awhile, the C.O. got so tired of this he called his instructors together, en mass, for what we assumed would be a pep talk to tell us how crucial our efforts were to the war, and so on. Instead, the message was a little different.

"I've got just one question for you guys," he barked, "What's the matter with

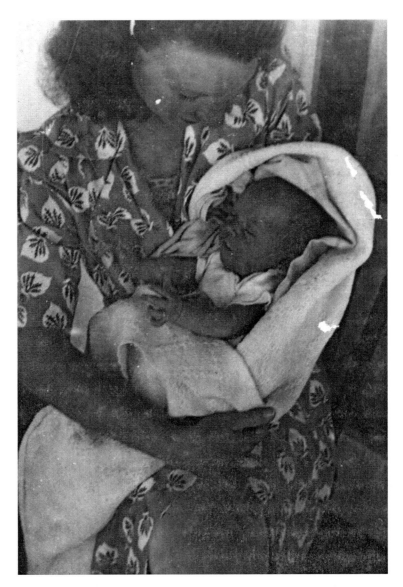

Maxine with daughter, Barbara, 1944.

you? Don't you like my base?"

We glanced uneasily at each other. We suspected it was a trick question.

"Well, if you don't," he continued, "I can make things a whole lot worse. So I don't want to see another transfer request come across my desk. Not one! Is that understood?"

We filed out, mumbling, but at least we knew now how to save a few hours each month: by not submitting paperwork that was headed straight for the wastebasket. At other times, in other places, such an edict would invite a visit from the Inspector General—even soldiers had rights (not many, but we had them) and requesting a transfer was right up there, as long as you put it through proper channels. Now, this particular commander was implying that he didn't care if you complained to the IG; he just didn't want to be bothered with our whining and sniveling any more, even if it got him fired. Maybe he, too, wanted a new assignment.

Although we didn't get what we wanted, we at least got a taste of it. Our commander told us shortly thereafter that two obsolete Navy fighters had been sent back from the fleet and would be stationed at one of our auxiliary fields. We could fly them, he said, whenever we wanted—provided it didn't interfere with our primary duties. One was a Douglas SBD Dauntless dive bomber like the ones that won the Battle of Midway. (In fact, this plane looked like it had been shot down at the Battle of Midway!) The other was a Curtis SB2C Helldiver—another single-engine, carrier-based attack plane that was obsolete when I graduated from high school. Most of us tried these airplanes a few times, but the drive from Marana to the auxiliary field was time-consuming and once we got there, one or both were usually down for maintenance—especially the Helldiver, which had a finicky electric prop. Checkout in each consisted of the crew chief standing on the wing, leaning into the cockpit, showing you how to start the engine, and that was about it. The Dauntless looked and flew pretty much like the AT-6, though those slotted dive brakes lining each wing could really slow you down. The Helldiver was older, but actually more fun to fly. It was a very honest plane and felt like a real war horse—if riding a Clydesdale into battle was your thing.

As I said, most of my instructing at Marana was in instrument flying, which meant the student flew in the back seat under a canvas "hood," controlling the aircraft by watching the gauges, while the IP monitored his performance and watched out for other airplanes. This was important training, and instrument flying makes all pilots better by teaching them to be more precise, even when the weather is good. However, it's also incredibly tedious, so whenever a lesson was through, I often invited the student to pull back the hood and we'd shake out the cobwebs by doing a few aerobatics. One maneuver I got very adept at was the "falling leaf." This isn't really aerobatics, but it's hard to do in a straight wing airplane—especially a trainer that is designed to give plenty of warning before a stall and get you out of one (drop the nose on its own) in case the student forgets what to do. Essentially, the trick is to slow the plane down, flying straight and level, until you feel the airframe begin to buffet—the signal of an approaching stall. Instead of dropping the nose and adding power, as in normal stall recovery, you enter a falling leaf by keeping just enough back pressure on the stick to "ride the nibble" and keep the wings level, maintaining a constant heading, without letting the nose drop or (horror of horrors) falling into a spin, which is entirely possible if you stall completely and are using too much rudder. Of course, an airplane in this mode begins sinking rapidly and rocks gently from side to side as you try to level the wings, hence the name: falling leaf. If I say so myself, I probably did this maneuver better, and could hold it longer, than any other instructor; although, I was probably the only one who cared enough about it, or got bored enough, to practice it regularly. It was just one way among many I used to stay sane while I watched my students graduate and win the war.

Toward the end of 1944, we finally got our wish: a transfer out of flight training and into combat assignments. Pete was transferred to March Field in California for "phase training" in the Consolidated B-24 Liberator—the four-engine, tricycle-gear heavy bomber that was the most widely produced aircraft of World War II. Bill was sent to Douglas, Arizona to train in the North American B-25 Mitchell—a twin-engine, twin-tailed medium bomber, also with tricycle gear, that was still in demand in Europe, although most Air Corps bombers (like Pete's) were now being sent to the Pacific. It had been a long haul, but both of us now seemed destined to see some action. Frankly, we *would've accepted command of an observation balloon as long as it got us into the war.*

WRY: I was mighty happy to be assigned to B-25s, though it meant yet another move for me and my family. The airfield at Douglas was pretty remote, even by desert standards, but that meant lots of open space and good weather for flying, and that's what counted most.

The B-25 was made by North American Aviation—a company that would play a big role in my future. They had a great reputation in aviation circles, having designed the P-51 Mustang, arguably the war's best fighter and one of the prettiest airplanes ever made. The B-25 was no fighter, but it was the next best thing: rugged and reasonably maneuverable and capable of just about any ground attack mission. This was also the first time I'd flown an airplane that needed a crew: in this case, a pilot, a copilot, a navigator-bombardier, a flight engineer (who doubled as the top turret gunner), and a tail gunner. It was a popular ship with the allies, too, being flown by the British, Russians, and even the Chinese.

At first, I flew the right seat, the copilot's position, while I learned the ropes. With two Wright R-2600 Cyclone radial engines, the plane was just about twice as complicated to operate as the old AT-6, and coordinating the activities of other airmen took a little getting used to. But while other would-be fighter pilots viewed this as an inconvenience, I accepted it as a challenge and got a kick out of seeing what the airplane and its crew could do. By the spring of '45, I was flying the left seat as pilot-in-command with a crew of my own, preparing to depart for "ETO" (the European Theater of Operations) when on May 8th, Germany surrendered— abruptly ending my plans for an all-expense paid tour of Europe.

Without missing a beat, they changed our assignment to the Pacific, where carrier planes and Air Corps bombers were tightening the noose on the Japanese homeland. Although most of the heavy lifting was being done by long-range B-29s and B-24s, medium bombers like mine were still essential for tactical interdiction— bombing trains, vehicles, and bridges behind enemy lines—and anti-shipping strikes. It was now that my checkered past caught up with me. Because I had spent so much time as an IP and had adapted so enthusiastically to the new environment of multi-motored, crew-operated aircraft, they made me an instructor again, dang

At the end of '44, Bill flew the B-25 Mitchell: one of the most versatile
aircraft of WWII.

it, and told me my new assignment was to teach Chinese pilots to fly the B-25s our government had so generously given them. And by the way, they said, unpack your bags. You're staying in Douglas, Arizona.

This, too, I took in stride, though I had to smile through gritted teeth and my salute was a little less snappy. It was hard enough to teach some Americans—native English speakers who were raised around cars, radios, and other modern technologies—how to fly the BT-13 and AT-6, but even the worst of these were aces compared to the average Chinese pilot. Not that the Chinese guys were stupid or uncoordinated or anything like that—they just didn't understand a word you said and many had never turned a doorknob before coming to the United States. Their ground school was all in Chinese, thank goodness, and they learned quickly about the airplane's systems and flight procedures—though a lot of them had trouble putting the two together. Our main means of communication in the cockpit was by pointing, grunting, and shaking or nodding our head—but we usually got our message across. When worse came to worse, we instructors were told to request a Chinese translator to talk to our students on the radio, but with so many planes and so many Chinese in the air at one time, the poor translator was run ragged and always seemed to be talking to somebody else just when you needed him most.

Fortunately, with the war in Europe over, our schedules were more relaxed and we found ourselves with a little free time. I finally had a plane with extra seats and enough range to make a recreational, cross-country practical, so I flew back east for that long-delayed visit with my sister and brother. Dave had been turned down for flight training because of color blindness, so he enlisted in the Army and, although barely the minimum age for service, was now a sergeant. I picked him up for a weekend in Richmond and was at the airport's operations office, preparing for the return trip, when the pilot of another B-25 came in to file a flight plan. He was in a big hurry to get to New England which, unfortunately, would take him right into the teeth of a big storm that was just passing out of Virginia and headed toward the northeast.

"You know, if I were you," I said to the other pilot after our weather briefing,

"I'd give it another day. That way, the front will be out to sea and you'll skate in there just fine."

"Can't do it," he replied tersely. "Gotta get up there today. We'll just stay low and do some scud-running. No sweat. Hope you have a good flight."

I shook my head and said he was a braver man than I was, then watched him head out the door with his parachute and two crewmen into the pouring rain. He took off and immediately headed north. It was early on a Sunday morning and since the weather in Richmond was gradually improving, Dave and I still had some time to visit. I didn't think any more about the other pilot until we heard later in the day that a B-25 had crashed into the Empire State Building, between the 78th and 79th floors, while trying to overfly New York City in bad weather. The crew was killed along with ten people on the ground, but it could've been worse. Because it was a weekend, there were few people in the building. Still, it was the first airplane-high rise disaster and some of the lessons they learned fighting that fire and managing that catastrophe were employed after the 9/11 attacks on the World Trade Center some 45-years later. That was another of my scary little brushes with history. It wouldn't be the last.

On August 14th, the atom bomb (plus the cumulative effort of a lot of hard-fighting guys in the air, at sea, and on the ground), brought 3-1/3 years of misery to an end. It was VJ Day. The Japanese had surrendered. World War II was over.

PJW: By the fall of 1944, the USAAF decided its biggest need was for four-engine heavy bomber crews, so that's where I was headed. By now the B-17 was gradually being replaced everywhere by the B-24, which could carry twice the bomb load twice as far, though the even bigger, longer ranged and faster B-29 was beginning to enter service. Unlike fighter squadrons, which could get by with a steady stream of replacement pilots and planes, bombers required the extensive training of an entire crew—and on the B-24, that meant eight to ten people—a group that not only had to know their individual jobs, but had to coordinate those activities with everyone else and in some cases take over those other jobs if a crewman was killed or wounded. Thus pilots had to know how to navigate over water and operate the Norden bomb site, as well as fire the waist gun and one of the turret-mounted machine guns that defended the ship. Other crewmen pitched in at other positions, but the demands on the pilot were a lot more than I'd imagined. Thus our "phase training," as it was called, was as much about learning to work as a team—in some cases pitching and catching *while* you were playing first base—as it was about taking off and landing a four-engine monster.

My first surprise upon arriving at March Field was to be told that, even though I was an instructor pilot with several thousand flying hours, my duty station would be copilot. That meant that the first pilot, or aircraft commander—the "AC," my boss in the air—would be a recent pilot training graduate who had just finished bomber school, adding maybe another 150 hours to the 100 or so he'd received from instructors like me. This didn't sit well with the other IP's who'd received similar bomber assignments, but it had a certain logic and, when you thought about it, was probably a smart way to go. For one thing, flying a big, multi-engine bomber is a lot different than zipping around in a single-engine trainer. These were serious war machines that often had unusual and dangerous flight characteristics. Old reflexes and old habits that might serve you well in an AT-6 would only get you into trouble if you relied on them at the wrong time, or under the wrong conditions. Second, flying eight or ten hour missions over thousands of miles of ocean, in all kinds of weather, was a lot different that beating around the pattern at the home 'drome or doing loops in the local practice area. Add to that things like bad guys shooting at you from fighters or on the ground, and you found you were in a whole new ball game. Besides, training a crew meant building a team, and that meant knowing each other's strengths and weaknesses and flying your missions accordingly. If the low-time aircraft commander was smart, he'd be happy to have an experienced IP in the right seat, ready to help him out.

Unfortunately, a significant number of the IP's that arrived with me at March decided that they wouldn't go along with the program and tried to transfer out. That immediately established bad-blood between the two guys who should cooperate the most on a plane like this: the pilots. Not a good way to go into battle.

Maybe I lucked out, but my AC—a first lieutenant named Burrell Fletcher (we called him "Buzz")—was former artillery officer who had seen combat as a ground-pounder and put in for the Air Corps. He was accepted and had just finished bomber orientation school when he was assigned to B-24s. Buzz was a southerner, like Bill, and pretty easy going, so we got along fine. He said up front that he appreciated my experienced and would make the most of it in the air. That philosophy was put to the test a lot sooner than we expected.

Among the many phase-training maneuvers we had to master were formation takeoffs, not only in daylight, but at night. These can be tough enough in single-engine airplanes, which on conventional runways might takeoff in flights of four. But when you're talking about B-24s, even a two-ship formation means *eight* big Pratt & Whitney R-1830 Wasp powerplants revving up, and that generates lots of prop wash. This "dirty air" then creates turbulence for the wingman and all the airplanes behind him. Just getting airborne under such conditions is sometimes the hardest part of the mission.

On this particular flight, we were downwind, just to the side and slightly behind, another B-24 which itself had to follow another pair of bombers off the runway. Buzz advanced the throttles, beginning our takeoff roll, and I covered his knuckles with my hand, which was standard procedure. Even on the ground I could tell the takeoff would be a rough one, because the prop wash began jolting us even before the airplane started to move. I kept my right hand on the yoke, the airplane's "steering wheel," to help the AC if he needed it.

The lead ship broke ground and started to climb. We lifted off, too, but didn't climb nearly as fast. The ship stayed on the deck, bucking and rolling as if in a thunderstorm. We just weren't gaining altitude, even at max power.

Now, the novice pilot's impulse at moments like this is to keep pulling back on the yoke, forcing the nose higher. Unfortunately, if the nose gets too high and the airplane is going slow—as it does on takeoff—the wing stalls and quits flying. When that happens, you drop like a rock, crash, and burn up. At this particular moment, with Buzz pulling back on the wheel, the airplane shuddering, our airspeed dropping, and our rate of climb passing zero on its way down, I knew we were headed "south." In a matter of seconds, we'd be a big smoking hole in the runway. I could see from the look on his face—that gaping mouth, those big round eyes—that he was quickly running out of ideas as well as altitude and airspeed.

Pete (kneeling, 2nd from left) with his B-24 crew at March Field, 1945. Captain Fletcher is on Pete's right.

Without saying anything, I gently pushed the yoke forward, just enough to get us out of the fast-approaching stall. He kept his hands on the wheel but didn't resist or pull back, despite the fact that the windscreen was quickly filling with runway. Our airspeed began to build. As it did, I gently pulled back on the yoke and our grateful bird began a modest climb. When we had a sustained, positive rate of climb, I raised the gear. The departure end of the runway flashed past and we were still climbing and accelerating. The lead ship in our formation now came into view, ahead and well above us, but we were closing. I gave the wheel a little wiggle and removed my hands. Buzz knew he had the airplane again. Instead of "Thanks, Pete," he merely gave the command, "Flaps up," which I was happy to obey. After all, that's what copilots do.

After we landed, the flight engineer (who sat behind and between the pilots, in reach of the throttle quadrant) came up to me and said, "Lieutenant Wurts, thanks for saving our butts. I guess we know who to count on when things get tough. As long as you're on board, I'll always feel safe in this airplane."

That was a great compliment, though I didn't have the heart to tell him that whatever bad happened to him in a crash would happen to me first, at least by a split second or two, so I was as motivated as anyone to keep our aluminum overcast flying. I also took it as a compliment to our aircraft commander, who could have ridden his rank and his pride into the ground, taking all of us with him, but he didn't.

My second near-miss in the Liberator occurred during another stage of training in over-water navigation. These missions were run strictly to benefit our navigator—in this case, Ed Berger, a novice second lieutenant—who plotted a series of courses over the ocean, which we flew for several hours, after which he'd guide us back to home base. Most pilots hated these, since there was nothing for us to do but periodically change altitude and heading and try to keep from falling asleep. We flew these missions with a minimum crew—no gunners or bombardier, not even any bombs—just two pilots, the flight engineer, the navigator, and enough fuel to get us out and back with a modest reserve. In this case, drowsiness turned out to be the least of our worries.

About 500 miles out to sea, our number one engine—that is, the outboard engine on the left wing—conked out; simply quit running, so we shut it down and feathered the propeller. We had practiced engine-out landings before, and the airplane flew fine on three engines—especially with a light fuel load—so we felt kind of glad for the diversion and a chance to earn our pay. Though we weren't quite finished with the navigator's profile, we aborted the mission and headed back toward March Field.

Unfortunately, about half-way back, the number two engine (the inboard engine on the same wing) also failed, suddenly leaving us with two engines on an airplane designed to work best with four. Even worse, when two engines fail on the same side, it means all your thrust has to come from the opposite wing. At high power settings and low airspeed—like making a go-around from a missed approach—lateral control becomes a real problem as those big propellers try to make the airplane do cartwheels; and when you run out of rudder to compensate, it sometimes does.

We now declared an emergency and told the navigator to plot an immediate course for the nearest airport, which at this point was Lindbergh Field in San Diego. The captain and I dug out our charts—neither of us had been there before, let alone landed a disabled airplane on its runway in the middle of the night. The oceanic air controller said he was dispatching an amphibious rescue plane—probably a PBY Catalina—to intercept us and escort us in, standing by if we had to ditch, but even on two engines we were a whole lot faster than a flying boat, so we knew that if we were going to make it home with dry boots, it would have to be on our own.

Fortunately, as I said, the airplane was light and we were able to maintain altitude and airspeed with no problems. We crossed the coast line and spotted the runway, and were told to make our landing east to west, which meant flying inland for a few miles then turning back, making our final approach over the city. Now, the layout of Lindbergh Field is very peculiar and certainly wouldn't pass muster if it was being built today. While the runway is fine, the final approach course descends at the same angle as the surrounding, sloping terrain. That means that as you descend and look out to the side, the ground appears to be staying level—especially at night, when your only outside reference, besides the runway, are city lights, which feel close enough to touch. This was very disconcerting to the pair of us, who were already a little rattled at the prospect of *maybe* having to make a go-around on two engines—a very chancy maneuver.

Long-story short, we landed safely after giving our right legs a workout on the rudder. We had to remain in San Diego over night, which was kind of a bonus, though we didn't have time to sightsee and were told to report to the terminal bright and early the next day to be picked up by an Air Corps shuttle plane for the short flight back to March. While we waited, the airport snack truck came around. We hadn't had breakfast, so we each bought rolls and coffee or some other snack. Our navigator, Ed—the "Magellan" whose mission got us into this pickle (though we could hardly blame him for failed engines)—bought a single-serving, packaged apple pie. We sat down on the ramp and were eating our breakfast when he complained, "Boy, these pre-made pies sure are terrible. This crust tastes like cardboard!"

He held up the pie and sure enough, he was right. He was eating the pie-plate as well as the pie.

Fortunately, we would not have to rely on Ed's "good luck" (over-water or at the snack bar) much longer. A few weeks before VJ Day, twelve other copilots and I—all former IP's—were told we had been promoted to First Pilot and would be transferred to Liberal, Kansas, for aircraft commander qualification training. This was good news, I suppose, but by then we'd been positioned at Gowen Field in preparation for departure to the Pacific, and I was perfectly happy to go overseas with the crew I'd trained with, even if it meant remaining in the right seat.

Still, orders were orders and it was not the first time Uncle Sam and I disagreed about the best use of my time. A special sleeping car for us was attached to a passenger train, and as we passed through Denver, our car was decoupled and placed on a siding to wait for a different train that would take us into Kansas. While we were waiting, we listened to the radio, and to our delight (and, I admit, with some mild but passing disappointment) we learned that the Japanese surrender was imminent. We'd already been told that all military bases would be "locked down" and all leaves and town passes cancelled as soon as the surrender was announced. The Army and Navy didn't want mass disorder—or mass desertions—of troops who suddenly decided they'd done their duty and it was time to celebrate or go home.

So I thought of Bill, cooling his heels on the blistering desert at Douglas, while we B-24 pilots "in transit" remained pretty much on our own with a big city out there just waiting to entertain us. Since there was nobody around to give or deny permission, four of us simply walked from the railroad yard into town, in uniform, and had dinner at a Chinese restaurant. While we were there, the surrender announcement came over the radio. You forget it was a world war until you see how other nationalities—in this case, Chinese waiters and bus boys—acted when they knew their homelands were finally safe. It was like New Year's Eve. They said our meal was on the house and when we went into the street, traffic was grid-locked with horns honking, people laughing and clapping, hugging and kissing. We started down the sidewalk and at the first car we passed, the driver rolled down the window and held out a bottle.

"Hey, buddies!' he yelled, "Step into the car and help us celebrate!"

Like obedient soldiers, we did, and the girls in the back seat made us feel even more welcome. It now occurred to us that, as four of maybe a hundred uniformed service men in the whole city of Denver, we had lucked into something good. We thanked our host for the drink and got out, only to be swarmed by more grateful citizens who gave us hearty hugs and handshakes and forced us to swig more booze from bottles and hip flasks, and honor their wives and daughters with a smooch. All I can say is that what you may have seen or heard about all the hoopla on VJ Day is completely and totally accurate. We didn't have the guts to tell the good citizens of Denver that it wasn't we four who stormed the sands of Iwo Jima or the beaches at Normandy. We'd done our part, yes, and were ready to do more but the world had finally said "enough!" To the happy crowd in Denver that balmy evening, we *were* their overseas sons and brothers and husbands—the ones they'd see again and the ones who would never come back. Even if we hadn't felt like celebrating, acknowledging their relief and giving them an object to express all those pent-up feelings seemed like a duty that went with the uniform. From one perspective, it may have been one of the more important things we'd done since putting it on.

✪ ✪ ✪

Wars start with a bang but seem to end with a whimper. After August 14, 1945, America and its allies still had millions of men and women in uniform, two conquered nations to occupy, millions of displaced people to care for, and a dozen shattered economies to rebuild. If U.S. servicemen and their families thought the weeks and months after VJ Day would be filled with champaign and caviar, they were sorely mistaken. In its own methodical way, and in its own sweet time, the military had to disassemble the massive juggernaut it had put together. Fortunately or unfortunately, we were still cogs in that machinery.

PJW: After our big night in Denver, a new train arrived to pick up our sleeping car. Thank goodness for those fold-out beds—we really needed them.

Around dusk, we arrived at Liberal, Kansas, a sleepy farming community and were met by a small crowd at the station. It had been a day or two since the big announcement, and people were still in a buoyant mood, but this was a pretty big gathering for a pretty small town and we wondered if some Hollywood celebrity or political big shot was on the train, so we asked a couple of locals about the gathering.

"Shucks," one friendly guy answered, "it's sundown! We always come down to the station and watch the train come in!"

Welcome to Middle America!

After a month or two twiddling our thumbs at Gowen Field (most flying was curtailed for obvious reasons—when that budget axe falls, it chops fast!), "First Lt. Peter J. Wurts" was presented with his discharge papers and a train ticket to Tempe, Arizona. It was Army policy to return all separating personnel to their point of enlistment, even if their immediate families, like mine, lived in another state. It was up to us to arrange our own reunion, pay dependent moving expenses, find housing, and go hunting for peacetime jobs. I was getting used to the Army taking care of us and kind of wondered what happened to F.D.R.'s "welfare state" that my Dad was always complaining about.

Welcome to the post-war world!

✪ ✪ ✪

WRY: With the war over, I thought my assignment as aerial ambassador to China would end. No such luck.

In the fall of 1945, I was transferred to Enid, Oklahoma, along with our contingent of Chinese pilots. With all that flat land and all those section lines to keep you oriented, you'd think flying there would be snap—which it probably was in spring and summer; but in the winter, it looked like Greenland: one of bleakest landscapes imaginable, with snow and ice for as far as you can see, and freezing rain made even driving to the base from our little, rented shack a big adventure. By now, Marian's mother had moved in with us, along with another IP and his wife who were looking for scarce housing. Since we couldn't train in bad weather, we spent most of our time in Enid trying to stay warm and avoid stumbling over each other. We were a tribe of hillbillies without the hills, and I'll tell you, it got old real fast!

Fortunately, my assignment in Oklahoma didn't last long. Like most other servicemen, I had the option of getting out, but I really liked flying and the military still had the best equipment around—plus, they paid me to fly it! So I decided to stay in. Fortunately, too, Uncle Sam still had plenty of work for me to do.

Early in 1946, Marian, our son Bill Jr., my mother-in-law, and I moved to Macon, Georgia—a decided warmer place. We qualified for base housing at Warner-Robbins, a huge facility where surplus warplanes arrived daily from all theaters for repositioning or decommissioning. The Army gave me two jobs. One was as an instrument instructor making sure the military pilots on base flew their minimum hours under the hood, or in the clouds, to stay current in instrument flying. My second job was something new and much better—as an operations officer—the guy who scheduled and coordinated the use of all the aircraft on the base. I felt like a kid in a candy store. Here I was, at one of the few places on the planet where famous planes of every type arrived each day, most with no specific assignment other than to look pretty on the ramp and be ready to fly when I (or a handful of other privileged pilots) decided to take them up.

The first plane I tried out was the legendary P-47D Thunderbolt, affectionately nick-named the Jug, made by Republic "iron works" (so-called because the aircraft they built were so durable—a polite way of saying *heavy*). Its powerplant was a single Pratt & Whitney R-2800, huge for its day, making the airplane designed to carry it one of the biggest fighters of the war. The RAF pilots used to kid their American counterparts: "If Jerry ever shoots at you in a Jug, just dodge around inside the fuselage." Like the P-51, which I also met at Warner-Robbins and would get to know real well over the coming years, it had a bubble canopy that gave a superb view in all directions. It wasn't a dog-fighter—most enemy planes could out-turn it; but for speed, rate of climb and dive, as well as high altitude capability, it flew almost like a jet. I thought it handled well and understood why, a decade later, it was still in service with a number of Air Guard units.

At the other end of the spectrum, both in performance and in my personal preference, was the venerable C-45, or Twin Beech, a small, twin-engine utility craft used for hauling VIPs and priority cargo, as well as proficiency training. It flew well for what it was, but that short-coupled fuselage was hard to handle on the runway, explaining its unusually large number of ground loops and takeoff and landing accidents. I found something to like with most airplanes, but this was one bird that—as far as I was concerned—probably should've been left on the drawing board.

One of my favorites, though, was the least glamorous bird on the ramp, the good old C-47 made by Douglas—the military version of their famous DC-3 airliner. Affectionately called the Gooney Bird because of her ungainly appearance, she flew like a lark, was as rugged as the P-47, and extremely reliable. Because of her conventional gear (the Goon was a tail-dragger), modest size and low stalling speed, she could haul a fair amount of cargo or passengers and still land just about anywhere. If you had to name one workhorse that helped most to end the war, the Gooney Bird was probably it. We used our C-47s whenever we could, taking the base's top brass, visiting dignitaries, and furloughed airmen all over the country.

Back on the ground, one of my earliest—and it turned out, one of my strangest—duties was to edit the miles and miles of combat camera footage that came in from our bases around the world, but mostly from Europe. Every time a fighter pilot pulls the trigger, it activates cine cameras in the wing. This film is developed right after each mission; partly to confirm or interpret the pilot's post-flight debriefing (enemy planes shot down, trains destroyed, that kind of thing) but also to glean other intelligence, such as troop or vehicle movements that the pilot may have missed but the camera caught. Not long before VE day, a new enemy aircraft, the first operational jet fighter, the Me-262, was first documented that way as it sliced through our bomber formations at astonishing speed, showing up clearly only on gun camera film. I mention all this because these reels and reels of combat footage at Warner-Robbins had to be checked for continuity, or anomalies, before going into the national archives. One day, we "movie critics" got more than we bargained for.

I had two assistants who worked with me—one to run the projector, the other to take notes and keep records. Both were WACs, or female members of the Women's Army Corps. They were sweet, cheerful ladies and very diligent so we got along great, despite the mind-numbing procession of grainy, jumpy, black-and-white pictures that usually showed little more than a few dark blobs against the clouds, distant farmland, and tracers. One reel, however, was totally different and it took us a full minute, jaws dropped, to figure out what we were seeing. Some enterprising ground crewmen servicing the planes at one of the bases had liberated a gun camera for a day, or overnight, to make a little home movie: an amateur "stag film" film (with the emphasis on *amateur*), apparently using GI's and local girls as actors. When it finally dawned on us what we were seeing, the WACs turned beet red, laughed, and covered their mouths (but not their eyes) in astonishment. Chagrined on behalf of all my male Air Corps comrades, I said my assistant could stop the film and rewind it—we pretty much knew what was on the rest of the reel.

I didn't make a big deal over the incident or report it to anyone. The MP's could have probably traced the film to its source and put somebody in jail—but I just took it off the projector, destroyed it, and pressed on with the remaining million cans of film we had to review. I figured troops like that probably had enough problems during their tour and didn't need more trouble from me now that the war was over.

I stayed on active duty until 1947, then decided to call it quits. Marian and I had a second child, a daughter we named Regina Ann, who was born in Marian's home town of Brooksville, Florida, where the Army deposited me after my discharge. Fuller offered me a job at the quarry, but somehow—now that flying was under my skin—driving a bulldozer just didn't warm my cockles.

By the end of the year, though, President Truman had created a new branch of the service called *The United States Air Force* out of the remains of the old Army Air Corps. Air power had played a big role—perhaps the decisive role—in winning World War II and with the Soviets beginning to crack down on their conquered territories, threatening their neighbors, the powers-that-be (wisely, for a change) thought that America shouldn't neglect this new and vital combat function. Air Force Reserve units sprang up all over the country, including one in Jacksonville, Florida, composed entirely of personnel recently discharged from the service. They only had a few well-worn AT-6s on hand for proficiency flying, but that was good enough for me. We made the move to Jacksonville and I signed again on the dotted line—but this time as a part-time reservist.

It didn't pay much, so to make ends meet I found work as a flight instructor (again!) at a civilian seaplane base and Piper distributorship called Skytel, located on the St. John River near the heart of Jacksonville. We flew J-3 Piper Cubs what, until the appearance of the popular Cessna a decade later, was the poster plane for private pilots after the war. Half our planes were on floats—canoe-shaped pontoons that allowed us to takeoff and land on water—and I had never done that before. Fortunately, one of my buddies from the AF Reserve, Warren Spratt, already worked at Skytel, gave me some orientation, and I picked up the drill pretty fast. Soon, thanks to the GI Bill that gave returning soldiers and sailors free money for higher education or occupational training, our classroom and planes were full.

About this time, a former Navy amphibian driver, a PBY Catalina pilot named Bill Haviland, arrived on the scene. Although he hadn't seen much action or achieved high rank, he was well-connected politically. His wife was heiress to the Colliers publishing empire, and that gave her husband, a savvy and ambitious guy, a lot of clout in state government. Because the National Guard had been around for hundreds of years and was always part of the Army, many state governors and congressional representatives felt that the new Air Force deserved a new Guard component of its own. Thus, about the time Army flyers gave up their khaki uniforms for Air Force blue, the Air National Guard was established. Because Bill Haviland liked to fly and knew all the right people, he lobbied state and national officials to create Florida's first Air Guard unit—equipped with P-51s, no less, though Haviland himself had never flown anything faster than a trainer. He was promoted from lieutenant to lieutenant colonel and given command of the unit. It was a fateful move.

I wasted no time transferring my paperwork from the Reserves to the new Guard unit. My fingers were itching to get a hold of one of those beautiful new Mustangs just back from Europe or the Pacific with hardly a scratch on 'em.

Life was good. I assumed it would stay that way forever.

3

LOGGING TIME
BETWEEN THE WARS

—

W e stayed in touch as best we could after the war, though we spent most of the mid-1940s at opposite ends of the country. We each had new families to raise: Bill with two kids and Pete with one. We both lived smack in the middle of our in-laws, too; Pete in Phoenix, near Mesa where Maxine's folks lived—as well as his own two brothers, who settled in Arizona along with his parents. Bill stayed in central Florida. Marian thought that was to be near her mom, who was now a family fixture, but we knew it was because of the flying. To tell the truth, despite his new job as a Phoenix policeman and investment in a surplus Ryan (a low-wing, fixed-gear trainer popular with civilians) Pete was getting antsy for a military cockpit.

PJW: After my discharge, I had to find something to do. I still loved flying, but flyers were a dime a dozen and I wasn't interested (at the time, at least) in going back into the active-duty AAF or trying to eke out a living as a commercial pilot giving lessons or taking bigwigs on chartered flights. And since these were the days before airline pilots got paid like doctors, those jobs didn't interest me either—assuming I could even get one, since so many former military pilots were flooding the market. I was a member of the Air Corp's active reserve, which had a couple of AT-6s at Luke, but the "organization" was so disorganized that I seldom went out to fly, settling instead on a vintage Ryan trainer (which I bought for little more than its scrap value) to satisfy my occasional itch to get into the air. The bottom line was I wanted to try something different, though I had no idea what that something might be.

In that frame of mind, I spotted a newspaper ad in the fall of '45 announcing that the Phoenix Police Department was hiring new officers. No experience was necessary—you just had to pass a civil-service exam that, as it turns out, was being given later that week. I'd known a few peace officers before the war—Arizona Highway Patrolmen, Mesa cops, and such—and they seemed like nice guys and always had great stories to tell. Plus, I was used to wearing a uniform and couldn't stand the idea of a 9-to-5 job in an office. So on the day of the exam, I showed up with my sharpened number 2 pencil and gave it a whirl.

There was a lot of competition—the room was full. In fact, some of the candidates were temporary patrolmen trying to qualify for full-time jobs! But they graded the tests and I came out on top—literally, first in the class. The officer running the recruitment called me immediately.

"Congratulations, Pete. You're now a Phoenix police officer, if you still want the job."

"Sure!" I said, wondering when I would go to the police academy, how long it would take, and how hard the training would be.

"Great," he said. "Stop by the civil service building tomorrow and we'll find a uniform to fit you. By the way, do you own a .38-special revolver?"

"Um, no..." I had returned my aircrew sidearm to the government.

"Well, no problem. I'm sure we can get one from the city auditor. Just be sure you show up on time for your first shift. You start at 10 PM this Saturday."

That was it. No classroom training, no weapons qualification, no nothing. Just put on your badge and go to work. What had I gotten myself into?

Well, Phoenix after the war was a bit like the old west in some ways, but law enforcement wasn't as casual as that phone call suggested. They assigned me to an experienced partner who gave me as much on-the-job training as each shift allowed; but mostly he told me to just watch what he did, listen to what he said, and do likewise. After a few months I eventually went through "the academy," which was a series of classes given by FBI agents to local police covering finer points of the law, including jurisdictional and constitutional issues, and a smattering of advanced police tactics. But when it came to using the tools of your trade: how to handcuff a belligerent, drunken prisoner, when and how to use your nightstick, and all that,

TOP: Pete takes a friend for a ride in his surplus Ryan. Once, flying against strong headwinds through Indio's Banning Pass, the Ryan actually tracked backward.

LEFT: Pete served with the Phoenix Police from the end of '45 to the beginning of '47.

it was pretty much left to the example and patience of your senior partner. While some of those lessons were scary and painful, the job had its lighter moments—occasionally both at once.

For example, my first felony arrest came during my probation. We answered a call about a double knifing; one victim was seriously wounded, the other man's injuries were superficial and he gave us a good description of the suspect. My partner told me to handcuff the injured man and take him back to the squad car (which was some distance away) and use the radio to call an ambulance and notify the detectives. While I did this, a guy matching the suspect's description popped out of the bushes and ran down the sidewalk. I dropped the mike and gave chase, tackling the guy and putting him, too, in handcuffs. I now had two men in custody, including the major suspect, all by myself when the detectives pulled up and piled out of their unmarked car. I felt like Rookie of the Year or Sergeant York as I gave them a debriefing and they took charge of the case. Later on, when I read the detective's report, it sounded like they arrived just in time to apprehend the suspect and took credit for the whole thing. Welcome to real-world police work!

I had to fire my revolver twice in the line of duty, which was a lot considering I only spent two years on the force and many officers (at least in those days) never unholstered their weapon except on the firing range. The first time was after a felony hit-and-run accident in which the driver of the car in front of us hit a pedestrian, knocking him a hundred feet and delivering what was obviously major traumatic injuries (in fact, the impact killed him) then bailed out of his car and tried to flee the scene. My partner and I abandoned our squad car and gave chase on foot. The suspect had a good lead and was pretty fast—faster than us, with all our equipment—so my partner drew his revolver and began firing. This seemed a little excessive; after all, although we knew the guy was guilty, we didn't know if he was armed, and he seemed more anxious to avoid arrest than commit more mayhem—but I was the rookie and my partner was the veteran and I was told to do whatever he did, so I drew my .38 and banged away. We didn't hit him—or anybody else, thank God (those .38-Special slugs were notorious for shooting through walls and scaring, if not injuring, innocent bystanders)—so I guess both we and the perpetrator got lucky. We put out an APB for the guy, but I don't remember if he was captured. Given our quick resort to deadly force, though, he probably avoided anyone who even *looked* like a peace officer until he could get out of Arizona.

The second and last time I fired my weapon on duty was in a gun fight worthy of the old frontier. My partner and I responded to an "all units" dispatch to a commercial building where a pair of major bad guys wanted for armed robbery and murder had been trapped by detectives and decided to shoot it out. Actually, the suspects were a man and a woman—a kind-of modern Bonnie & Clyde—passing through Phoenix from out of state. At least 15 officers responded, screeching to a stop and fanning out behind their squad car doors. We didn't have rapid-fire, high-capacity rifles in those days, let alone a SWAT team—just our service revolvers and a pump-action 12-gauge shotgun (often called a "riot gun") in each car—so we had to blast away with what we had which, despite our numbers, didn't seem to be enough. Still, like so many professional criminals, these two were dangerous but not suicidal. When it was clear they were surrounded with no way out, they threw out their guns and surrendered. They were extradited and probably spent the rest of their lives in prison, or on the short list for some gas chamber.

One of my scariest calls didn't involve gunplay at all—at least on my part. We were dispatched to the Phoenix railway station after the conductor of an inbound train reported a passenger behaving erratically. When we arrived, two detectives were already on the scene, waiting for the train to pull in. They hadn't been called, but sometimes detectives just hung around train and bus stations, since those were good places to spot wanted criminals. Anyway, the train stopped and the conductor, seeing our uniforms, showed us the car, described the suspect, and told us what seat he was in. He said the fellow was acting "very weird" and he (and a lot of passengers) just wanted him off the train.

My partner, a great guy named Clarence Meyers (who became a good friend and helped me get back into aviation), and I entered the car from one end, the detectives from the other. The suspect was sitting in the middle of the car, saw our uniforms, then immediately drew a large knife. He jumped into the aisle and started running the other way, slashing people on either side as he went. Clarence was in front of me—a tall, wide-shouldered man—and drew his gun, a .45-caliber semi-automatic like the ones issued by the Army. Unfortunately, these big-bore man-stoppers were forbidden for police to carry, and I was about to find out why. He chambered a round and was about to drop the slasher but his auto-loader had jammed. By this time, I had my revolver out, but I couldn't get around those broad shoulders and get a clear shot. The next thing I heard were two loud *bangs* and the knife-wielder was on the floor, mortally wounded. A detective at the other end of the car had shot him. We checked the injured citizens but none of the wounds seemed bad, though they all got medical attention. I never found out what the guy's problem was. He may have been wanted for some serious crime or he may have just gone nuts. You got both kinds in this job.

On the lighter side, police work, like flying, can be characterized as hours of boredom punctuated by moments of stark terror—or humor—so when things got slow, especially on the night shift, we found ways to amuse ourselves. One of my first partners, Fred Green, and I used to drive the squad car to the city limits, take our flashlights, and hunt rabbits with our official "riot gun." Occasionally, a citizen would phone the police and report "gunshots in the area." Because it was in our sector, we got the call and knew what it was. After a decent interval to simulate an investigation, we told the dispatcher we didn't find any evidence of foul play— which was technically true—and if the citizen called again, to tell them it must have been a car backfiring.

Sometimes, our sense of humor involved our colleagues who, more often than not, repaid our practical jokes in kind. Late one night, we spotted a paddy wagon parked at a doughnut shop—two officers we knew were having coffee. It was an opportunity we couldn't pass up. The doughnut place was across the street from a bar, which had just closed, so their trash bin was full of empty liquor bottles. We each grabbed an armful, entered the paddy wagon from the passenger's side, then stacked the bottles between the driver's seat and the door, so when it opened, the bottles would tumble out, crash onto the pavement, and (with any luck) draw an embarrassing crowd. We then tiptoed back to our squad car, which was parked down the street, and watched everything unfold as planned. After the last bottle broke, the officers naturally looked around and saw us drive off, so we were sure they knew who to blame. The next night, we returned to our squad car after breaking for dinner to discover that the whole front seat had been removed. We paused for a second, looked at each other over the top of the car, and had exactly the same thought. *Those guys are probably watching us right now! Let's not give them the satisfaction!* So we just got a box of road flares out of the trunk, put it on the floor behind the steering wheel, and drove back to the station. Since this was the night shift and the motor pool office was closed, we just left the seat-less vehicle in the parking lot and took another squad car to finish our shift. We could only imagine what the mechanics thought when they discovered the car the next morning; but nobody in the briefing room brought it up, least of all our "victims" who were only paying us back.

Most of the time, though, patrol duty kept us busy. Like flying, it demands your complete attention if you want to do it right. We were "first responders" to everything from traffic accidents to missing children, and the best stories were the ones that ended happily, though that wasn't always the case. One of my most satisfying moments came when I was driving home after a shift, still in uniform, and discovered two cute little kids—they couldn't have been more than four and five—walking down the sidewalk holding hands. Sweet as they looked, something told me things just weren't right: they weren't smiling, they were shabbily dressed, and I didn't see an adult within a mile of them.

I waited for a break in traffic then made a U-turn and pulled up to the curb beside the kids. I got out and identified myself as a policeman, which they could see by my uniform, and smiled and pleasantly shook each of their hands, which were filthy. The older one was a boy, the younger one was a girl and was his sister. The boy asked about my gun and I said it was "just for bad guys" and I asked if they were okay. They didn't answer, so I asked where they lived—were their parents around? Still no answer, so I asked them to come with me into the office of a nearby motel and had the desk clerk call the station. As it turned out, there was an APB on the kids—put out by their parents as missing children. Their address was a nearby public housing project.

I thanked the clerk, put the kids in my car, and drove them home. I escorted them to the front door of the apartment where they were greeted by a very worried mother. The father, who looked like he'd had a drink or two, seemed indifferent to the whole thing. The kids seemed happy enough to see them, though, so I didn't suspect child abuse—though their condition sure bordered on neglect. I asked the parents if I could come in and speak to them for a moment, and they agreed. I then read them the riot act about parental responsibility and told them that the next time a peace officer found their kids wandering in the street, I'd personally arrest them for child endangerment. I left feeling better, but with a nagging suspicion that I, or some other policeman, would be seeing them again.

One of my last calls was one of my worst. It was prom night in Phoenix and several high schools were having parties. We were called to an accident where a furniture van had run a red light and "T-boned" a sedan containing a teenaged boy and girl. The students had been drinking, there was no doubt about that—we saw a beer bottle they'd been sharing in the floor under the crumpled dashboard—but it didn't seem to have played a role in the accident. Witnesses said their car had entered the intersection normally—not speeding or driving erratically—when the moving van simply barreled out of the dark and creamed them. Both were pinned in the seat and suffered massive head trauma (their brains were clearly visible through partly crushed skulls) though both were still conscious and able to speak. The boy tried to tell us what happened but we just told him to stay quiet and wait for the ambulance. The girl, her pretty prom dressed soaked with her own blood, managed a sickly smile and asked for a cigarette. I didn't smoke but my partner did, so he obliged her. He put the lit cigarette between her lips but she died before taking a drag.

It was not the first fatal accident I had seen, and it wouldn't be the last, but it was the saddest—as these things always are when kids are involved. It probably registered somewhere in my subconscious that I wasn't cut out for twenty years of this. Busting bad guys is one thing, but police do a lot more for communities than catch bank robbers, and a lot of what they do, while necessary, is just plain awful. I didn't start looking for a new job, but my attitude by then was such that if the right opportunity came along, I'd sure take a closer look. As it turned out, that opportunity came sooner than I expected.

WRY: Warren and I had been flying for Skytel for about a year, having a ball with those little floatplanes, when the owners of the business decided they wanted to sell. Because the G.I. Bill picked up the tab for most of our students, business was booming and they were making a lot of money, but they were businessmen, not instructors, and when one of the original partners left, the other decided to cash out.

Warren asked if I wanted to go in with him to buy the business and I said, "Hell yes!" until we opened our wallets and moths flew out. We could each borrow a few thousand dollars from friends or family (I raised my share of the ante, $5,000, by borrowing from "good old Mr. McDonald," who had become a fine family friend), but at best our combined assets were only half of what we needed. We agreed that each of us would find an additional partner for our venture.

Warren came up with Frank Wilkinson, a former Navy man who lived in Jacksonville. He was a great guy, but not a pilot, which meant we'd have three-quarters of the cash we needed but only two who understood airplanes. The first person I thought of, naturally, was Pete. I picked up the phone and told him about our plan. He knew I'd been flying for Skytel and while he'd always listen politely to the stories of my adventures, he never seemed particularly interested in going back to general aviation, at least as a salaried instructor. Now, maybe because it was a chance to own the business or for some other reason, he got real excited and said to count him in. I think he was already packing his bags when he hung up the phone.

PJW: Bill's offer to become a partner in Skytel couldn't have come at a better time for me, emotionally, or a worse time, financially. Maxine and I had just bought our first house in Phoenix—in fact, we had just closed escrow and she was pregnant with our second child. I was off probation at the Department and had recently been reassigned—"promoted," they called it—off the night shift and was beginning to work civilized hours. Unlike most cops, though, I enjoyed the night shift. There was usually more action, at least until the bars closed, and working regular hours meant you had to deal with the Department's brass as well as the politicians and lawyers at the courthouse—for me, a real pain in the neck. Plus, Maxine had never lived in the south, though I had spent a lot of time in Florida as a kid, and the move would be very disruptive. Still, she knew I was getting stressed as a cop and that my first love would always be flying, so she agreed to give it a try. I borrowed the necessary $5,000 from my Dad, bless his heart, who also undertook to sell our new house in Phoenix—which went for less than we paid after you figured in the transaction costs, but it was worth it. Before you could say, "Switch on!" and "Contact!" we were packed and on our way.

*T*he seller of our new business was a fast-talking used car dealer named Jack La Rue. He had financed the purchase for his old partner, who happened to like airplanes, so when his friend got tired of aviation and moved on, La Rue had no reason to keep the operation. He liked the money the business made, but couldn't care less about the airplanes. He may also have been worried about the liabilities associated with flight operations, but that concern wasn't even a blip on our radar. We just wanted to fly and have a piece of the action. Now we had to figure out a way to make that happen.

Of course, we weren't seasoned businessmen, and when it came to negotiations, La Rue, a real sharpie, was out of our league. To compensate, Pete invited a friend of his from the Phoenix police force—a big guy but very distinguished looking, with gray hair and a calm, commanding manner—named Clarence Meyers to visit Florida and pose as our "financial advisor." After being introduced to La Rue, he sat in a corner and said nothing, just making notes and occasionally scratching his chin. At the end of each session, we thanked La Rue for his proposals, then said we'd talk them over with "our advisor." La Rue never knew what Clarence's background supposedly was, and maybe felt too intimidated to ask. Anyway, whenever we came back from one of our private "consultations" and told La Rue that his proposal, whatever it was, had to be better, he always gave in. We think Clarence saved us more money and got us more concessions just by sitting there and looking distinguished than a whole battery of high-priced lawyers.

Our new enterprise was a wonder to behold—a going, growing concern. Our hangar, operations building, and launching ramp were built on a former swamp, which was lousy for just about everything except float plane operations. It was right by a footbridge that connected our site to downtown Jacksonville, so it was easy to get to, and real estate developers would've grabbed it long ago had our conditional use permit not contained a "propeller-driven water craft" clause grand-fathered in when swamp buggies, not float planes, ruled the river. Our staff included 16 flight instructors—most former military—

Skytel Sea Plane Base in Jacksonville, FL.

plus three office girls who were in charge of payables, receivables, and smiling sweetly when our customers had a complaint.

We had 21 airplanes, almost all J-3s, about half of which were fitted with detachable pontoons, or floats, allowing them to take off and land on water. The land planes were kept at a small auxiliary field, called Mile Branch, which we leased from the Navy. For awhile, we kept a surplus Stearman and a nice little amphibian called a "Seabee"—a plane with a pusher prop and a boat-shaped fuselage with retractable wheels—there for students who wanted instruction in bigger aircraft. The runway at Mile Branch was only 1,500 feet long, but that was plenty for a Piper Cub and allowed us to issue land- as well as seaplane-ratings to our students—a big marketing advantage over the competition.

Located in the boondocks, just getting to Mile Branch was an adventure. It was surrounded by swamps filled with poachers and moonshiners. More than a few of our planes had potshots taken at them as we buzzed back and forth from Jacksonville. The locals thought we might be "damn revenoors" flying low and slow to sniff out their stills. They obviously didn't know much about airplanes. That's the only way J-3s fly.

One of our private pilot groups must have set some kind of record. It was composed entirely of ex-Navy personnel all of whom worked during the day. That meant they took their classroom and flying instruction only at night, including their check rides. Warren Spratt, our designated CAA examiner (a senior civilian instructor empowered by the Civil Aviation Administration to give pilot certification flight tests on their behalf), said ours was the first school to conduct an entire pilot training cycle at night, and we had no reason to doubt him.

Anyway, our business was booming and the four partners—Bill, Pete, Warren, and Frank—quickly made enough money to pay back our investors, with interest. We also had enough left over to invest in a luxury we had put off for far too long. Since early 1942, Detroit had stopped making new automobiles and commercial car production in the U.S. had resumed only in the last few years. We all felt our hard work and shrewd investing deserved some kind of reward, so one day when the weather was bad and all flights were cancelled, we gave the staff the day off and went into town to treat ourselves and our families to a new car. Part of the fun was that none of us told the others what kind of car we were buying—we wanted that to be a surprise when we all showed up for work the next morning; although as it turned out, two of us would be more surprised than the others, and *a whole lot sooner.*

Pete went out and bought a Buick. Bill bought a new Ford. Warren and Frank went to a different part of town and drove their new Studebaker and Dodge, respectively, proudly off different lots. The problem was, they left the dealerships at about the same time and lived in approximately the same part of town. As they neared their neighborhood, they came to an uncontrolled intersection at precisely the same time and, being too busy tuning the radio or testing the windshield wipers or whatever, they banged into each other in the middle of the street. It was a good fender-bender: not enough to hurt them, but it drew a crowd. They both got out, as drivers usually do at such moments, and examined the damage to their beloved cars. When they finished, they turned to "that other idiot"— intending to sort out who was at fault—and recognized each other from Skytel. All they could do was stare for a second, then clap each other on the shoulder and sit on the curb, laughing hysterically until the police arrived. The crowd must've thought they were nuts— two guys banging up their brand-new cars, then laughing, not fighting, about it. Frank at least had an excuse to be inattentive—he wasn't a pilot; but we never let Warren—our ace flight examiner—forget the incident, or live it down.

Of course, driving while distracted can happen to anyone; it's what's doing the distracting and how you handle it that counts. Warren, it turns out, had a special flight later that week to scatter cremated ashes, or "cremains," over the Atlantic for a bereaved widow. Apparently the urn containing the ashes had been shipped to Jacksonville from out of state and the widow arrived with them in a parcel post box still wrapped with brown paper and string. It was late in the day and a tropical storm was moving in, so Warren— with as much compassion and sensitivity as he could muster—invited the lady along, advising her that with bad weather approaching, they'd have to expedite the ceremony.

They took off from the St. John River, and Warren, with one eye on the weather and the other on his sobbing passenger, pushed the little plane, one of our J-3s, as fast as it could go. All the way, the lady kept crying and relaying stories about her husband; it was obviously a very emotional moment for her. When they arrived at the designated scattering spot, Warren (seated in front) turned to face her and said the dispersal could begin. Unfortunately, the urn was still in the package, wrapped up tighter than a drum. The widow pulled at the strings but couldn't get them loose.

"Madam, I'm sorry," Warren said, tension rising in his voice as the black clouds *loomed ahead, "But we've really got to get this done!"*

"I can't, I just can't do it," the widow said.

"Here, give it to me. I'll take care of it!" Warren snatched the package just as rain began to pelt the plane. He gave the string a tug, saw that it was hopeless, then cracked the Cub's side door and threw the whole box out toward the whitecaps. He didn't wait to see it splash, but racked the plane into a diving turn back toward the mainland.

We were there when he landed and helped the widow out of the plane and into her car. She was still sobbing inconsolably as she drove away.

"Wow," one of us said to Warren, "that must've been some ride!"

"You have no idea," he answered.

PJW: Owning Skytel was like having our own private air force. CAA rules were minimal and we could pretty much do what we wanted. No two days were alike. We often flew our J-3s in formation, though mostly for our own amusement, since it wasn't part of the training curriculum. On one occasion, we got 16 ships airborne—all with ex-military instructors—and formed a gaggle which we flew over downtown Jacksonville. True, they weren't fast-and-flashy like military fighters, but 16 airplanes of any type will get your attention when they're flying close together. We considered it cheap advertising.

Once, however, our bold and intrepid airmanship almost cost us a plane. One of our senior instructors, an old Navy man, led a flight of three J-3s in a V-shaped formation along the St. John River a fair distance from the town. The river was often clogged with Hyacinths—a pretty flower that grew on the surface, but caused real problems for boats and power craft, like ours, that could get tangled in the stalks and leaves. It had been brought to Florida anonymously by someone returning from Asia. A few seeds or live plants were dumped in the water and they quickly took over the river. The state had been battling it ever since, and in this section of the river, we never landed because Hyacinths usually stretched from bank-to-bank.

Anyway, I was on one wing with an IP on the other while our fearless Naval aviator led us down the river at wave-top level. Every once in awhile, just for fun, he would drop down and let his floats skim a patch of open water, then pop back up a foot or two to clear the Hyacinths. He did that for a mile or so and I didn't think much about it. We wingmen held our altitude, keeping an eye on each other and a lookout for other airplanes, when our leader suddenly disappeared.

After blinking at the other wingman a second, I leaned forward and looked up, thinking perhaps our leader had somehow zoomed above the formation. He wasn't there. I twirled my finger at my companion and we peeled off in opposite directions. Just as I turned, I noticed a huge spray of water coming down on the river behind us. As the foam and mist cleared, a yellow J-3 on aluminum floats bobbed back to the surface, propeller still turning. The pilot gunned the engine and the little plane rocked back on its tail, then quickly gathered speed, shedding water as it went. A few seconds later it was airborne and skimming again down the river. The other pilot and I circled back and rejoined on his wing.

When we got back to the base, the other guy asked him, "What the hell happened to you?"

"Just snagged some weeds I guess," the Old Salt answered. "Everything was running okay, so I just took off."

That was the first and only time I'd seen an airplane become a submarine, then convert back to aeronautical use. They just don't make them like that any more—on either side of the controls.

WRY: Our students were an enthusiastic bunch. One of the biggest challenges for most beginners is flying at night, a little of which was required for a pilot's license even in those days. Our problem was that the J-3 was designed for day, contact (visual) flying only. It didn't have exterior position lights or navigation lights (heck, even small boats have those), or cockpit lighting. It didn't even have an electrical system, not even a battery for starting the engine. We also lacked an illuminated landing area—pretty helpful for putting a plane down in the dark. Our solution was to jury-rig all of these things ourselves.

To make the airplane nightworthy, we had our mechanics install a motorcycle battery under the pilot's seat and run nav lights out to the wing and tail. This would keep our planes from bumping into each other as they flew "the pattern"—really just a mile-and-a-half wide patch of sky over the river near the base. The battery didn't have enough juice to power a landing light, so we did without it. Personally, I told my students to make sure they were lined up over open water, then set up a slow but steady rate of descent—maybe a hundred feet per minute, until they hit the water—although we never used the word "hit" to describe a landing. To help our students see the instruments, such as they were, we rigged a red tail light from a bicycle over the panel, then powered it with a plain D-cell battery. Even then, they didn't have much to look at: just an airspeed indicator, altimeter, and magnetic compass—called a "whiskey" compass because it was just a magnetized compass card floating in a sealed liquid case.

We solved the "runway illumination" problem by floating a highway flare on a tiny buoy in the middle of the channel. This was a cheap and practical solution, but chancy. Any landing requires the pilot to orient the aircraft with respect to the landing surface, making sure that the plane arrives at the touchdown point going the right direction at the right airspeed, with enough room ahead to avoid any obstacles. In contact flying, this means you need to see the runway and position yourself beside it (called flying the downwind leg), then make a gentle, descending turn (base leg) onto final approach, landing into the wind to keep ground speed at a minimum. Good airports—like municipal fields and military bases—had substantial lighting that showed the outline of the runway, the final approach threshold, taxiways, and so on. With only a single flare pot and the distant lights of the city as a frame of reference, our students had to imagine all this in the watery darkness below. They didn't seem to mind; in fact they thought it was lots of fun. This was in stark contrast to most military fighter pilots—many of them WWII vets with lots of experience— who used to complain about the Air Force's periodic night flying requirements, and *they* had modern fighters with excellent lighting, electronic navigation aids, and a well-designed runway to land on. "If they want us to fly at night," they grumbled, "they should give us night fighters!" which were special aircraft, usually multi-engine, fitted with even more elaborate gear, like radar. So here were our Skytel students, who had little more than 20-hours of daylight instruction in a J-3 Cub, cranking their little planes around our flare pot night after night, with no accidents or incidents—and they loved it! We just had to make sure that our one highway flare stayed lit and they had extra flashlight batteries on the airplane.

One of our most hard-working and conscientious students was none other than Pete's Dad, Burkhardt Wurts—or "Sir" as Pete called him; "Mr. Wurts" to the rest of us. Pete's parents used to winter in West Palm Beach so they were familiar with Florida and enjoyed having a relative to visit. Since they stayed for several months, it gave Mr. Wurts Senior enough time to sign-up for, and complete, his private pilot's training. Although Pete's Dad had always been supportive of his son's aviation pursuits, he never showed much interest in flying himself, so his decision to enroll came as a surprise to us both. Pete thought he finally got curious enough about airplanes to see what all the shouting was about; or maybe, as a Skytel investor, he just wanted to see where his money had gone. Personally, having gotten to know Pete's Dad pretty well, I think he just saw it as a chance to share an activity with his oldest son, an activity he knew his son really loved. Whatever the reason, Pete insisted on giving his Dad every lesson himself, until it was time for his "graduation" flight check, which I administered as a friend of the family. Mr. Wurts Senior passed with flying colors.

My two main memories of the episode were his Dad's appearance; he always flew in a gray suit, necktie, and fedora, no matter how hot the weather. The other was Pete's demeanor during the whole experience; he was a nervous wreck.

PJW: I was glad I decided to teach my Dad to fly, though at the time I thought it was probably one of the dumbest things I'd ever done. As I've said, he was always a very formal man, though kind and considerate—a father that inspired affection as well as respect and obedience, though not always in that order. I could've asked another instructor to give him lessons. Bill certainly volunteered to do so, and I knew they got along well, but somehow I figured this was something I just had to do myself.

My mother, Muriel, was curiously silent about the whole adventure. She seldom came to the base and never watched him fly. I'm sure she was happy that my Dad and I were finally spending some time together after the long separations of the war. But I think she would've been happier if we'd taken up golf, or some other hobby less prone to disaster. My father may have had qualms about flying too, though he never showed it in the air. However, after receiving his private pilot's license, he just put it in a drawer and never touched a stick and throttle again. I

Pete gives his Dad instruction in the J-3. "I can't believe I just said that to my father!"

think he just wanted to prove that he could do it: not to me, but to himself.

The worst moments of his training came, as they did with any student, when he just couldn't get some maneuver right, no matter how many times we tried. The J-3 is a pretty simple plane; in fact, it's not much more than a lawn chair attached to a leaf-blowing motor, and I wasn't exactly preparing my Dad to shoot down Germans. Still, standards are standards and I wanted him to have the best training possible. I also found myself, in the heat of the moment, falling back on old habits learned after thousands of hours in BT-13s and AT-6s, where I had to deal with some world-class yo-yos who managed to slip through the Air Corp's cadet screening process.

"Okay," I'd say calmly, cooly, and respectfully, "let's make a steep level turn to the left."

He began a turn to the right.

"No, to the *other* left," my voice was a little firmer.

The plane tentatively dipped a wing to the left.

"Did you clear the air first? Remember how we check for other aircraft before we turn?"

The wing came up and I watched that familiar face—eyeglasses pinching that wonderful, bulbous nose, felt hat planted squarely on that close-cropped, Prussian haircut—lean into the left window and look around.

"It's clear," he rumbled in reply.

"Okay," I said, "let's turn. Sixty degrees. Nice and level."

He managed a tepid, shallow bank of about 15-degrees—but at least in the right direction.

"A *steep* turn," I repeated.

The angle of bank increased to a whole 25 degrees.

"A steep turn! Sixty-degrees! Like I showed you! And don't forget to add power!"

I grabbed the stick in the rear seat and snapped the wings to the desired angle, then pulled back to maintain altitude and jammed the throttle forward to hold our speed. The extra G pushed us deeper into our lawn chairs, a symbol of my despair as I thought, *Oh, Jeez—that's my* father *up there! What am I saying?*

Fortunately, he was a quick learner (or maybe he just got tired of my carping—we never charged him for a lesson, so maybe he assumed he was getting what he paid for) and seldom made the same mistake twice. Actually, he had a lot of aptitude for someone taking up flying so late in life, and I was always thankful that he never ran into the kinds of serious problems that sometimes grounded other students or caused them to quit. He soloed successfully—to my mother's great relief—and Bill gave him his flight check. I saw a hint of a smile on his face when he received his private pilot's license, then he folded it up, put it in his pocket, and—to the best of my knowledge—never looked at it again.

About this time Bill Haviland—now "Colonel Haviland"—organized the P-51 squadron at Jacksonville, Florida's first Air National Guard unit, and we both ran, not walked, to join it. With the shooting war over, most veterans just hung-up their flight jackets; the last thing they wanted was to risk their necks in high-performance planes now that they had families, new jobs, and mortgages, so most of that first bunch were pretty dedicated fliers. The two of us were so gung-ho, in fact, that we took demotions to second-lieutenants just to get into the cockpit. A lot of vets, too, didn't like the "Mickey Mouse" they remembered from military life—the hierarchy, the regimentation, the paperwork in triplicate—but that was pretty much overlooked in the new Air Guard. Sure, we still had uniforms and saluted superior officers, but discipline was relaxed and we could do pretty much what we wanted, especially in the air, as long as citizens didn't complain and we brought our airplanes back in one piece.

PJW: Although I'd spent lots of time in the AT-6 and had logged a few hours in the Dauntless and Helldiver (which nobody would ever confuse with mighty warbirds), I really didn't have much experience in fighters before joining the Florida Guard. These other planes were similar to first-line WWII fighters with big engines, conventional gear, and could be flown by one pilot; they just didn't have the romance and reputation of the war-winning P-51 with its streamlined, liquid-cooled Merlin engine, six wing-mounted .50 caliber machine guns, and low-drag laminar flow wing: a marvel of engineering and one reason the Mustang was so fast. It also had a notoriously high sink rate on final approach, didn't particularly like tight turns, and could swap ends if the aft fuselage fuel tank was full and you tried a high-G maneuver right after takeoff, so you had to be respectful of its quirks and foibles.

But like most young pilots my age, I was full of confidence and knew the Mustang was the airplane I was born to fly. I buckled on that parachute and put on my old leather helmet and cranked up that big Merlin (what a beautiful, distinctive growl!) and taxied out to the runway and lined up for my first takeoff. To be honest, I was expecting a more exciting ride than I got. That big, four-bladed prop produced a lot of torque; but frankly, the P-factor (or force that tries to pull a nose-high, prop-powered airplane off the side of the runway) was worse in the AT-6. I found the Mustang to be a real pleasure to fly and although it was SOP to make a "wheel landing" in the bird (that is, to contact the runway with the main gear first with a good margin above the stalling speed) I felt comfortable enough to make my first touchdown in a three-point attitude, just above a stall, which impressed several veteran P-51 pilots watching from the tower. Actually, the plane deserved most the credit: she was a real sweetheart in the air.

WRY: We had a great time in those P-51s, beating up the sky in mock dogfights and practicing air-to-ground gunnery. So between spending my weekdays skimming the water in our J-3s then defending the free world from Navy fliers and other Air Guard pilots on the weekends, I was in hog heaven. And just when I thought things couldn't get better, they did.

I said our commanding officer, Lt. Col. Bill Haviland, was a great politician, but that's an understatement. I didn't know how great until he announced one day in 1948 that our unit was one of three Air Guard squadrons in the country (the other two being in Nebraska and Maine) to get the new F-80 Shooting Star—the USAF's first operational jet fighter. Even better, ours would be the new C model, a version superior to the F-80As and Bs operated by the active-duty Air Force.

After brief, separate tours at Williams AFB in Arizona for F-80 transition

Pete after an early fam ride in a Florida ANG P-51.

LEFT: Bill (standing, left) checks his aerial gunnery score. Jack Nunnally (standing, right) also flew with the *Florida Rockets.* Another *Rocket,* Bud Haefel (kneeling) survived an airshow collision only to be killed in Korea.

BOTTOM: Higher, faster, but not necessarily farther: F-80s replace the Florida Guard's P-51s. Pete stares at all those "clocks and thermometers" during transition at Williams AFB, Arizona.

A cockpit view of the *Florida Rockets*—the FL-ANG's precision aerial demonstration team.

The men behind the magic of the *Florida Rockets,* from L to R, Bill Yoakley, Harry Howell, Bill Haviland, and Jack Nunnally. Bill and Harry wear infantry-style helmet liners—the new Air Force didn't have enough modern flight helmets to go around.

training, Pete and I (along with a couple of other experienced IP's) returned to Jacksonville ready to familiarize the other pilots with the unique and wonderful—and in many ways, much easier—world of jet-powered flight. The differences between a piston-powered plane and a jet were dramatic. While that big prop on the Mustang gave many pilots fits, there was no torque, or P-factor, in a jet, you could take off and land with both feet flat on the floor, using the rudder pedals primarily for nosewheel steering on the ground. There was also no vibration in a jet, so you whistled along at speeds unthinkable in a P-51 without a whole lot of shaking going on. The biggest drawback was acceleration. Despite all the thrust of that jet, it took time for an idling engine to "spool up," or reach a high enough RPM to put that thrust to work. With the Mustang's huge propeller disk, all the power of that big Merlin was instantly available to the pilot—pretty handy when you had to go around or hold airspeed in a turn. And since everything in the F-80 was done at a significantly higher speed, you had to think even farther ahead of the plane, though that same high speed meant the controls were more sensitive, making formation flying much easier.

Before long, we got so skilled in the new bird that Haviland—always on the lookout for a good PR opportunity—decided to form our own precision flying team, which he called the *Florida Rockets*. The only other group doing aerobatics in jets was back at Williams, where a few instructors had formed an F-80 "aerial demonstration" team called *The Acrojets*, which later became *The Thunderbirds*, the Air Force's analog to the Navy's *Blue Angels*, who were still flying piston-driven, carrier-based fighters. We thought our team was superior to either of these groups, flying tighter formation, making more dramatic maneuvers, and even throwing in a special solo routine by yours truly in a crowd-pleasing P-51.

My portion of the show didn't last long—about five minutes—but I used every second of it to do things even experienced P-51 drivers would never think of. After takeoff, I'd climb to 50 feet above the runway, roll inverted, and count to nine: "one thousand one, one thousand two," and so on, since that old Merlin would lose oil pressure after ten seconds of negative G. Just before that could happen, I'd roll upright and zoom into a Cuban 8—literally, a figure eight laid on its edge, with the airplane looping up one side, then instead of completing the loop, rolling over and doing a second loop in the opposite direction. Instead of a single roll, though, I'd give it two or three extra rolls between loops. Zooming down after the last loop, I'd pull straight up, rolling clockwise all the way, then when I ran out of airspeed, I'd fall off on one wing. After another inversion or two, I'd make a high-speed pass in front of the crowd, pull up, drop the landing gear during a slow roll, then pitch out and touch down at just above a stall, braking to a stop inside a thousand feet.

Pete, who flew one of Haviland's wings with the Red Rockets, always got very nervous when I did this part of the show—especially flying inverted at low altitude over the runway. Of course, while the maneuver wasn't for everyone, it looked more dangerous than it was because I took a lot of precautions when preparing the act. To be sure I could really nail that altitude when I was upside down, I'd practice over a level cloud deck whenever the weather cooperated. I'd put the spinner of the prop into the topmost cloud layer, then roll inverted and count to nine. If I couldn't see anything while I was upside down, then broke into the clear when I rolled right-side up, I knew my altitude control was okay. After doing this exercise until it became second nature, I got pretty good at both timing and holding level flight while inverted at low altitude. It was a stunt, I admit, and pretty useless for combat, but like any trick, it amazed a lot of people and worked only because of practice, practice, practice.

One viewer's appreciation was expressed in a most unusual way. The *Rockets* were flying at an air show in Terra Haute, Indiana. For some reason, I couldn't bring my usual P-51 up from Florida, so I asked to borrow a bird from the local Guard unit. This wasn't really kosher; I intended to put their plane through some paces that weren't exactly in the flight manual, so I didn't tell them what it was for. But the show must go on and we had a VIP in the audience, General Hoyt Vandenberg, the first commander of our new United States Air Force.

So I did my act, taxied back to the ramp, and shut down. Before the prop stopped turning, an Air Force Sergeant in dress blues was on the wing, shouting into the cockpit as I rolled the canopy back.

"Lieutenant Yoakley, General Vandenberg wants you to report to him immediately!"

Uh oh, I thought. *This is it.* Somebody with the Indiana Guard complained about my risking their bird, or the commanding general, in his wisdom, thought my routine showed more guts than brains.

I unstrapped and jumped into the sergeant's jeep. We dashed back to the grandstand where General Vandenberg was seated in a box with various dignitaries. I walked up and saluted smartly, grateful that I already had a civilian job to go back to.

He returned my salute and said, "Young man, that was the finest piece of flying I've ever seen. Keep up the good work." He then offered me his hand and I shook it. I saluted again and did a precise about-face, feeling like I'd just received the Medal of Honor. If any of the Indiana Guard headquarters types seated around the general had complaints about my methods, they sure weren't going to mention them now!

PJW: I flew with the *Rockets* a fairly short time. Bill stuck with them as left wingman (and was indispensable with his fabulous solo act in the P-51), as did Bud Haefel, who flew on Haviland's right. Jack Nunnally and Harry Howell, both fine pilots, alternated at slot (the center position, in close trail behind and slightly below the flight leader), and even our Guard unit's active-duty Air Force advisor, a Major Walker, joined in from time to time. I dropped out partly because I was busy with Skytel and couldn't put in the practice I felt was needed to stay proficient in our elaborate routines. I was also pretty uncomfortable with Bill Haviland flying lead. We got along personally, but he'd spent most of his career flying low-and-slow in a PBY. While being fine for its job as a sub-spotter and rescue ship, it just didn't develop the quick reflexes, judgment, and fine touch needed to perform jet aerobatics. And, contrary to popular belief, flying lead is the toughest position of all. It requires a lot of advance planning and a smooth hand on the controls, and poor Bill Haviland, in my opinion at least, came up short on both. Once, these shortcomings almost cost him his life.

On the last day of an airshow in Miami (a bad day for aerobatics anyway, with broken clouds and a lot of low-level turbulence) Haviland was leading the

TOP: Bill waits to perform his solo routine in a trusty P-51D. In the lower right, a newly arrived F-80C.

LEFT: Program for an air show in Terra Haute, Indiana, featuring the Florida Rockets. The artist apparently had to draw the new F-80 without ever having seen one.

Rockets out of a loop and abruptly leveled off to make a high-speed pass over the grandstand. Bud Haefel, who was an aggressive flier and had a habit (again, in my view) of flying formation a bit too close, couldn't react fast enough and clipped Haviland's tail, ripping off the horizontal stabilizer. Haviland's plane immediately dropped to the runway and skidded a long way on its belly, crossing a field, then a highway, then another field, scattering parts all the way. When it finally came to rest, only the cockpit was intact. Haviland—a big, strong guy to begin with—must have prayed like a son-of-a-gun during that long slide, because he climbed out with only minor bruises. It was a miracle that Bud, too, didn't crash, or that people on the ground hadn't been killed or injured. If you're going to have a terrible accident, I guess that's the way to do it.

After the emergency vehicles had come and gone and the gasping crowd went home, Havliand took Yoakley aside and said, in effect, *Look, the Air Force is going to want to investigate this right away, so I want you to fly me up to Philadelphia right now in the B-26 for an appointment I have tomorrow.* They returned to Jacksonville two days later. I won't say that Haviland was trying to dodge responsibility for the accident, and certainly if the authorities descended on the scene the way they usually did, our unit commander wouldn't be going anywhere for awhile, so maybe he was right to leave for an important meeting while he had the chance. All I know for sure is that I always felt a lot safer when our leader led the squadron from his desk instead of a cockpit.

WRY: Pete had real qualms about Bill Haviland, and nobody ever accused our intrepid leader of being Pilot of the Year, but I figured I could cope with our CO since I never expected more from him than he could deliver. Sure, he flew "square loops," his barrel rolls dished out, and his eight-point rolls usually had six to ten sloppy pauses, but who's counting? I figured when it came to formation, I could stay on my toes and avoid anything really catastrophic, though I'm sure that's what poor Bud Haefel thought, too, before that awful collision at Miami.

Of more concern to me was his style of leadership—what command is all about. Case in point: when we first got F-80s, he told Florida state officials that our squadron would fly in mass formation—some sixteen planes—over Tallahassee for the Governor's Day celebration. We started out in deep yogurt, an omen of things to come. Tallahassee wasn't that far away, and Haviland thought our wingtip fuel tanks made the airplane look clumsy, so he ordered maintenance to remove them. Next, after getting airborne and milling around a bit trying to get our gaggle together, we arrived over Tallahassee but he couldn't find the reference point to begin the flyby. When somebody mentioned this and pointed out we were running low on fuel, he laconically replied, "Don't worry guys, I've been lost here before."

We made a couple of passes over what may or may not have been the reviewing stand then cut out, lickety split, for home base. Our fuel was getting critical now, and after a couple of inbound pilots declared fuel emergencies, the Jacksonville tower closed the field (a nice facility with two parallel main runways and two secondary, diagonal runways) to other traffic and told us to land any way we could. Two ships flamed out in the pattern and had to make dead-stick approaches. Several more ran out of gas on the runway, or taxiing to the ramp. Through skill and cunning and a heap of good luck, I myself had enough fuel to park the airplane and shut down the engine just before it ran out of fumes.

Not all of our adventures in the FL-ANG were so hair-raising, though we sometimes didn't find out about a close call until after the fact.

The Navy was very cooperative with our unit—at least initially—allowing us to use their surface targets out in the ocean for air-to-ground gunnery, and their well-equipped Naval Air Station at Jacksonville (NAS-JAX) to practice GCA's—Ground Controlled Approaches in which a radar operator at the airport talks a pilot down through the clouds using heading and glide slope information. On one of these missions, Pete brought along a camera and took some snapshots of Bill flying in formation. It's a good thing we were both fantastic pilots used to tucking that wing in close. While "lead" was snapping pictures, we flew straight through a large formation of propeller-driven Navy fighters (probably Bearcats or Bobcats or Hep Cats or whatever they called them); it was hard to tell because they flashed by so fast on either side. The Swabbie flight commander got on guard channel immediately (the radio frequently always left open for emergencies) and warned all other flyers in the Western Hemisphere that a "couple of Air

Force dummies" were tooling around Navy airspace not watching where they were going. We could honestly say that we didn't know what he was yelling about. We hardly saw a thing.

Another time, we took off after refueling at Reading, Pennsylvania, into a thick deck of clouds. We knew we'd be in the soup a long time, so we filed separate flight plans and Bill departed a couple of minutes before Pete. We climbed on instruments for quite a while, talking to each other on "company frequency" (our unit's operations channel), air traffic control being minimal to non-existent in those days. Since he was ahead in both distance and altitude, Bill called out any changes in the weather he thought might be of interest to Pete. At 30,000 feet he broke out on top into dazzling sunlight. A few miles ahead, he saw another jet fighter glinting in the sun.

"Hey, Pete," Bill said, "Looks like we got company—another F-80 going in the same direction. Wonder if he's one of ours."

"I dunno," Pete replied. "I'm on top, too. Let's join up and find out."

So Bill closed on the "bogey" and saw from the fuselage markings that it was not only an F-80 from the Florida Guard, it was Pete's airplane. He had somehow managed to overtake Bill, pass him in the clouds, and reach cruising altitude first. It was the first time we'd accidentally encountered each other in the air, but it wouldn't be the last.

PJW: 1948 and 1949 turned out to be tougher years than we expected. The cold war heated up with the Soviet takeover in Czechoslovakia and their blockade of Berlin, necessitating a monumental airlift that saved the city and averted war. It was obvious that the nation was going have to spend a lot more on the military—again—so Congress cut back on their extraordinarily generous package of veterans benefits. The Gray bill, an amendment to the G.I. bill that funded 90 percent of our students, refused to subsidize any occupational training that was not directly required by an employer, so overnight we found ourselves with a lot of empty cockpits and idle airplanes. The market for seaplane services wasn't exactly dead, but it wouldn't support the crowd we had assembled; so, since Bill and I got our "flying fix" regularly with great airplanes at the Guard, we negotiated a severance package and sold our interest in the company to our partners.

Of course, we weren't rich and couldn't stay idle for long. My second child, Charles Jay, was born in 1947, doubling the size of my family, and I had to bring in more cash than part-time flying could pay. Because of my Dad's background in the retail gas business, I knew something about running service stations and through his contacts at Sinclair Oil, Bill and I obtained a franchise. We bought an established gas station and changed the sign to "W&Y Service Station," though "Florida's Flying Gas Jockey's" would've been more accurate. We knew we'd have to stay open 24-7 to compete with other dealers, so we hired a mechanic and a couple of helpers (one of them an airman from the Guard) and split the day into two 12-hour shifts.

A big part of our business came from a nearby Hudson dealership, who hired us to apply the protective undercoating that came as an option with each new car. They also liked to deliver new cars with a full tank of gas—a surprise "thank you" gift for the customer. Usually, the salesman who sold the car would bring it in and give us a "ticket," or voucher, to fill the tank. On the sly, they'd usually say, "Hey, put half of it in the customer's car, the rest in mine." Since the cost was the same to the dealer and the buyer wasn't expecting anything, we did what we were told. Most of those salesmen came back to buy gas from us anyway, so I guess you could say our cooperation with their scheme was a kind of customer service.

Of course, we still preferred flying with the Guard to pumping gas, so we went out to the base as often as we could. That meant we frequently reported for our shift at the station wearing our flight suits or khaki uniforms. Once, an Army colonel, a spit-and-polish West Pointer we both knew, pulled up (in uniform) to buy some gas and the attendant on duty happened to be me, also in uniform. Well, he was not to happy seeing a commissioned officer (even a lowly lieutenant) washing his windshield and checking his oil like a grease monkey. Through the glass, I watched him slowly turn several shades of purple. When I came up to collect for the gas, I expected him to chew me out, but instead he just shook his head and drove off. We never saw him again. I guess he had something against the free enterprise system we were all defending.

It didn't take long before Bill and I realized we were working ourselves to a frazzle at two jobs, neither of which was putting much money in the bank. We decided to sell the franchise and attracted a buyer down from Canada. Though the

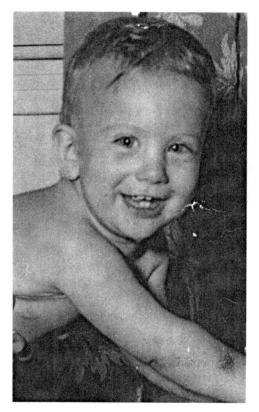

LEFT: Pete's son, Jay, increased the Jacksonville population by one in December, 1947.

BOTTOM: The famous "W&Y Service Station": a short-lived Jacksonville landmark.

The W&Y's "flying gas jockeys" wait to serve you. That's Pete (L) and Bill (R) in white jackets.

station was breaking even, sales could be better, so we asked a bunch of guys from the Guard—pilots and ground crew—to stop by when our prospective buyer came in to inspect the business. For the first time since we'd opened, we had a line of cars around the block. The pigeon—I mean, the prospective owner—was so impressed he made us an offer on the spot, which we accepted.

I should've quit when I was ahead. Now that I was free of the station, the sales manager at the Hudson dealership, who apparently liked me a lot (why not, after all that free gas?), asked me to work for him. I'd never sold a car in my life, but I needed a job and said yes. Big mistake. The first (and only) car I sold was to Bill—a top-of-the-line red convertible which we both liked so much, I bought one, too. My next customer was so impressed by my patter about the Hudson's reliability that he went over to the used car side of the lot and bought one there—though the salesman was good enough to split the commission. My third candidate was manager of the men's clothing section at a local department store. He, too, wanted a top-of-the-line convertible and I was determined that this one would not get away. I treated him royally—took brochures to his house and schmoozed him at his office. In the end, I bought a new suit from his store and he never bought a car.

I knew I was going to make a fortune. The problem was, it wouldn't be mine.

WRY: About the time we transitioned from P-51s to F-80s, I also transitioned out of my marriage to Marian. The bloom came off the rose sometime after the birth of our second child. Maybe it was all that sudden domesticity or forced togetherness with her mother or whatever, but maintaining the relationship became a very low priority for me and I behaved accordingly. It was not my finest hour, since Marian was and remained a kind and decent person who cared about me a lot, though I refused to see it. She was a wonderful mother as our two children, growing up later with another man to call Daddy, subsequently proved.

In the meantime, I let my eye wander to a cute bunch of girls who came down to Mile Branch to watch the airplanes and flirt with the pilots, one of which was me. The leader of the pack was a little Dixie dazzler named Dorothy Webb, called Dottie by her friends, who was hotter than a 50-cent firecracker lit at both ends. I took her up in the J-3 for a spin—literally—and she loved it so much she signed on to get her license. When the time came for her flight test, Pete returned the favor I'd extended to his Dad and gave Dottie her check ride, which she passed like a pro.

The more Dottie and I saw of each other—flying, swimming, going to parties—the more we liked it and as Marian and I began thinking about divorce, Dottie and I began talking about marriage. My life was about to change again—but not exactly in the way I thought.

4

COMBAT OVER KOREA: FIGHTING AMERICA'S "FORGOTTEN WAR"

*O*ur easy days in Jacksonville ended abruptly on June 25, 1950, when North Korea invaded her sister state below the 38th Parallel. We had a few days to scratch our heads, look Korea up on a map, and wonder how Washington and the rest of the world would react to what had until now been the unthinkable—another shooting war coming so soon after the last one.

By the end of the month we had our answer. President Truman ordered USAF and Navy forces to give all possible support to the beleaguered Republic of Korea (ROK) which had already lost its capital of Seoul. With Japan nearby and still bristling with men and machines from MacArthur's occupation, American reaction was swift but inadequate. Some ground troops arrived in early July but were immediately pushed back. Even our theater commander, General William Dean, was missing in action by the end of the month. Before long, all U.S., ROK, and British troops had retreated to the "Pusan perimeter"—an embattled enclave on the southernmost tip of the peninsula. Neither one of us had visited the Alamo, but from the pictures of Korea in the newspaper, it sure must've looked like Pusan.

The scuttlebutt at the Guard was that our lazy days as weekend warriors were about to come to a screeching halt. MacArthur engineered a brilliant end-run around the North Koreans, flanking them to the west by an amphibious landing at Inchon, but it only bought our ground commanders time, not victory. The Reds retreated and Seoul was recaptured. In fact, our soldiers and Marines marched all the way to the Northern capital of Pyongyang and took that, too, before the Communist Chinese began pouring south over the border. By early fall, what began as a nasty regional conflict now started to look like World War III, especially when the Soviet's first-line jet fighter, the high-flying, fast-

turning MiG 15 began to appear south of the Yalu River, giving allied aircraft fits.

Our F-80C Shooting Stars were the hottest jet fighters America had in production, and if there was one thing the generals needed in Korea, it was more first-line war planes and veteran pilots to fly them. It wasn't a question of if our unit would be activated—Federalized and made part of the active-duty Air Force—but when. Where we'd be stationed was another matter. Airbases in Japan were in good shape, but the few fields in Korea that could handle jets had been thoroughly trashed as they were lost, then recaptured, by allied troops. The only thing we knew for sure was where we'd be doing the fighting. Our first look at those maps made our blood run cold. Korea looked like one big mountain range in search of a rice paddy. It took guts just to deliver air mail in terrain like that. Dropping bombs and strafing troops—low-down and dirty, right on the deck—looked like suicide.

Still, we were both trained as aerial warriors and this was our chance to prove it. When the call came down from the Air Force Department for replacement F-80 pilots—well before the top brass had decided where to deploy our unit—some of us raised our hands and did what no smart soldier is supposed to do; we volunteered to be first in the pipeline.

PJW: Around the middle of October, 1950, Bill and I arrived with other replacements at George AFB on the high desert of South California for tactical training in the F-80. For most of us it was a refresher course. We'd shot up ground targets and practiced air-to-air gunnery in both the F-51D and F-80C, the latest model of the Shooting Star, which made our planes and our skills in high-demand for Korea. Of course, we were *all* active-duty pilots now. Like so many other aspects of peacetime, stateside flying those old distinctions were among the first to go.

For me, preparing for deployment was stressful beyond belief. There would be bad days in Korea, but few were as hard as those spent ferrying our couple of dozen F-80Cs to California, where they were prepped for overseas. The trip from Florida was bad enough, with long hours in a cramped cockpit and frequent stops to refuel (range was not the F-80's thing), but we had to return to Florida that same day. Actually, it was the same night, the original "red eye" special. Going east, we hitched a ride on our twin-engine C-47, the work-horse cargo plane of WWII. It

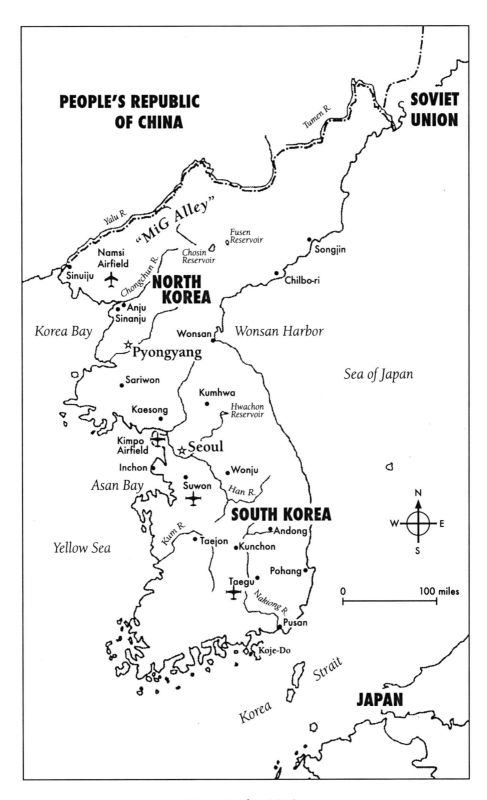

PEOPLE'S REPUBLIC
OF CHINA

SOVIET
UNION

Tumen R.

Yalu R.

"MiG Alley"

*Fusen
Reservoir*

Namsi
Airfield

*Chosin
Reservoir*

Songjin

Sinuiju

Chongchun R.

**NORTH
KOREA**

Chilbo-ri

Anju
Sinanju

Korea Bay

Wonsan

Wonsan Harbor

★ Pyongyang

Sea of Japan

Sariwon

Kumhwa

Kaesong

*Hwachon
Reservoir*

Kimpo
Airfield

★ Seoul

Inchon

Wonju

Asan Bay

Suwon

Han R.

SOUTH KOREA

N

Yellow Sea

Kum R.

Taejon

Andong

Kunchon

W   E

Pohang

S

Taegu

Naktong R.

0   100 miles

Pusan

Koje-Do

Korea   Strait

JAPAN

Korea in the 1950s

was a nice enough airplane to fly, but for military passengers it was the pits—just a slower and less comfortable version of the civilian DC-3. The overnight flight was crowded, with no "amenities" like cabin heat or individual seats. Exhausted from the flight west, we ferry pilots tried to stretch out wherever we could. Since there was never enough room on the troop benches, we'd try to sleep on the cargo floor, and that steel deck got pretty cold and hard after the first four or five hours. Needless to say, most of us pilots arrived as walking zombies: dead tired with bad attitudes and worse colds. Complicating things was worry about my family, including untangling from civilian life in Jacksonville and moving my wife, four-year old daughter—and now a brand-new baby boy—to the badlands around George AFB, where dependent housing was scarce to nonexistent. And the payoff for accomplishing all this was a free trip to a place I'd barely heard of and the privilege of getting shot at for reasons that weren't entirely clear. Before long I decided I needed a day away from the treadmill, so I just crawled into bed and tried to *get well*—get that porcupine out of my throat and the sandpaper out of my eyes, break that fever and see if I could simply get my hands to *stop shaking* before I had to grab that control stick again.

Bill, on the other hand, seemed to thrive on all the chaos. His divorce to Marian had come through, sad as it was, and he married Dottie, who Maxine and I adored. I suppose he took things in stride, too, because while I had been out trying to sell cars, he took a full-time job with the Air Guard: part of the cadre that managed the move while we part-timers packed up our civilian lives. He'd recently been promoted to captain and now outranked me, so when on base and in uniform I'd have to salute him. As I soon discovered, though, he'd earned that extra bar—and more. A true warrior—not the weekend-warrior type or a guy who bores holes in the sky just to collect a paycheck—he is a gifted pilot whose highest calling is to lead good men in battle. I like to think I rose to that challenge myself when we got to Korea, but for Bill the jump from reservist to active-duty combat pilot was a shorter leap than it was for me, at least in the beginning. Thank God one of us had that running start.

WRY: Pete and I took our families to California. For him and Maxine, it was kind of a homecoming, since they'd grown up out west and gone to college in Arizona.

Heck, after flight training in Southern California and Arizona, not to mention active duty in Douglas, I was practically a native myself. For Dottie, though, moving west was a big adventure. When we couldn't find housing on or around the base, we started looking up in the hills, along the highway connecting Victorville to San Bernardino. We found a pretty little area in a woodsy town called Crestline, which was great except for the three-hour drive—one way—to go to and from the base, and that was when the highway wasn't closed due to snow or an overturned truck. It didn't take long for Pete and me to figure that our time was better spent in the BOQ (bachelor officers' quarters) on base, studying the manuals, and commuting to Crestline once or twice a week to recharge our batteries and to remember what married life was like. In a way, that initial separation was probably good training for everyone. The day would soon come when our two lovely ladies would have to get by with 3,000 miles of ocean between them and their husbands, with no guarantee of a happy reunion.

*T*ravis AFB was the main staging area for men and equipment headed for Korea. With all the military transports and chartered civilian airliners crowding the ramp, it might as well have been Chicago O'Hare or LAX—it was one big and busy place.

We departed Travis in late December 1950, and arrived at Tachikawa airport outside of Tokyo. Replacement pilots from the Florida Air Guard usually went over with the MOS (military occupational specialty) of "jet pilot, single engine" and since we were current in the F-80C, we figured our new home would be with the 8th Fighter-Bomber Wing, which ran jet fighter ground-support operations in Korea. That's where we wound up—but not at the beginning—at least for Pete. Getting squared away organizationally taught us a lot about how the new "blue-suit" Air Force really worked, especially in a combat zone.

PJW: Bill and Ed Farley, another replacement pilot, took an earlier flight out of Travis so I arrived a few hours behind them. When I got there, it was late on a Friday afternoon. We were told that after in-processing we wouldn't have to report for duty until the following Monday, so we had the weekend to ourselves. None of us had been to Japan and we were anxious to see the sights, so Bill and Ed stood around checking their watches and tapping their toes while I tried to expedite my paperwork.

Things were fine until I got to a gruff old Master Sergeant who shoved a stack of forms at me and told me to fill them out. Up to now, in-processing had been mostly a matter of "sign this" and "initial here" but this guy wanted me to write down all the military aircraft I'd ever flown, where I'd flown them, and the amount of time I had in each. I thought, "This is ridiculous—don't you guys have this on file someplace?" and I may have even said something like that out loud. Anyway, my MOS clearly stated "jet pilot," so who cared how much time I had in an AT-6 or BT-13? I rolled my eyes at my companions, who thoughtfully reminded me that there was a train getting ready to leave for Tokyo, then sloppily began filling out the forms, telling the Air Force what it already knew. After a few minutes, I decided to make a long story short and just wrote down: "a few thousand hours in single-engine, fighter-type aircraft, such as the P-51" and slid it across the desk. The old sergeant glanced at it, pulled out his rubber stamp, and said, "Great. We'll put you in the 51ˢᵗ Fighter Group flying F-51s flying out of Pusan. Be here at 0600 hours Monday with your gear."

I said, "Wait a minute—I'm an F-80 pilot. You know—jets! I think there's been a mistake!"

The old sergeant looked at me over his glasses and replied, "Yes sir, lieutenant sir, and you're making it by standing here arguing." The big rubber stamp slammed down. "Next!"

To make a long story even longer, I was "officially" a P-51 driver again—for about two weeks. I spent the whole time trying to sort things out at Tachikawa while Bill went on to Itazuke AFB, near Fukuoka on the southern island of Kyushu, from which all the F-80s of the 8ᵗʰ FBW operated during that phase of the war. I never went to Pusan. I never strapped on a P-51—at least until after Korea. I just played the game, filled out my forms, and learned that a good fighter pilot should never pass up an opportunity to keep his mouth shut. I also learned it was wise to never make trouble for Master Sergeants, who—at least when it came to personnel—clearly ran the Air Force.

✪ ✪ ✪

WRY: Ed and I waited around the airport while Pete sorted out his paperwork and we finally got into Tokyo. Downtown was in surprisingly good shape, considering the pounding it took in the war. I was impressed by the Ginza district. It seemed very ancient but well-preserved, as if wrapped in some bubble that made it impervious to time and bombs. I expected to see more people in western clothes—like Asians wear in American cities or the Japanese who worked at our base, but most wore traditional attire, especially the women. At Tachi and Itazuke, the Japanese workers were used to Americans and were quite friendly. The town people were friendly, too, but more reserved. Where Pete, Ed, and I felt uncomfortable was in the countryside, where you'd see some big guy in an old, threadbare Imperial Army jacket pitching hay into an ox-cart, giving you the "evil eye." These people reminded us that the Big One hadn't been that long ago and the wounds of war take time to heal. We never really had any problems with them, but it was kind of unsettling knowing you had "allies" like this covering your back.

Anyway, I reported for duty with the 80th Fighter Squadron, an F-80 outfit that was one of three jet squadrons under the 8th FBW. Pete wound up in the 36th Squadron, same wing, so once they fixed his mis-assignment, we lived at and flew out of the same bases for the rest of our tour. Because I was a captain with a lot of flying time, they made me a flight commander right away, leader of "D Flight," a four-ship formation, after demonstrating in a few combat missions that I could hack it. Ed got re-assigned to a transport squadron, but he didn't squawk about it. There would be days ahead when both Pete and I would envy his assignment.

My squadron was called the Headhunters. Pete's was called the Flying Fiends, but if you take a look at their patch, you'll see why everyone else called them the "Puking Pups." This was back in the days before camouflage dominated war-plane paint schemes, so our ships were pretty colorful. Aside from a bright aluminum finish that made it easier for enemy gunners to spot us, we wore our squadron's heraldry on the vertical stabilizer: three jazzy stripes swooping up from the fuselage. Pete's squadron, the 36th, had red tails, our squadron's tails were yellow. That term never set too well with us gung ho types, but there were only so many colors in the paint box and that's the one we drew. I like to think we Headhunters gave the term

LEFT: Contrary to popular belief, Pete was not the model for the famous "Puking Pups"–mascot of the 36th Fighter Squadron.

BOTTOM: An airman walks past Headhunters Operations: the 80th Fighter Squadron—Bill's unit.

TOP: An F-80 equipped with oversized Misawa tip tanks hauls two napalm canisters into battle.

BOTTOM: The air strip at Taegu. If you think the flight line is bad, you should see the latrine.

"yellow tail" new meaning during those years—especially to the North Koreans and Red Chinese.

We began flying combat in January, 1951. For the first few months, we operated out of Itazuke in southern Japan, which meant our fully loaded ships had a long way to go before we could even think about dropping bombs. There was no aerial refueling in those days, and our first-generation jets were real gas guzzlers, so much of our takeoff gross weight was in fuel. The first thing the ground crews did was throw away the factory drop tanks, mounted under the wingtips, and install much bigger custom-made tanks, called "Misawa tanks" after the Japanese manufacturer. These 265-gallon tanks gave us an extra 15 minutes over a target, or an additional safety margin for getting home. We were happy to have both.

Because it took so much time to reach a target, we usually landed after the day's first mission at Taegu, a hastily constructed staging base about 70 miles north of Pusan. There, we would re-arm and refuel, then go out on another mission before returning to Itazuke. Taegu was a real dump, but when a plane is shot-up or low on fuel, it could be a beautiful sight. One of the worst things about it was the runway. The surface wasn't concrete, but PSP—the pierced steel planking used widely in the Pacific during WWII. It was better than dirt, but not by much, and those interlocking planks really rippled under a heavy airplane. Sometimes, watching a fully loaded F-80 take off, we could see the PSP oscillate around the airplane as it gathered speed, like the bow wave around a boat. Occasionally, a piece would pop up and strike the tip tanks, which hung down pretty low below the wings. Even if the plane didn't catch fire, lifting off with a hole in your gas tank was a lousy way to start a mission.

WRY: Taegu was like a busy truck stop on a major interstate highway. All kinds of aircraft pulled in for all kinds of reasons—mostly for fuel and ordnance—but some because of battle damage or malfunctions and had nowhere else to go. Also like a truck stop, we pilots used the brief layover to answer the call of nature. The latrine at Taegu was one of wonders of the Asian world. Basically, it was one long trough—about 50 or 75 feet—with evenly spaced holes in the floor. There were no urinals or toilets—you just stood or squatted and took care of business. This was a challenge during winter, when you were wearing a heavy flying suit, G-suit (special "chaps" that inflated to push blood from your legs back to your head in tight turns or fast pull-ups), long-johns, sidearm (or in my case, two sidearms: a .45 Army automatic in a shoulder holster and a more reliable .38 Special in a hip rig), life vest, and assorted other goodies designed to make you and the airplane heavier. Just getting set up over your spot was an accomplishment. But the biggest treat was the latrine's enormous water tank, positioned at the end of the trough and used to flush the system. It constantly filled with water and when it was nearly full, tipped over against a beam. Now, this was a clever and efficient system, but its designers overlooked one thing. You never knew exactly when the tank was going to tilt and when it hit that beam, it sounded like a 500-lb bomb going off behind you. Needless to say, to a frazzled pilot seeking relief between missions, this was an unwelcome intrusion on our reverie—particularly since Taegu had a well-known problem with enemy infiltrators who liked to roll hand grenades into buildings. As far as I know, they never attacked the latrine. They never had to. That big water tank gave enough people heart attacks.

PJW: Combat flying wasn't quite what I expected. I was no stranger to airplanes or military flying, but nothing quite prepares you to fly and fight at the same time— especially when people down there are trying to kill you. Our first missions out of Japan were in winter, which meant the weather was terrible most of the time. We usually got up about 3 in the morning to get briefed for a 5 AM takeoff. The idea was to catch the enemy just before dawn, when they were most vulnerable and we were harder to see. We'd go out to the airplanes in the pouring rain, do the pre-flight walkaround inspection, then strap in and get the canopy closed before the cockpit filled with water. Still shivering, we'd start engines and taxi out, then take the active runway for a formation takeoff, usually two ships at a time. This procedure gave us plenty of time to think such heroic thoughts as "What the hell am I doing here?" and "What headquarters genius gave us *this* frag order?" Most of all, waiting to go with rain beating down on the canopy, visibility practically zero, a ceiling of a hundred feet and a long climb through freezing clouds before breaking out on top (when you'd scramble for your sun glasses to avoid colliding with your leader—our helmets had no visors), you figured your reward for doing all this was descending through equally stinking weather at the other end only to get shot at for your trouble. At times like that, waiting to release the brakes, you thought mainly about what little you had to gain and how much you had to lose, so you checked the instruments one more time and wondered if that slight wobble in the RPM meant a compressor blade was about to go or if that little dip in hydraulic pressure meant a pump was about to fail. You know most of your buddies out there are thinking the same thing, so you ask yourself, "Maybe I should abort early and avoid the rush?"

But you don't. You go anyway. You do it partly because everybody else is going and partly because you're in for a hundred missions and if you don't fly today, you'll have to fly tomorrow so you might as well get it over with.

So you spool up the engine, wait for the leader's nod, then release the brakes. By the time you've got flying speed and rotated, you're retracting the gear and flaps, and you're too busy to think about anything except what's happening *now*. It will be that way for the next hour and a half, until you feel those oleo struts compress and hear that lovely sound of concrete or PSP under the wheels. Another day in paradise.

M any of our missions were close air support for ROK or American ground troops. A forward air controller—usually a USAF fighter pilot pulling temporary duty in an AT-6 spotter plane with a non-pilot observer in the back seat— would mark the target with smoke, giving us an idea of its location. We'd then quickly analyze the surroundings, taking terrain and weather into account, then select an attack course to deliver our ordinance—usually 500 or 1,000 pound bombs, 5-inch HVARs (high velocity aerial rockets), or napalm (jellied gasoline). Rockets weren't very accurate and didn't do much damage when they hit, but that napalm was really effective against troops and vehicles—even buildings—leaving a swath of sticky, burning gasoline half the size of a football field. We could also make strafing passes with the six fifty caliber machine guns massed in the F-80's nose. Because these were ganged together on the airplane's centerline and not on the wings like the P-51's, we could throw a lot of lead at a target over a wide range of distances—pretty handy when the bad guys are shooting back at you.

Other missions included interdiction, where we would try to cut the enemy's supply lines by bombing roads, railroad tracks, tunnels, and bridges—hopefully catching the trains, vehicles, and troops that were using them. We also flew flak suppression missions, where we would attack the enemy's anti-aircraft batteries before a wave of allied bombers, usually B-29s, approached from higher altitude. Before the F-86s arrived, we sometimes flew escort for these bombers, to defend them against the MiGs, which showed (if nothing else) that somebody at combat central control had a sense of humor. The bombers would come in between 20,000 to 30,000 feet and we would try to stay above them, usually with about a 15 knot spread between our maximum mach number and stalling speed. A level turn under those conditions, even in a shallow bank, caused the aircraft to shudder, so we didn't have much room to maneuver. Of course, the MiGs were always 10,000 to 20,000 feet above us and could attack whenever they liked. If they did, our only tactic was to turn into them—they didn't like those massed .50 calibers and were understandably anxious to avoid them. With all that energy, though, they could break off an engagement at will just by diving away. Early on, a few F-80s tried to dogfight with MiGs but our pilots ended by walking home—or worse. The MiG-15 could turn tighter, climb faster, and hit harder (with its pair of 23 mm and one 37 mm cannons) than any plane in our inventory at that time, including the relatively few carrier-based jets the Navy put into the air. That's how things stood until the F-86, rushed into production, arrived in the middle of 1951. Until then, all we could do about MiGs was use our speed and eyeballs to avoid them, concentrating instead on doing what Uncle Sam was paying us for: cause the enemy on the ground as much grief as we could.

Before long, we got pretty good at it. The trick was to stay high until you were sure of your target, then go in fast and get out even faster. Sometimes your wingman would attack in echelon, just off the leader's wing, but mostly they would attack in trail: behind and slightly below the leader. For strafing and skip bombing, you had to fly low—and we mean very low, often just a few feet off the ground both coming and going—at very high speed. Pulling up from an attack was dangerous because it presented the bottom of your airplane to enemy fire, so the man behind you had to be Johnny-on-the-spot, guns blazing, to keep the defenders' head down. If your wingman wasn't there to support you, bad things could happen—as they sometimes did even when everything else went right.

✪ ✪ ✪

PJW: Experience means making small mistakes now so you can avoid bigger ones later on. Close calls and false alarms fall into this category, but that doesn't make them any less scary.

On one of my early missions I was assigned as wingman to an element leader. That meant flying "number four" in a typical four-ship formation. In fingertip formation—that is, with each plane holding a position like the fingernails on an outstretched hand—that put me in the position of the little finger, with the element leader (called "number three") between me and the flight commander, who is called "number one" and flies in the position of the long finger of a hand. From this vantage point, the flight commander can navigate the formation and watch where everyone is going. *His* wingman, called "number two," flies in the position of a hand's index finger, opposite the element leader. This is an efficient and useful way to move four airplanes around the sky without bumping into each other, but as I was about to see, it has its drawbacks.

Now, I'd flown a lot of close formation and flying four isn't too tough if the flight leader is reasonably smooth and plans ahead, because when he turns, there's a slight delay before number three, the element leader, perceives his movement and can follow. That delay gets exaggerated as it is passed down the line to number four, like playing crack the whip. If the flight commander is abrupt on the controls or if there are several airplanes between the leader and "tail-end Charlie" (which in this case was me), close formation can be a challenge.

This particular mission was led by a Captain Downey, who had just returned from a month's duty as a forward air controller helping the Army direct our strikes. He was a good pilot, but a bit rusty in the F-80—and, even worse from a formation standpoint, was a bit rough on the controls. The weather was bad, as usual, and we had to climb through a lot of it on the way out and descend through even more when we got to the target. Because we had no electronic navigation aids (after all, the enemy could use those, too) all our missions were planned and flown by DR ("dead reckoning"), which meant using airspeed and wind information to compute time and heading to target. If the target was socked in, we'd pick the elevation of the highest terrain within a certain radius, usually about 25 miles, then add a thousand feet for safety and that would become our minimum descent altitude. If we didn't break out of the clouds and see the target by the time we hit that altitude, the flight would abort and return to base. Sounds simple—and it usually was—but a lot of things can go wrong.

Today, takeoff, climb-out, and cruise went well. When we started our "jet penetration" (rapid descent through the clouds with speed brakes out) over the target, the weather got really nasty. The clouds were so thick and dark that I had trouble even seeing the fuel tank on the tip of my element leader's wing. Add to that an uncomfortable amount of turbulence and you've got the makings of an exciting ride, even with no enemy on the ground to shoot at you.

I was too busy watching my element leader to sneak a peak at my altimeter, but I knew we were getting low—quite close to our minimum descent altitude. All of a sudden, my element leader's wing tip popped up and disappeared into the soup. I figured Downey had changed heading abruptly and his element leader had to scramble to keep up, which meant I had to be psychic to stay with him, or turn blindly toward the formation hoping to re-establish visual contact. Well, I wasn't about to yank my airplane toward three F-80s I couldn't see, so I gently banked in their direction, using my wingtip as a "curb feeler," hoping that if they had rolled out, I would have just enough time to avoid a collision and rejoin.

Unfortunately, the clouds just got blacker as I turned, still descending, with no hint of an airplane in sight. Under these conditions, a second is an eternity, so I followed SOP for lost contact and rolled wings level, slightly dropping the nose. As I did, I popped out below the clouds and saw the most horrible sight I'd ever seen. Looming three-quarters of the way across my windscreen was the biggest, ugliest, snow-covered mountain I had ever seen—every crack and gully and plane-grabbing boulder stood out in sharp relief. Even worse, it's peak was lost above me in the clouds. We had somehow not only dropped below the highest terrain in the area, but below our safety margin as well.

Out of the corner of my eye I spotted a wedge of air—the edge of the mountain—to the right, away from the direction the flight was turning. If I banked *now*, I could avoid crashing so I retracted my speed brake, slammed the throttle forward, and pulled hard toward the open space. It then occurred to me that the rest of the flight was still headed for that wall of granite. I got on the radio and yelled, "Lead—look out! Big mountain ahead of you!"

After a second, a laconic reply came back, "Roger, four, we're aborting."

Downey didn't even sound like he'd broken a sweat. Still, I half expected to see the orange glow of their impact as I cleared the mountain and began a steep climb to safety. I never rejoined the flight—never even saw them and used my own navigation to return to the field. Back on the ground, I learned the flight had broken out of the clouds just before I did, saw the high terrain, and changed course to pass the mountain on the other side. They, too, aborted the mission and landed without incident. Downey didn't make a big deal of what happened; partly because he thought I was still with the formation and my panicky radio call was mild criticism of his leadership—which in a way it was—and partly because he may have realized that his rough stick work made it impossible for any guy at the end of that "whip" to stay with the flight under those conditions. I really don't know. The scary part is that if I'd continued to look for the flight while we were in the clouds—a dumb move to begin with—my gentle bank in their direction would have flown me smack into that mountain. The moral of the story, I guess, is to trust your leader but don't forget to fly your own airplane.

After a month of learning the ropes, the 36th squadron CO made me a flight commander, like Bill. That meant I was not only responsible for getting my airplane and weapons over the target at the right time, heading, and altitude, but making sure three other pilots did the same, and hopefully get everyone back in one piece. That sounds like a lot of responsibility—and it is—but since so much of combat is the result of random chance, you learn pretty quickly not to beat yourself up too bad if things don't always go right.

On one mission, my wingman, Bob White, was attacking in trail behind me. I had just pulled up and broke hard from the target when I looked back to see how Bob was doing. A small amount of smoke was streaming from his fuselage; he had obviously taken a hit, but it didn't look too bad. He pulled up, but instead of following me, he began a slow climbing turn in the opposite direction. I immediately got on the radio and asked if he was okay. No answer. Since there are lots of reasons to lose radio communications (equipment can fail or get damaged) other members of my flight began trying to contact Bob, who was obviously in trouble. Again, no answer. His aircraft continued its slow roll, wings passing the vertical, and started to split-S toward the ground. He was still trailing smoke, but had no visible flames or any other kind of obvious damage. Our calls now became urgent appeals for Bob to bail out. He never did. Without answering, his plane continued its graceful roll right into the ground, going up in a tremendous ball of flame.

We were all quiet for a few seconds and it struck me just how awesome—even sublime—Bob's terrible last moments appeared from a distance. I suspect he had been killed by the same burst of ground fire that had punched a hole in his plane, which would explain why he never answered, bailed out, or regained control. Maybe that's what made his last moments so astonishing—this wonderful guy and this beautiful machine with polished aluminum and its proud red tail glinting in the sun—just soaring effortlessly toward its fiery doom, like a Viking's funeral pyre. If Bob suffered, it wasn't for long. That was reserved for the rest of us, who could only watch from a distance and replay it again and again in our minds.

Another mission, about midway through my tour, shows the consequences of doing the right thing in the wrong way—fortunately, with less tragic results. Our wing commander, a square-jawed WWII combat vet named Colonel Tipton, occasionally came down from headquarters to fly missions with various squadrons. That's great—a commander needs to know what his troops are up against. But in combat flying, recent experience counts a lot and Colonel Tilton, while an excellent pilot, wasn't particularly current. He was also no fool, so when he decided to accompany my flight (I was a flight commander by that time), he didn't pull rank and said he would be happy to tag along as my wingman.

The mission started smoothly, though I noticed on the way out that the colonel's formation flying was a little rusty. Over the target (I forget now what it was, but defensive fire was pretty heavy), I signaled the flight to go trail and rolled in for a strafing pass. From this point on the mother hen doesn't have much time to watch the chicks—you pretty much expect everyone to do their jobs—so I concentrated on putting as many rounds on the target as I could. As I pulled up and started to jink away (a "jink" is an abrupt, yank-and-bank maneuver intended to make you a lousy target), I heard and felt a terrific *crash* in the front of my plane. It felt like somebody had slapped me in the face (literally, my head jerked to the side) and bits of hot metal *pinged* around the cockpit. Immediately, smoke began to billow from behind the instrument panel.

I rolled out but continued to climb while I assessed the situation.

"Pete—you okay?" somebody asked on the radio.

"I don't know. I think I got hit on the nose."

I didn't specify if it was my nose or my airplane's nose—both were pretty prominent targets—but nobody answered or seemed to be particularly concerned, so I assumed I wasn't trailing flame or losing parts. The airplane was flying normally, though noisier than usual because of the fist-sized hole that had just been gouged into the armor plating in front of the instrument panel (thank you, Mr. Lockheed) by a 20 mm exploding shell. The armor absorbed most of the energy and kept any serious shrapnel from chewing me up, but bits of metal cut my cheek and scratched my oxygen mask, as well as chipping paint and cracking glass around the cockpit. But everything still worked, and that was the important thing. We went around for a few more passes before fuel got low and we headed for home.

Back on the ground, Colonel Tipton admitted I may have been hit because he was late coming onto the target—not by much—but it gave enemy gunners enough time to cook off a few well-aimed rounds at my plane's unprotected belly. He congratulated my flight for clobbering the target then went about his wing-commanding business, flying another mission in a week or so with another unsuspecting—I mean, suitably honored—flight of F-80 drivers. I couldn't feel too sorry for myself, though. I thought about Bob White, whose "bad day at the office" turned out to be a whole lot worse than mine.

WRY: We were still flying out of Itazuke when I witnessed what would be the first of too many horrible takeoff accidents. Hank Compton, a buddy of mine in the 80th and a fine young pilot, was on strip alert with three other yellow-tailed F-80s. That meant they sat in their airplanes, which were fueled, armed, and ready to go on a moment's notice in case radar or ground observers detected any threat to the base. This is SOP in any war zone, although we were far enough from North Korea and

TOP: Lt. Hank Compton and his "lucky" F-80 from the 80th Fighter Squadron. After a takeoff accident killed two wingmen, his ship survived to land with a wing and a half.

TOP: An F-80 from the 80th FBW makes a rocket-assisted takeoff from Suwon. Those JATO "bottles" saved a lot of lives in hot weather.

BOTTOM: The wreckage of Darlington's aircraft after a takeoff accident at Kimpo. Badly burned, he returned to finish his tour.

TOP: A C-47 lands near the control tower at Kimpo field.

BOTTOM: Hard-working Korean women repair the runway at Kimpo. Sharp rocks and bare feet don't mix, but that didn't stop them!

China to make a surprise enemy attack unlikely. Still, our alert crews got scrambled on occasion—mostly for false alarms or, I suspect, just to keep us on our toes.

Anyway, the winter weather was terrible, as always—really down on the deck and raining hard—so the chance of even friendly aircraft coming or going wasn't good. Nevertheless, the alert horn sounded and Hank cranked up his engine and was soon lining up for takeoff with the flight leader and his wingman. They entered the clouds as soon as they raised the gear and immediately thereafter we heard and saw a tremendous explosion at the end of the runway. The leader, it seems, got vertigo or lost power or something right after takeoff and simply augured in during a steep turn to the right, taking the wingman with him. Hank was on the left wing, however, and had a fraction of a second more to see what was happening as they dropped out of the clouds. He leveled his wings and pulled back on the stick just in time to keep from crashing but not before his right wing hit a steel utility pole, sheering both the pole and wing in half. Still, his airplane kept climbing. After a minute or so, Hank was on top of the clouds and radioed a report on his condition. He was advised to bail out, but he said no. He could control the aircraft, wasn't on fire, and nothing else seemed to be wrong, so he decided to stick with the plane. As he circled the field, burning up fuel, the weather began to lift. In a half hour or so, it was above landing minimums and he made his approach, carrying extra speed on final since he had only one aileron and couldn't use the flaps. Amazingly, Hank greased it in, pulled off the runway, and taxied back to the ramp. I think Lockheed engineers still have a framed picture of his plane hanging somewhere in their hallowed halls, though nobody back at the plant probably believed the story behind it.

As the weather warmed up, our high-gross takeoffs got even chancier. The Air Force was just getting JATO (jet-assisted takeoff) bottles—basically, disposable rockets mounted to the fuselage to help a heavy plane get airborne—but they hadn't yet filtered down to our unit. All we could do was engage the F-80's water-injection system, which gave us a bit more thrust, but it was seldom enough to do the job on a really hot day. As a result, we had a lot of takeoff accidents where the pilot rode a race horse that just wouldn't leave the gate.

One unlucky guy like that was a 36th squadron pilot named Darlington. His ship accelerated okay but couldn't get airborne and ran off the runway. He went through some trees, ripping off the wing tips, then hit some berms, breaking the fuselage, trailing fire all the way. By the time they got him out, he was pretty badly burned. Still, old Darlington was a tough cookie. After emergency treatment in Japan, he went stateside for a series of painful operations and a lengthy recuperation. Believe it or not, he volunteered to come back to Korea and complete his hundred missions. I'm sure the top brass and his family weren't too thrilled about that, but they were still desperate for jet-qualified pilots so they put him back in the saddle. Before I finished my tour, Darlington had come back to finish his. You've got to take your hat off to a guy like that. He could have quit when he had the chance, bow out gracefully as a hero, having paid more than his share of dues, but he came back out of loyalty to his buddies and his commitment to the job. That kind of courage doesn't grow on trees and I always felt honored just knowing the guy.

Of course, as the months went by, we would lose other exceptional people, and most of those stayed gone. Two of them were brothers—identical twins, in fact—named Merv and Irv Taylor. Both were excellent pilots and flew with me in my flight. They were also great guys, friendly and trustworthy and willing to go the extra mile both in and out of the cockpit. Halfway through my tour, Irv was shot down and killed. Knowing there is often a special bond between identical twins, I asked Merv if he wanted to lay off awhile, take some extended leave or visit his folks in the states or something, but he said no, he just wanted to finish his tour. In a way, you can't blame him. From the moment Irv died, Merv was fighting the war for two.

*J*ust as we got the hang of flying out of Japan, UN ground forces recaptured enough of Korea to make operations possible out of bases closer to the 38th Parallel. By this time, President Truman had fired General MacArthur and replaced him with Matthew Ridgeway. Unfortunately, the Red Chinese had now jumped into the war with both feet and launched a spring offensive. This resulted in a series of actions known as the Battle of Imjin River, which would involve both of us deeply before it was over.

✪ ✪ ✪

WRY: In March of 1951, the Army had retaken Seoul and with it South Korea's national airport, Kimpo. Partly because of my background in construction and flight operations, I guess, the bigwigs at 8th FBW tapped me and a few others to go in as an advanced party to set up the field. I'm not sure what we expected to find, but what we saw was a lot worse than we wanted. The field was really messed up; buildings were damaged or destroyed by bombs and artillery, the runways were cratered by repeated dive bombing by both sides. Our job was to prepare the field and get our aircraft in there as soon as possible, since operations so much closer to the bomb line, or front, meant faster support for our ground troops and longer loiter times over the target. Our only problem was materials and labor. There wasn't enough of either. To fill-in the cratered runway, we needed crushed rock by the ton, and those earth movers and road graders that were still functioning had long ago been requisitioned by the Army—though we occasionally got one on loan when our top brass heated their fannies. We also discovered that the local Korean men didn't care for manual labor, so they sent their wives and daughters to the field when our call went out for workers. As a result, we hired several hundred Korean women in rubber shoes (and sometimes barefoot) to clear debris and crush rocks, often by hand, using big stones to make little stones and to move rock and dirt around in baskets, often strapped to their backs.

After all was said and done, we began landing ground crew, support equipment, and airplanes in less than a month—fast even by wartime standards, and miraculous considering what we had to work with. I'd like to take credit for that, but it was all due to those hard-working Korean women, bless their hearts.

My prized possession during this period was an Army jeep I'd appropriated at Itazuke "for official use only," though it wound up taking me and a bunch of other guys, including Pete, on a few sight-seeing tours whenever we had the chance. I knew that if I ever turned the dang thing in for maintenance—even to have the oil changed—I'd never see it again, so I called it "Hobo," which was painted on the side, and took care of it myself. After all, Pete and I had been outstanding grease-jockeys at the old W&Y Gas Station in Jacksonville, so those skills came in mighty handy.

One of my first excursions in the jeep was to drive with another officer to Inchon Harbor—about 15 miles from Kimpo—to supervise the unloading of supplies and equipment earmarked for the Air Force from a big Navy LST (short for Landing Ship Tank). It was a cargo vessel that could bring heavy gear close to shore without a dock. While we were there and had the time, we did some sightseeing in Seoul, recently liberated from the Reds. If we thought suburban Tokyo looked beat up, it was Beverly Hills by comparison. The damage to Seoul was incredible. What hadn't been bombed, burned, or pockmarked by communist weapons the previous summer had been pummeled when UN forces retook the city. Maybe the locals expected the real estate to change hands again before spring was over, I don't know, but many human and animal bodies remained unburied, the stench attracting packs of dogs and carrion birds. All in all, it was a sight I'd have just as soon skipped, but we would all see much worse before things were over.

PJW: I had mixed feelings about moving to Kimpo. Bill and his crew had done a great job doing the impossible—getting a demolished airfield going after two invading armies had kicked it back and forth like a football. Being closer to the bomb line meant we could spend a lot more time over targets, though the soldier and Marines still preferred to see Navy Corsairs and Skyraiders overhead than hear the whine of our jets. Those old carrier-based prop planes could haul a lot more ordnance than us and stay on station a whole lot longer. Because they flew slower, their gunnery and bomb delivery was generally more accurate—pretty important when working close to the troops—though jets were better at interdiction, getting far behind enemy lines faster and getting on top of most targets before they saw or heard us.

The worst part of Kimpo was its location. Being close to the front, we heard artillery all night long, which made sleeping difficult even when we were dead tired. Perimeter defense was pretty good, and our workers had dug fox holes near every tent, but saboteurs—people today we would call terrorists—got through with alarming regularity, partly because there was no way to tell a North Korean from a South Korean, and any bad guy who wanted to infiltrate the base could do so with the locals who worked on the field. As a result, I traded part of my whiskey

TOP: Bill (far right) takes some Headhunters out for a spin in *Hobo*.

BOTTOM: Equipment to restore Kimpo arrives via a Navy LST at Inchon.

TOP: On the road from Kimpo to the capital at Seoul.

BOTTOM: Downtown Seoul.

TOP: Fred Poston (another FL-ANG pilot), Bill, and Pete on a visit to Seoul. Fred stayed in the Air Force after Korea and retired a three-star general!

OPPOSITE PAGE, TOP: An old bomb crater made a great swimming hole for South Korean kids who hung around Kimpo.

OPPOSITE PAGE, BOTTOM: Pete traded his whiskey ration to an Army sergeant for a Russian-made "burp" gun, which he kept under his bunk in case North Korean infiltrators got too close.

TOP: Bill's bunker outside his barracks at Kimpo. Because of "Bed-Check Charlie," we got to know our foxholes pretty well.

BOTTOM: A blast bunker near some Quonset huts at Suwon.

ration (I only drank beer in those days) to an Army sergeant in exchange for a Russian-made "burp" gun, a small submachine gun he had liberated, along with some communist ammo, and kept it under my bunk. I don't know if that broke any Air Force regulations, but it could sure throw out more lead than my old Phoenix Police Department .38 Special, which I carried in the airplane. I'm sure if I'd ever had to use it, the top brass would've forgiven me. As it turned out, I never even fired it for practice; but I always felt better knowing it was under my pillow.

More annoying, but less dangerous, was "Bed-Check Charlie," a North Korean pilot who often buzzed our base in the middle of night in an old fabric-covered, Soviet-made Polikarpov Po-2 biplane. Looking and sounding like the Stearmans we used for primary flight training in WWII, the Po-2 would swoop out of the darkness and drop hand grenades or shoot small arms randomly around the base. The anti-aircraft batteries that surrounded the field were designed for more sophisticated targets, so when confronted by a "bandit" who barely showed up on radar, there wasn't much they could do but fire at the sound of the engine, which meant they always missed. Unfortunately, although we pilots eventually learned to sleep through distant artillery, the sound of those big 40 mm anti-aircraft guns booming a stone's throw from our tents knocked us out of bed every time. Although he was later credited with destroying a parked, unmanned F-86 at Suwon, I never heard of anyone getting hurt in "Charlie's" attacks, and I admit it took a lot of guts for those North Korean pilots to put their head in the lion's mouth like that night after night. But if one ever got shot down and captured, he wouldn't have lasted long—that many Americans were eager to string him up.

The last time I heard Bed-Check Charlie was when a friend in the 36th, a fairly new replacement named Jack Henderson, and I were watching a Martin & Lewis movie being screened on a sheet near my quarters. Jack knew I was about to rotate home, to be stationed at Luke AFB near Phoenix, and he wanted me to deliver a message to his girlfriend who lived in the area. I said, "Sure, be happy to—what's the message?" just as Bed-Check Charlie chugged over. The projector went dead, all the area lights went out, and that big Quad behind our tents opened up. We ran for different fox holes and by the time the all-clear sounded, Jack was nowhere around—probably went back to his quarters. I didn't think much about it, since he had an early mission the next day and undoubtedly wanted some sleep. We'd finish our discussion later.

Unfortunately, "later" never came. The next day he got shot down on a dive bombing mission—not by ground fire, our biggest risk, but by a MiG nobody saw until it's nose cannons tore Jack's plane to pieces. He bailed out and spent the rest of the war as a guest of the North Koreans.

Near the end of the summer of '51 our group transferred to Suwon about 50 miles southeast of Kimpo. The MiGs had been having a field day since they arrived the previous November, ripping through our B-29 formations and shooting down our low-and-slow ground attack aircraft, like the Navy Corsairs, and even the low-and-fast ones, like our F-80s. The Air Force had rushed the North American F-86A Sabre into production and now they began to arrive in large numbers. Their fuel was as critical as ours, so the top brass wanted to station them as far north as possible, giving them maximum time in "MiG alley" as the area just south of the Yalu River was known. That meant the "MiG killers" needed our space on the ramp, so we got booted to a smaller airfield farther south. Our flying time to targets was a little longer, but Bed-Check Charlie came by less often and, after we learned to ignore the artillery, we finally got a good night's sleep.

WRY: On moving day, I loaded my little jeep and drove down to Suwon. The quarters there were better than the tents at Kimpo but not as comfortable as the quonset huts in Japan. The barracks were framed-out at the bottom and covered with canvas on top like tents at a summer camp. It was now getting pretty hot so we were happy we could open up the sides and let in some air. At Kimpo we had plenty of locals—mostly women—to clean our quarters, do laundry, and keep things tidy. I, however, wound up with a 16-year old houseboy, Lim Yung Sot, who was one hard worker and a really nice kid to boot. We became good friends, despite his poor English and my almost non-existent Korean. His family lived somewhere in Seoul, but I never met them. If Lim was any guide, they were probably good people. I think they appreciated his having an American "big brother" to look after him at the base, just as I enjoyed having a semblance of a "family" to come home to at the end of the day, so I always tried to treat him right.

Lim helped me pack and when it was time to go, he presented me with a little reed mat his father who, I assume, earned his living as a basket maker and had woven the mat as a going-away present. It wasn't real big or fancy, but very artistic and well made. I have to say, with all the death and violence and other nonsense going on around us, it was quite a moving gesture. I gave him a big hug and wished him and his family the best of luck.

Two days later, after all our aircraft had been repositioned and we were ready to resume operations, Lim showed up at my barracks in Suwon. He greeted me with a great big smile and a few belongings rolled up in a ratty blanket. My surprised face must've startled him.

"Lim, what in blazes are you doing here?" I asked, or words to that affect.

He answered in his familiar, fractured English that he'd come down to make sure I got moved in safely and was properly settled.

"Well, that's great," I said, "but what about your family? Don't they need you up in Seoul?"

"Is okay," Lim answered.

"How about your father?"

"Is okay," Lim said.

"Lim, does your Dad even know you're here?"

"Is okay," he made a big circle with his thumb and forefinger.

So I became the only pilot at Suwon with an imported houseboy. Frankly, I was glad to see him. We still had problems with infiltrators and even the "friendlies" sometimes caused us grief. In one case, Lim literally became a life-saver.

I said that Korean women did most of the non-military work for us on base, doing cleaning, laundry, and so on, and that's true. The problem was, their men—particularly those in the ROK army—didn't always understand the American way of doing things: namely, a day's pay for a day's work and that's it. The South Korean Army, and presumably the North as well (and maybe even the Red Chinese), had adopted something like the Japanese "comfort girl" program used widely in WWII and thought nothing of dragging the nearest young woman, and any of her sisters or girlfriends who caught their eye, off to their camp to live virtually as slaves, rendering sexual as well as domestic services, not just behind the lines, but in the trenches as well. One day I noticed that one of the Korean girls who worked in our barracks, a sweet little thing about 19 or 20, very quiet, but always pleasant and very efficient, had just up and disappeared. None of the other girls would talk about it, but Lim explained she was in "Big trouble!" She had been kidnaped by a ROK soldier who was passing through with his unit on their way to the front.

I asked Lim if he could show me where the soldier had taken her, and he said yes, they were only a short walk from the base, so I buckled on my .38 in its single-holster cowboy rig (complete with bullet loops), and followed him. After about ten minutes we came to a small South Korean encampment—really just a circle of tents—but that was as far as Lim would go. He pointed out the kidnapper, standing by a tent, so I left Lim by the road and marched up to the soldier looking as mean and ornery as I could, which wasn't hard under the circumstances. A dozen or so of his buddies—not exactly crack troops, but armed with rifles—blinked up from their bowls of rice or naps and seemed disinterested in my presence. I didn't see anyone who looked remotely like an officer, or even a noncom.

The man Lim pointed to was a rather skinny Korean standing near the flap of a tent. I marched up to him like Hopalong Cassidy. Most of these guys were intimidated by any American, let alone an officer with wings who was obviously pissed off and carrying a gun. As soon as I got to the tent I saw our housekeeper cowering inside. I grabbed the girl by the wrist and put the other hand on my revolver, still in its holster, then got in the guy's face like a Marine Corps drill instructor. I shouted, "Mine! Mine!" holding up her wrist to make my intention clear. I was not leaving camp without the girl.

Fortunately, the soldier didn't want a confrontation. He lowered his eyes and slunk back into the tent, mumbling something in Korean I didn't understand: either cussing me out or apologizing for his mistake, which he now realized was a big one. I led the girl outside and became a little concerned that the other soldiers might now resent my presence, but they still ignored us, which was fine by me. I took the very relieved looking girl out to the road and with Lim, returned to the base. She continued to work around our barracks unmolested. According to Lim, the soldier who abducted her never came back, and none of the other girls in our area were ever bothered by ROK units again. I guess word got out there was a new marshal in town: the Americans.

The tempo of the air war picked up with the Red Chinese offensive. I spent a lot of time at 80ᵗʰ squadron operations, which was a stone's throw from the 36th's, and usually got a peek at the teletyped frag orders for both as they came down from central control, called "Mellow" on the radio. There was a lot of new activity along, and north of, the bomb line—roughly the 38ᵗʰ Parallel. As our missions increased, I spent more time at runway control, or mobile control, a kind of supplementary control tower that monitored air traffic around base. Runway control was always manned by a rated officer and an experienced noncom and had radios to keep track of our aircraft in the pattern as well as the occasional allied or Navy aircraft, or planes from other bases, coming in for emergency landings.

On one of my first visits to runway control, a twin-engine Air Force B-26 (made by Douglas and later called the A-26, used with great effectiveness in Vietnam) came in with "one burning and one turning" and made a superb single-engine landing. Knowing we had to keep the runway open, the pilot eased the damaged bird off to the side and parked it on a patch of bare ground. I jumped into *Hobo* along with a sergeant who was with me and zipped over to the crippled plane. The crew was climbing out as we got there.

"Hey, fellas" I called, "how 'bout a ride?"

"You bet!" the pilot yelled back and piled into the jeep with the rest of his men as if his pants were on fire, which they weren't. "Let's get the hell out of here!"

I had shut off the jeep's motor, so I cranked it back up and leisurely put it in gear.

"NOW!" the B-26 pilot shouted.

I glanced at his aircraft. The shot-up engine was still burning but the fire seemed contained. I knew the guy was shaken—any pilot would be after a close-call in the air—so I tried to say something reassuring, like "the fire truck is on the way" and "we'll take good care of your airplane" or some damn thing like that.

LEFT: Bill's faithful houseboy, Lim Yung Sot (L) with a friend. Lim followed Bill from Kimpo to Suwon just to make sure he got settled okay.

BOTTOM: The local "laundromat" outside Suwon.

The Korean housekeeper who was kidnapped by ROK soldiers. Bill rescued her from a short and unpleasant life as the platoon's official "comfort girl."

"Jesus Christ!" He grabbed my shoulder, "We still got a full load of bombs on that thing! Get the hell out of here!"

I popped the clutch and we laid rubber. A few hundred feet from the aircraft he yelled, "That's far enough!" and he was out of the jeep before it came to a stop. A short distance away was a pile of gravel saved for runway repair and he dove behind it along with the rest of his crew. I truthfully didn't understand the rush, but the sarge and I followed. Just as we hit the dirt, everything turned orange and we heard an enormous explosion in front of us; the concussion felt like an atomic bomb. When we looked up, bits of metal and rubber and God knows what else was falling around us. Where before had stood one moderately damaged B-26 there was now a big smoking hole, with one engine mangled beyond recognition a few dozen yards from our "bunker" and the other somewhere an equal distance in the opposite direction. I suppose there was enough left of the tail to read the airplane's serial number if you fudged a couple of digits. I mean, there was *nothing* left of that bomber!

A bit contritely, I drove the crew back to ops to get them checked over for injuries and arrange for a Gooney Bird to take them back to their base. I felt like saying, "So, other than that, how did the mission go?" but kept my mouth shut.

For my money, the most remarkable thing that happened at runway control involved recovery of an AT-6 forward air controller that had been shot up pretty badly directing ground strikes in the north. We didn't get any distress calls, just a familiar American trainer wobbling in on the northern horizon. We tried to make radio contact, but got no answer, so we figured their receiver had been damaged. The pilot may have been injured, too, because the airplane was really all over the sky. It made one low pass over the field, gear down as if intending to land, then pulled up and went around, which was probably wise, since he was set up to land really long and probably would've gone off the end of the runway. He made another circuit of the field, barely able to hold wings level, and made a skidding turn onto final. I'd trained enough novices to know that was the classic setup for a stall-spin accident; pulling back on the stick to get you through the turn while pressing too much rudder trying to line up with the runway, the airplane suddenly stalls and with all that yaw, you do a snap roll into the ground. But this guy made the turn, got the nose up to almost a three-point landing attitude, and bounced it in. His brakes must've been gone, too, because he just kept rolling until he stopped straight ahead on the runway.

In a flash, the sarge and I were in our jeep and out to the airplane. If there was a wounded man on board, we wanted to get him out fast, but we also wanted to clear the plane off the runway because nobody could take off or land with a damaged bird on the centerline.

We pulled back the front canopy and saw instantly that the pilot was unconscious and probably dead. He had been almost cut in half by heavy caliber ground fire, and if the bullets hadn't killed him outright, he certainly bled to death on the flight back. How the hell, then, did the airplane manage to land?

We stepped back on the wing to the rear cockpit to check on the observer— usually an Army officer or noncom that coordinated aerial attacks with the ground units. To our astonishment, the young guy (I don't remember his rank, but he sure wasn't a pilot) was in good shape, though his face was white as a sheet. It seems he was spared when his pilot got hit and suddenly found himself several thousand feet in the air with nobody to drive him home. Without a radio or a flying lesson, he brought the damaged bird back to friendly territory, learning how to control it on the way, located an airfield, and made a crude but safe landing in a high-horsepower tail-dragger that lots of student pilots still couldn't master after hours of instruction. He was either the luckiest young soldier in his outfit or the unluckiest, I could never figure out which, but he sure had an aptitude for flying, though I doubt if he ever went near an airplane again.

PJW: Some of our most successful missions resulted from targets of opportunity: trucks or tanks or troops or trains you just happened to catch in the open at a time when you had plenty of ammo, ordnance, and fuel. Frequently, these "bonus" targets appeared just before dawn or right around dusk, when the enemy thought it was safer to move. At first, they hid their artillery and vehicles during the day under haystacks, thinking we couldn't see them, which of course, we couldn't. But those caissons and trucks and tanks left tracks, which you could spot a mile away, so we just rolled in and blasted every haystack or barn that had tire tracks leading up to it. When they knew we were onto their system, they began running vehicles up to a haystack or a building, then backing them away and planting anti-aircraft guns inside or around the shelter, giving us a nasty surprise. After awhile we got so we could usually spot an ambush and go after something else. It was a game of cat and mouse, but some cats—and mice—were cleverer and luckier than others.

On June 16, 1951, almost two weeks after my daughter Barbara's seventh birthday, I was leading a flight of four on an armed reconnaissance mission in the Song-bung-ni area. The communist spring offensive had bogged down but they were still trying to force a breakout against our 8th Army in central Korea. In this case, we caught hundreds of Reds in broad daylight working feverishly to construct a bridge across the Imjin River, smack in the middle of one of their major supply routes. As lead, I spotted the activity first—it was pretty hard to miss—and ordered the flight to follow me in, first with napalm against the vehicles and structures, and then for strafing passes at whatever targets remained.

I rolled in and the poured the coals to the plane, seeing the construction was heavily defended by automatic weapons set up on both banks and in the surrounding hills. There were plenty of targets, so I pickled both napalm canisters, knowing the guys behind me would do the same. I pulled up abruptly and zoomed for altitude, rolling over to see if my guys were all right and how much fire we'd put on the target. That napalm really does the job—much of the river was covered with burning, jellied gasoline and the bridge structures were completely enveloped in flame; so I cranked the plane around, dove for the deck, and made several more passes, firing my .50 caliber machine guns, going for the troops who had jumped from the structures and were swimming for the shore. Intelligence later looked at our gun camera film and figured we not only knocked down the structures, preventing completion of the bridge, but killed or wounded at least 50 North Korean soldiers working on or defending the site. The group commander liked the pictures so much he put the flight commander—me—up for a DFC, the Distinguished Flying Cross, which was later awarded.

How did I feel about killing so many "bad guys" so close to my daughter's birthday? To tell you the truth, not much of anything. Sure, I would rather have been with my family at the beach or listening to a ball game on the radio, but that's not the hand I'd been dealt. If somebody (me and my flight, for instance) hadn't stopped those poor guys—many of whom, I'm sure, had families of their own— they would've eventually killed a lot of our troops and not thought twice about it. I guess that's the key to aerial combat. Until you get hit yourself, it's all pretty detached. You just hope it stays that way until your turn in the barrel is over.

WRY: One of the first things I learned about combat is that, despite the challenge and excitement, it isn't a game. Shooting at people from an aircraft feels pretty impersonal, but nothing puts the "you" in "uniform" quicker than having somebody shoot back at you, or killing one of your buddies. That doesn't make war a vendetta. If you take it too personally, you'll go crazy. But it means when your personal survival is at stake, not to mention the survival of the guys around you and the bigger issues of the war, you take it very seriously and do what's required to win.

For their part, the Reds got pretty clever and ruthless about hiding targets. Villages were always a problem, because when intel reported enemy troops in a populated area, you could be sure that at least a few of them—if not most—were taking refuge among civilians. That was sad, because whenever we hit a village, we gave it everything we had and usually leveled the place. A lot of North Koreans hated the communists, so our information about where their troops were hiding was usually good. Our analysts figured that on average we got ten enemy soldiers for every noncombatant we killed, but that didn't make such missions easier. You just had to remind yourself that these villages made good massing points for enemy ground troops, and if you didn't stop them there, they'd bust loose on your own troops or friendly villagers, take them by surprise, and casualties would be much worse. So all you thought about was nailing the target, getting the job done right, and getting everybody back in one piece.

Different targets had different personalities. Iron bridges were hardest to hit because it's like shooting at a skeleton. With all those open girders, space between supports, and so on, there just wasn't much "there" to hit. With bombs, even big thousand pounders, a near miss was as good as a mile, so you dive bombed the road bed then went for the support structure. But the North Koreans got pretty good at repairing bomb damage. Almost overnight they could get a pretty beat-up train trestle or highway bridge back into service. It was very frustrating to be fragged the same target again and again, but that's what it took to keep some of those arterials out of action.

Napalm was just about everybody's favorite—except those on the receiving end. It was extremely effective against ground troops (even those dug in or in bunkers), vehicles, buildings, you name it. That jellied gasoline exploded on contact and spread out like a dropped jar of mayonnaise, sticking to everything. Delivered properly—released at high speed just a few feet off the ground—it was the most effective weapon we had.

Tanks weren't immune to napalm, but if they were moving, they could sometimes wheel away or drive through it, so you'd have to hit them again. I learned that the famous Russian T-34 tanks that equipped the Red armies, while fast and durable, had an Achilles heel, provided you knew where to find it. I discovered that you could take them out with .50 caliber fire if you approached them from behind and ran a few rounds into the air intake used to feed that big engine. The plenum chamber inside was filled with steel baffles—probably to protect the fuel from enemy fire coming in at ground level. But rounds entering from above, at an angle, would bounce around and with some luck, start an internal fire that would either explode the vehicle or cause the crew to abandon it, post haste. If I do say so myself, I got pretty adept at tank-busting, as did the rest of my flight. I like to think those T-34 drivers got kind of worried and started "checking their six" when they saw our yellow-tailed Headhunters circling them like hungry hawks.

One anti-tank mission stood out in particular. I was leading a four-ship formation that caught a column of T-34s marshaling in a narrow valley, preparing to move out, most likely, as part of the Imjin offensive. I signaled my boys to follow me in, but two were hit almost immediately by automatic weapons. I asked if they could continue but their damage was too great, so I ordered them home while they still had airplanes to fly. That left the job to me and my wingman so we hunkered down and went to work.

The first pass was head on. We dropped our napalm and right away took out a third of the column. Instead of coming around for another pass the same way, I pulled straight up, rolled 180-degrees, and split-S'd back in the opposite direction, taking those T-34s from the rear with our massed .50 calibers. We got some good primary and secondary explosions, but the terrain was real tight and there were plenty of targets—tanks and supporting vehicles—left, so we just looped over them again and again until we ran out of ammo. After that, there was nothing more we could do but waggle our wings at the survivors in a kind of "catch you later" salute and head home. Debriefing the mission, I told the intelligence officer that, despite the abort of two planes, results had been excellent. We didn't know how excellent until they finished examining our gun camera film, which confirmed that a large number of vehicles had been destroyed, breaking up the planned attack. The fact that we pressed ahead with half our flight gone and hung around until those ammo belts ran dry must have impressed somebody higher up. Word came down later that they'd put me in for a DFC, which was subsequently awarded. I was just happy to be around to receive it.

Iron bombs were another matter. We had two ways of delivering them: skip bombing (basically, just lobbing them like an underhand softball from high speed at a very low altitude), and dive bombing, which was a lot more accurate but more dangerous, since you had to come in at a steep angle and passed through the defender's killing zone. In a high-speed dive, too, it was easy to misjudge distance, particularly pulling up toward high terrain; I discovered just *how* dangerous on a mission that spring. Our bombs were armed by a little propeller mounted on the nose of each bomb case. When the bomb was released, a small wire running from the bomb to the pylon under each wing allowed the propeller to turn in the airstream, converting the bomb from a great big paperweight to a quarter or half-ton dose of pain for whoever was underneath it. Because of this, one of the worse things you could see while tooling around in formation was that little propeller spinning before you'd pushed the bomb-release button. The second worse thing you could see was a bomb that didn't release when it was supposed to: a "hung bomb" that was armed and ready to fall, but didn't.

I had only one hung bomb during my tour, and that was one too many. Just my luck, it was a thousand-pounder that wouldn't release, so heading back from the target, I had the onerous duty to inform *Mellow* that I was coming back with a hot

TOP: Russian-made T-34 tanks knocked out in battle between Inchon and Kimpo.

BOTTOM: Tank-Killer Yoakley and one of his victims.

one. I tried everything in the book to release that booger—from high-G porpoising to fiddling with the circuit breakers and recycling the pickle switch—but that big boy just wouldn't let go. Halfway back to the base, I was left with a fateful decision: either to try to land with a hot bomb that, if it went off, would take me and the airplane with it and probably close the runway for a week, or point the bird out over the ocean, slow down, trim it up, roll back the canopy, and go over the side, making a "nylon letdown." (Ejecting would've been a bad idea, since the shock of the canon shell expelling the seat might have been enough to set off the bomb.)

While I was trying to figure out which was the lesser of these evils, the airplane gently banked to the left all by itself. I looked out at the right wing and the bomb was gone. It had taken pity on me and fallen off. I racked the bird into a tight turn just in time to see a big explosion below me in an empty field.

Well, no sweat. Wonder what's for dinner?

*L*ife in a combat unit is a lot different than military flying during peace, or even wartime flying in the states. On a combat mission, things are all business; but when you're done for the day or flying for other reasons, the "rules" are pretty lenient and dictated mostly by personal preferences and common sense. For example, when an aircraft came back with battle damage, which was much of the time, the maintenance crews worked like crazy to get it airworthy, but it often required a functional flight test to make sure it was ready for action. Many pilots wanted no part of this. They figured their job was done after combat and didn't want to risk their necks on a maintenance flight or any other kind of non-combat "joy ride." But we loved to fly—and liked it even better when nobody was shooting at us. And let's face it, there was not a lot of entertainment options in central Korea in the early 1950s, so we volunteered regularly for maintenance test hops. The other guys didn't know what they were missing.

PJW: Most of the maintenance flights were short—just around the pattern to cycle the landing gear or check the controls—like local area flying back in the states. However, the ground crews always asked us to stay aloft for at least 45 minutes or more, preferably above 15 or 20,000 feet, so we complied whenever we could, sometimes finding another F-80 or Navy plane on a similar hop that we could form up with or rat-race. It wasn't until after one of these hops that I found out why they wanted us to cruise so high. Since we only used internal fuel on our maintenance flights, the big drop tanks were always empty—or so we thought. In reality, the crew chiefs would load them with cans of beer, depending on the "cold soak" at altitude to chill them, since the base didn't have ice-makers or refrigerators. When we got back, the ground crew swarmed over the tip tanks like bees collecting honey and distributed the cans before they got warm. As the "bartenders" who made it all possible, we usually got a can or two for our efforts. It beat the heck out of reading a dog-eared magazine in a bunk.

On one occasion, I took a maintenance flight up through a cloud deck. Brilliantly clear on top, I spotted another F-80 descending slowly toward the field, obviously getting ready to land. As it banked away from me, my eagle eyes spotted its yellow-tail: a Headhunter from our rival squadron.

Knowing their pilots were always grateful to receive much-needed flying instructions, I decided to bounce him. I goosed my red-tail and climbed to his six o'clock position, ready to dive on him out of the sun. However, this particular Headhunter was pretty sharp, because he turned into me almost immediately and the "fight" was on. We spiraled around in an ever-tightening Lufberry circle, neither of us gaining an advantage, until we were just about to enter the clouds, where such games were too dangerous. We both rolled wings level and pulled abreast.

"Skytel, is that you?" a familiar voice came on the radio.

It was Bill. We had used that call sign—our own private identification code—to check on each other at various times during our tour. Since we flew in different squadrons, we were assigned different targets, but often found ourselves in the air at the same time. When we knew that one of us was heading out or coming back, we'd sometimes use the code-word *Skytel*—often broadcast in the blind—to check on the other's progress, or safety, or just to let each other know we were both still alive and well and up there doing our job. I waggled my wings in recognition and followed Bill into the pattern.

On the ground, we met at the "O-Club" (a collection of rickety wooden chairs and torn sofas inside a drafty tent) and reviewed our chance encounter.

I asked Bill, "How the heck did you know that was me?"

"I dunno," he answered. "The plane just flew like it was you."

That was either the biggest compliment or cleverest insult I ever received.

WRY: Pete and I used to go up all the time just for the hell of it on maintenance tests or ferry flights. Once Pete even escorted General MacArthur's transport into Korea so the Supreme Commander could qualify for that month's combat pay—anything to stay in the air and keep from getting stale.

On one maintenance hop out of Kimpo, I went out over the water, did whatever the crew chief asked me to do, then wifferdilled around a bit and started back to the base. Below me and about 10 miles offshore I spotted a lone U.S. Naval vessel—a corvette or a destroyer. So, seeing as how it was a pretty day and I was full of vinegar, I decided to give them an air show. I firewalled the throttle and picked up speed, quickly approaching the vessel. A few miles out, I did a few loops and Cuban 8s, then dropped to just above the whitecaps to give them the thrill of a high-speed pass. Funny thing was, I was the one who got the thrill. Just as I pulled abreast of the ship, their anti-aircraft guns opened up on me.

I was surprised, to say the least, but had done enough combat flying to know I needed to stay at wavetop level and get the hell out of there as fast as I could. I won't say the Navy has lousy gunners, so I'll assume those were just warning shots to scare me off—and thank goodness they missed. When I was safely out of range, I pulled up and went back to base. I made no attempt to contact the ship by radio, nor did I report their lack of hospitality and failure to appreciate fine airmanship to Air Force authorities back at Kimpo. In fact, I simply landed the plane, made a quick walk around inspection looking for bullet holes or shrapnel tears that might endanger the next pilot (there weren't any) and sauntered into squadron ops, hanging around a little longer than necessary, reading the weather charts and clipboard notices, waiting to see if any irate messages came in from Mellow or the Navy. None did. I can only assume the corvette's captain was as disappointed with the encounter as I was, and put his crew through a lot of extra gunnery drills over the coming weeks. There's a war on, didn't they know?

✪ ✪ ✪

*U*p to now, we felt like a handful of Guard guys (with help from the regular Air Force, of course) fighting the war all by ourselves. We stayed in touch with the Florida unit and learned that, instead of being deployed to France as they expected, sipping wine and eating cheese under the Eiffel Tower, waiting for the Warsaw Pact to attack Western Europe while American eyes were turned on Korea, they were being shipped to Misawa in the northernmost part of Honshu, Japan. This was probably to help protect Japan from a Communist Chinese incursion, or even to stand by for an attack on the mainland, if needed, since nobody at the time knew exactly where the Red Chinese intervention was going, and MacArthur himself wanted to nuke a dozen Chinese cities, including Peking, which was one reason Truman fired him.

Anyway, we felt sorry for our old compatriots who'd had the rug of a cushy European assignment pulled so rudely out from under them, so we looked seriously into hiring a Japanese marching band to meet their ship at dockside and play the Marseillaise as they stepped off. No, really—we did. It turned out to be impractical as well as too expensive, so we let the idea drop. But we couldn't think of a group of guys more deserving of such a welcome.

Meanwhile, morale among U.S. fighter-bomber pilots in Korea was low. Not only were our losses pretty high—one or two planes every day or so due to enemy action or accidents—but the newly arrived F-86s were getting all the glory for "winning the air war" at 30,000 feet while we continued to slug it out above the treetops. The newspapers loved to write about our vaunted F-86 "MiG killers" who were establishing a kill-ratio of 10 enemy planes for every Sabre Jet lost. But if you factored in the number of F-80s downed, plus the other fighter-bombers lost from allied countries and the Navy, that ratio dropped quickly to the range of 3- or 4-to-1. That number didn't make the history books, but was sure the one we thought about every time we saddled up. Not all of us even made it much past the end of the runway.

WRY: Toward the end of summer at Suwon, hot-weather operations in our fully loaded jets were getting to be a real problem. Sometimes when I didn't have a mission, the sergeant I worked with in operations and I would drive out to runway control to watch the takeoffs and landings. There wasn't much we could do if anything went wrong, but when Headhunters were flying, I was always interested in seeing how "my boys" were doing.

On one occasion, a good friend of mine and a frequent wingman in my flight—a fine young pilot named Mark Castellani—released his brakes for a high-gross takeoff on a very hot and humid day. His airplane accelerated slowly and I could tell almost from the start he was going to have a tough time making it into the air. About halfway down the runway he raised the nose to takeoff attitude, but the aircraft didn't budge. After another thousand feet or so, it began to skip and chirp along the runway, trying desperately to get airborne. It continued that way, skittering over the ground—buoyed up by ground-effect (riding on compressed air under the wing) then settling back down—way past any point for a successful aborted takeoff. A few seconds later he ran off the end of the runway, plowed through a pile of trash, then bounced briefly into the air, engine roaring, before dropping in a cloud of dust.

By this time, the sergeant and I were in *Hobo,* racing toward the crash. We knew there was a little village about a quarter-mile from the runway; the Air Force had asked its few inhabitants many times to move, but they always refused. Now it looked like the inevitable had happened. The only question was how lucky or unlucky all involved would be.

I drove like a maniac, following the dust and debris. When we got to the village, we saw the F-80 had rammed through the central square—probably a few feet off the ground, still struggling to get airborne. A dozen or so little kids—we later found out they had all been eight to ten years old—had been playing there when the plane sliced through them, killing them all. But at that moment, our first duty was to Castellani so I gunned the jeep past the carnage to where the F-80's fuselage had finally come to rest.

The cockpit was still intact, but that was about it. The wings were gone and raw fuel was everywhere, not to mention unexpended ordnance, but miraculously, there had been no explosion or fire. Castellani had blown the canopy, so getting at him was no problem. Without thinking, I reached in and began unfastening his seat belt and shoulder harness. Though covered with blood, he groaned so I knew he was still alive. His ejection seat was still armed so between that and all the fuel, my main priority was to just get him out and away as soon as possible.

I said, "Take it easy. We'll get you out." When the harness was off, I loosened the chin strap to his helmet and gently pulled it forward. As soon as I did, I saw the back of his head was gone—just brains exposed to the air. I didn't say anything—what could you say?—so I eased him back onto the headrest. The medics would have to deal with it.

"Don't worry," I said. "Relax. Everything will be okay."

By this time, the sergeant had run over to the village a few dozen yards away to see about the civilians. I stuck with Castellani, though there was nothing I could do except talk to him and try to keep him conscious and wonder what was taking our emergency crews so long. Normally after a runway accident, our ambulances and fire trucks (not to mention Air Police and even a few senior officers) would be swarming over the scene, but this time I didn't see hide nor hair of them. Maybe it was because there had been no explosion or fire ball—nothing gets your attention around an airbase faster than a loud *boom* and a rising column of black smoke—and I was sure mobile control and the tower had seen the whole thing. For whatever reason, though, our emergency vehicles were taking forever to get there. When an ambulance finally arrived a few minutes later, I helped the medics lift Castellani out of his seat, onto a stretcher, and watched them roar away. I learned later that he had died not long after arriving at the base hospital.

I jogged over to the village and a tragic scene got worse. The kids had been hit without warning—even a jet at max power doesn't get your attention when you're used to living by a noisy runway. Most of their little heads had popped off as their bodies were crushed by the wing, many leaving their little shoes right where they'd been standing. The Sarge and I just stared at each other, knowing we should do something, but what? We looked around quickly for somebody in charge—a headman, mayor, old mama *san* or papa *san*—anyone who might know the kids and their families, but we didn't see a soul. Maybe the women were in the paddies or working on the base, leaving the kids on their own, we had no idea. The only Koreans we saw were a few men in a nearby field where Castellani's plane had killed an ox. They were arguing about something—probably who would get which parts of the carcass—they sure didn't seem to care about the kids.

Castellani's wreckage at a village near Kimpo. A dozen kids and one fine pilot lost their lives in that tragedy.

"Well Sarge," I said, "let's do what we can and get the hell out of here!"

Together, we placed the remains as neatly as we could in a part of the courtyard that seemed cleaner and less damaged than the rest. We weren't policemen or rescue workers or the Red Cross or anything like that; we just wanted to leave the bodies with a little dignity for the relatives who'd find them. After a couple of minutes, when that awful work was done, we checked again for some responsible person—still, nobody home—so we got back in the jeep and raced to squadron ops. I found our Korean interpreter and told him what happened, suggesting he get to the village ASAP and help whoever showed up to cope with the grisly scene. By then the fire trucks and base security were responding to hose down the fuel and remove the ordnance. I have no idea what the Air Force told the families and I never went back to find out. I just hoped that the survivors found a better, safer place to live.

Our biggest air battle came early in May, when the first phase of the Red Chinese offensive was halted near Seoul. This was a raid of epic proportions, just like something out of a WWII newsreel, where strike fighters and bombers from all allied services participated: a total force of about 300 aircraft. Our target was Yong Dang Dong near Sinuigu, an airfield just north of the Yalu River.

My flight's assignment was flak suppression, which meant we went in first and either knocked out the anti-aircraft guns or made the crew keep their heads down while the other aircraft maneuvered overhead. Although I didn't have too many opportunities to enjoy the show, the sight of so many aircraft filling the sky was spectacular.

Our primary weapon against the flak guns were 500-lb bombs set with VT's, or variable timed "proximity" fuses that detonated 50 to 100 feet above the gun position, spraying the battery with hot shrapnel and a fiery concussion that would crack cement. It must have been hell for those guys on the ground, but they were trying to knock us down and it was our job to stop them. When we ran out of bombs, we strafed them with our guns, which in that environment meant running in at high speed, as close to the ground as we dared, then popping up for a few seconds to jab the nose down and squeeze off a few bursts. After that we either pulled up and jinked out of range or stayed on the deck and sought cover of the terrain until we got set for another run.

We did a lot of damage and silenced a lot of guns that way. Every ship in my flight took some hits, mostly from small arms, though all of us got back. Coming off target, we got bounced by some MiGs, which was to be expected given our proximity to one of their big bases. This time they intended to attack us and I let them get real close before signaling the flight to break into them. They *really* didn't like to see those massed .50 calibers pointed in their direction, so they broke off and climbed like scalded cats to an altitude where we couldn't follow. It's always frustrating to look up an enemy's tailpipe and know you can't do a thing about him, but MiG fighting wasn't our job. That was up to the '86s.

Inability to get MiGs was only one factor that tended to depress morale. Pete and I were pretty gung ho, mostly because we had a lot more flying time than the younger pilots and it's easier to fight the enemy when you don't have to fight the airplane. Besides, a lot of guys didn't really know why we were in Korea and while the vast majority of them just hitched up their britches and did the job, a few had real problems getting with the program. To me, this is the big difference between plain old "morale" and combat spirit. I wanted guys in my flight who put the mission first and not everyone did. Ground aborts weren't uncommon, but once you sucked up the gear you were pretty much expected to hold up your end of the log. I had a couple of guys on various missions who aborted after takeoff, giving one excuse or another, but I knew damn well it was because they got cold feet. Even worse, when this happened over enemy territory, I had to dispatch another wingman to escort a weak sister home. Air Force policy was to never leave a damaged or malfunctioning airplane to fend for itself. This was a double whammy, since it not only cut the combat strength of my flight in half, it royally pissed me off—neither one of which I enjoyed.

One of my pilots was a real pain-in-the-ass in this regard. I put up with him because he at least got through to most targets and although you couldn't count on him to do much when he got there, he went through the motion of delivering his ordnance. At minimum, that gave the enemy somebody else to shoot at while the rest of us did our thing. But on one instance, this strategy almost got me killed.

I was leading my flight in an attack on a target nestled in some hills. The terrain wasn't too bad and the target wasn't heavily defended, but you still have to stay on your toes or you're in for a nasty surprise. I was just about to release my external stores when four, 5-inch HVARs sailed past my canopy from behind the plane. I knew immediately what had happened—the joker behind me lost his nerve and just pickled his ordnance and peeled away, not caring, particularly, that I was in his way. I now had to make a quick decision. I liked to get close on any attack, and this yo-yo had just distracted me when all my concentration needed to be on the target. Even worse, we carried eight rockets per ship, and I had no idea if he had fired another four just to make sure he wouldn't have to come back. If he had, and I pulled up, I might very well fly into them. Almost as bad, by firing early and turning away, he left the bottom of my plane undefended and a lot of good men had met their maker that way.

Anyway, all those thoughts passed through my head in a split second and I quickly broke off target. Climbing safely, I asked rhetorically on the radio if there was anyone in my flight stupid enough to fire with another F-80 in his line of sight. For some reason, nobody answered. Back on the ground, I chewed the guy out royally and asked what he had to say for himself. He acted surprised and said, "Hey, why are you so upset? I saved your life!"

That was the last straw. I went to the squadron commander and told him I didn't want the guy in my flight. I added that if the group commander was smart, he'd never let the guy get close to an airplane again. A few days later, the guy who "saved my life" was off flying status and assigned to a desk which, in retrospect, probably made both of us very happy.

PJW: Though some missions were tougher than others, the pressure of flying combat was pretty constant. You never knew what to expect, so you tried to be ready for anything. Some hairy-sounding frag orders turned out to be a piece of cake while some milk runs turned into massacres, though thankfully that didn't happen too often. You just had to stay sharp and pay attention to what you were doing.

During the summer of big battles that stopped the Red Chinese offensive, I led quite a few flak suppression missions to pave the way for our B-29s, many of them in the area around Pyonyang. These were dive bombing attacks that started at about 15,000 feet and ended up on the deck. My wingman and I usually separated, on purpose, so that we could take on different targets. In this case, I was attacking east to west, which meant my egress after the bomb drop would take me out over a broad tidal flat on Korea Bay.

The attack went well and after releasing the bomb, I kept the plane down on the deck and picked up about 550 knots, near red-line for that altitude. It was late in the day and that was our last pass, so it felt pretty good to be zooming into a pretty sunset while putting miles fairly quickly between me and some guys I had just made very angry. But I was getting low on fuel and the base was 150 miles to the south, so I needed to start climbing and turning soon. Just as I raised the nose I saw some puffs of dust kick up about a mile ahead of me and just to the left, on top of some low hills on the edge of the mud flat. About the same time, little white dots sparkled on my windscreen then lengthened into tracers as 40 mm shells from a North Korean Quad tried to bracket my plane.

This quickly ruined a nice sunset. Normally, I would've just moved the stick a little and sprayed the hill with .50 caliber rounds—no ground gunner in the world would keep firing into that. With luck, I might even knock out the position. The problem was, I was too low to even *think* about banking the airplane. If a wing dipped more than a few degrees, it would've dug into the mud and done the enemy's job for him. If I pulled up, I would've presented him with a perfect target, the belly of my beautiful silver airplane shining brightly in the setting sun.

So there I was, roaring along like a bat out of hell, being shelled point-blank by the enemy's most effective low-altitude, rapid-fire anti-aircraft weapon, which I was approaching rapidly, and I couldn't do a thing about it. Even my wingman was too far back to help. In fact, he was probably already on his way home.

The distance from me to the Quad was now down to a hundred yards. The airplane was doing fine—I hadn't been hit—and by 30 or 40 yards I could see the individual crewmen manning the gun, trying frantically to swivel those four big barrels around, still blasting away. It was scary and frustrating and kind of amusing all at the same time, like I was just a spectator watching this horrible show, but I felt I had to do something. After all, I could now see individual faces of the gun crew and they could read the tail number of my airplane. So without thinking—out of nothing more than nervous tension—I just raised my hand and waved.

Now, I can't say that this unexpected gesture made the gun quit firing, but I believe that staccato pounding skipped at least one beat. I flashed past and as quickly as I'd appeared, I was gone behind some hills. The tracers stopped and I zoomed up, twisting and turning. At a safe altitude, I rolled out on a heading for home. On the way back, I wondered what those guys were thinking. "Did you see that stupid American? He just waved at us! What an idiot!" Of course, they might also have thought I was America's most fearless pilot—to simply *wave* at them as I flew within a stone's throw of their position. Yep, Fearless Pete. That must've been what they called me.

Not all missions ended so cavalierly. On another action north of the bomb line, I led two flights (an eight ship formation) on a pre-dawn sweep over mountainous terrain looking for targets of opportunity. We arrived in our sector at about 15,000 feet, maybe a little higher. At that altitude, in the dark, we could fly with our plane's navigation lights on, making formation flying easier, though for obvious reasons we turned them off for an attack.

At about 4 AM, I spotted a reddish glow in a canyon a short distance ahead of us. Railroad tracks cris-crossed the area, but so did railway tunnels, and enemy trains usually parked inside them during daylight to avoid being seen from the air. That didn't always save them, since many of our skip-bombing runs were aimed at lobbing 500- or 1,000 pounders into the mouth of the tunnels. If we hit a train inside—great. If we didn't, the resulting explosion often brought the hillside down, which meant the Reds would spend days clearing away the rubble and restoring the track. This time, the tell-tale glow could only mean one thing—we'd finally caught a locomotive, underway and in the open.

I put the formation in trail and rolled in for a closer look. The canyon floor was fairly wide and an attack presented no special problems as long as I followed the rails. Best of all, the locomotive was hauling quite a few cars and chugging up a

An F-80 with flak damage after a mission to Pyongyang.

Pete (right) and Bud Haefel show how you don't need a plane to do some fancy flying.

shallow grade. It would be five or ten minutes, at least, before it could take refuge in the nearest tunnel. We had them cold.

I led several passes with guns and rockets, shooting the length of the train. As always, we picked up some automatic weapons and small arms fire from the cars, but it was ineffective. Best of all, the locomotive blew up, stopping the train, and we got several big secondary explosions from the cars; they had been hauling a lot more than *kimchee* and cheap Russian cigarettes. The 8th FBW liked the results. After analyzing our gun camera film, they put me in for a second DFC, which was awarded awhile later.

*C*ombat is like hitting your head with a hammer—at the time you'd rather do something else and when you stop, it feels great. We were tearing through our hundred-missions at a pretty good clip, although Pete sprained his ankle playing volley ball and lost two weeks flying to mend. A lot of good men got equally close to rotation but never completed their tours. Bud Haefel, our buddy from the Florida Rockets who'd survived that harrowing air show collision with Bill Haviland in 1948, flew with the Headhunters and got shot up pretty badly on one mission. We'd been having some trouble with the F-80's ejection system; it didn't always fire, and when it did, the parachute sometimes got tangled with the seat, so a lot of guys didn't trust it. Bud was one of them. He brought back a badly damaged plane he probably should have abandoned, made a good belly landing, then skidded off the end of the runway, hit a berm, and blew up. Sad ending for a great guy we'd known a long time, but at least it was quick.*

Another great guy with a little better luck was Jim Kiser, intelligence officer for the 36th. He didn't fly much, but when he did it was often with Pete, and they frequently enjoyed a cigar and a beer together after a mission. He had been Air Force permanent party in Japan, living there with his wife and child when the war broke out. Pete thought so highly of him, he recommended that Jim take over his flight when we rotated home. Unfortunately, Jim didn't get the chance. His plane went down about sunset during a skip-bombing mission against a bridge close to the Chinese border. Always an aggressive wingman, he pressed his attack too closely and the blast from his own bomb hitting a girder shattered his plane, though Jim was able to bail out. Again, the ejection sequence caused him trouble and ripped open one of his knees, but the chute deployed as advertised and lowered him gently into a tree on a rocky hilltop. The bad news was, the hill was surrounded by North Korean soldiers, who swarmed over it looking for the Yankee pilot who just ruined their brand new bridge. Jim hid among some boulders while the rest of the flight strafed the troops, but their fuel was low and it was getting dark, so soon they headed for home. We learned the rest of Jim's story after the war. He tells it more or less like this:

"I found a crack in one of the boulders and squeezed through it. I knew the North Koreans were all around me, swarming over the hill like angry ants, so I drew my .45 pistol and pointed it at the opening. One soldier walked in front of the crack but faced the wrong way. If he had taken just one glance in my direction that muzzle flash would've been the last thing he ever saw.

"After dark, I tried to hike to the China Sea where the Navy was operating, but I ejected so fast I hadn't had time to pull my feet completely off the rudders, so I clipped one knee on the instrument panel, laying it open to the bone. As a result, I couldn't move very fast, and every step was painful. I'd also lost a lot of blood and passed out a couple of times. I finally collapsed in a rice paddy with my head against the berm. Good thing, because I passed out again and would've drowned if I'd fallen flat.

"I came-to feeling a nudge against my ribs. It was a North Korean soldier poking me with the barrel of his rifle, shining a flashlight in my face. Without thinking, I grabbed the rifle and pulled it forward. He wasn't expecting that and lost his balance, falling on top of me. While he struggled to regain the rifle, I reached down and pulled a knife from my boot. This knife wasn't intended for hand-to-hand combat; we all carried them in case the dingy under our seats accidentally inflated in the cockpit—we needed something to deflate it fast to keep control of the airplane. But I knew it was there and just acted instinctively. I stabbed the guy several times until he rolled off and lay still.

"I knew I had to get out of there, so I used the rifle as a crutch until it dawned on me that if the soldiers found the body and discovered me with the rifle, they would kill me on the spot, so I threw it away. Just before dawn, I found a beat-up little shack and crawled inside, planning to hide until nightfall when I could again head for the coast. Unfortunately, my shelter was a woodshed and a North Korean woman discovered me in the morning. She screamed and got the soldiers, who captured me. I didn't get any medical attention until we arrived at a P.O.W. camp, and even then I would need more surgery back in the states. It was a long march to the camp, with captured G.I.s and South Koreans

Pete's friend, Lt. Jim Kiser (standing, second from right), was downed by his own bomb blast on his 81st mission but bailed out successfully. He spent the rest of the war in a North Korean P.O.W. camp. This photo (showing a Chinese guard at left) was stolen by Jim as it lay drying on a rock and kept hidden until his release.

joining us every few miles. Once, our column got strafed by a flight of F-80s. I looked up from the ditch at the side of the road and saw a red tail on one plane as it flashed by. I had been attacked by my own guys! I always wondered if that pilot ever knew who he'd been shooting at."

WRY: On March 19, 1951, shortly after the Red Chinese launched the second phase of their spring offensive, I led an armed reconnaissance flight over North Korea in the vicinity of the Chosin Reservoir. The calendar may have said "spring" but the weather was still winter, with layers of thick cloud everywhere. My element leader was a great guy named Willie Wall who had flown with me on numerous missions. Conditions were exceptionally bad in our assigned area, so absent X-ray vision, all we could do was fly between cloud layers and peek down through occasional holes to try and spot enemy activity on the snow-splotched ground.

Through one of these "sucker holes" I spotted a few vehicles and troops snaking their way along a winding mountain road about 2,000 feet below the peaks and a thousand feet above the valley floor. My initial reaction was, "Great! We finally found a target!"—doubly good because the road was carved into a rock wall and gave them no place to hide. On the other hand, the surrounding terrain was like a fortress. Getting at them would be risky; we'd be attacking a low-value target with no guarantee of success. Rather than risk losing the whole flight, I told my guys to orbit above the nearby hills while I made an exploratory pass. I had second thoughts about that too, but as it turned out, they came too late.

I approached the road at high speed from the mouth of a long, narrow valley. We carried rockets but using them would've been a bad idea: explosions on the cliff wall would've thrown debris into the path of the aircraft, so I elected to use guns. I fired a few short bursts, but the road was so winding and the terrain so jagged it took a lot of concentration just to put a few rounds on target, so I banked away and started looking for a way out. That's when I began to have those second thoughts. A big mountain loomed in front of me, with a saddle-back between peaks about a thousand feet above the road. I flicked the stick toward it and pulled back. The throttle was full bore and in the cold air, the engine delivered a lot of thrust, but it was early in the mission and the plane was still loaded with rockets and fuel and I could tell instantly I wouldn't make it. The saddleback was seconds away—a slope, not a sheer wall, thank God, because the only question was how hard I would hit. Instinct told me that if I hit the slope with the flat underside of the airplane, like a slap with a hand rather than a blow by a hammer, I might just be able to limp away. Right before impact, I jerked the nose up.

A terrific *bang*—like a piano dropped from a skyscraper. The inertia reel on my shoulder harness locked and my head snapped forward. My hands dropped from the controls then bounced up into the air. I immediately grabbed the stick and throttle and heard an explosion on my left; a couple of underwing rockets had gone off. I looked over just in time to see half my left wing break off and disappear in flames behind me. But the airplane was still flying. I felt like I'd been punched by Joe Louis, but I was alive. The rocks and weeds and patches of snow that filled the windscreen a second ago were suddenly gone, replaced by a deepening valley and a beautiful bowl of sky. I worked the stick. The airplane wallowed like a washtub in a hurricane, but at least it responded for the moment. I was suddenly aware that I was holding full right aileron and full right rudder just to stay pointed in the same direction. I didn't have to pull back on the stick. I was not only climbing, but accelerating. I tried to retard the throttle, to reduce speed, but it was jammed wide open. I knew I had to keep the speed down The plane was really shaking and I didn't want to lose more parts, so I raised the nose. The airspeed dropped a little and rate of climb increased.

I thought I entered the clouds, but it was the cockpit filling with smoke. I couldn't see or breathe so I blew the canopy. The cockpit cleared with a blast of frigid air. About this time I became aware of a voice on the radio. I glanced over my right shoulder. There was Willie Wall on my right wing.

"You're on fire, Bill," he said, his voice an octave higher than usual. "Get the hell out of it and get out now! It's just a matter of time till it falls apart!"

My right wing looked like a washboard, the left was half gone, and I didn't even want to think about the tail. I didn't want to bail out, not just yet, not if I didn't have to, not over North Korea, not over these goddamn mountains.

"Hell no," I answered, "I'm going to get down to the Navy. I'll fly it as long as I can, then get out when I lose control. What do I look like?"

"Well—" his plane dropped back and down a little, "The bottom of your fuselage is gone. The engine is hanging down. Don't ask me what's holding it on. Your tailpipe is crushed but you got power. Your nose is all bashed in and everything under your wing is on fire."

I glanced down at my map, still clipped to my thigh and fluttering in the wind. I was 80 miles from Wonsan Harbor, less than ten minutes flying time if I could hold everything together. Mission briefing said the Navy was conducting operations down there, shelling the enemy coast.

"I'll try for Rei-to island," I said. I'm sure I sounded like a soprano myself. "Call Monte Carlo." That was the Navy's code name for the task force. "Tell 'em I'm on my way."

"Roger," Willie complied.

Glancing out at him, partly for reassurance, partly to see how my right wing was doing, I noticed his plane was in a slightly nose high attitude. That meant we were either slowing down or climbing. I glanced at my airpseed indicator. It was approaching 450 knots and accelerating. What hadn't broken off at impact was bound to blow away if I flew much faster, but that flattened tailpipe was acting like a nozzle on a water hose and with the throttle jammed open, there wasn't much I could do except keep the nose up, which meant keep climbing and getting colder. At least more altitude meant more insurance for clearing the peaks along the coast and having some gliding distance over the water in case that tough little engine decided to quit.

After what seemed like forever, I saw a blue smear on the horizon and a flotilla of ships off to the right. We were passing through 10,000 feet and I didn't want to go higher, but every time I relaxed back pressure on the stick the ship started to vibrate and accelerate.

"Approaching 500 knots, buddy," Willie said. "Better start thinking about—" Before he finished, the .50 caliber guns in my nose shorted out and began to fire— all by themselves—and my left wing, what was left of it, started shedding its skin. A fraction of a second later it folded at the root and the nose dropped like an anvil. I was already lifting the ejection handles.

The 500 knot wind blast hit me like a Mack truck. I unlatched the lap belt and kicked the seat into space. Tumbling, I noticed then that everything I had worn below the lap belt—including my flying boots—was torn off, making a chilly trip even colder. I slapped at the D-ring on my parachute harness, but my fingers were too cold and numb to grasp it, so I shoved my flattened hand through the opening and yanked it with my wrist, and—nothing. *Oh shit—I got a streamer!* I looked down at my bare legs and saw the risers—the lines that attach the harness to the parachute—tangled around my legs. I kicked like a madman until the opening shock jerked me parallel to the horizon, then eased me gracefully into a swaying arc below the nylon canopy. I have to tell you, I've seen some pretty women and beautiful airplanes in my time, but that big old circus tent above me was the most gorgeous sight in the world.

I let out a deep breath and glanced down to enjoy the view. There was a Navy chopper below me, closing fast. I waved at the pilot (as if he might see my arm but miss that big canopy!) and he waved back—another reassuring sight—then the ocean smacked me in the face. It wasn't so much the impact as the temperature. That water was *cold!* I inflated my life vest, which popped me back to the surface, and wiped the water off my face just as the canopy drifted down beside me. Again, those damned risers covered me like an octopus. To be honest, this was the first time in the whole miserable adventure that I really got scared. We'd all heard about pilots ejecting safely over water only to be dragged down by their parachutes, and those blasted risers were thicker than sea weed. I fought like a maniac for what seemed like an hour, whacking away at those lines, until a canvas sling lowered by the helicopter hit me on the head. I looped my left arm through it, and tried to insert my right arm but the pain in that shoulder was excruciating. I just couldn't do it. I was about to fall back when I became aware of rising from the water so I just held on. A second later strong arms hauled me into the helicopter and, after what seemed like another hour of the helo playing tug-of-war with the wet parachute, the crewman freed my harness and we watched it drop away.

"Thanks, fellas!" I croaked. Kinda stupid, I know, but heartfelt.

"Don't mention it!" he shouted into my face. The name tape on his jump suit said *Moore*. I would later learn that his first name, like mine, was Bill. "You okay? You hurt anywhere?"

Captain William R. Yoakley

Bail Out over KOREA

"I took a good look at the Communists on the way down and strafed them good. They were all on one road. Clobbered them all—and then started the pull-out."

12

ABOVE AND OPPOSITE PAGE: *Flying* magazine's cover story about Bill's "Bail Out Over Korea," from the August, 1951 issue.

The captain's wingman yelled. 'Get the hell out. It's just a matter of time till it falls apart.'

BIG, blond Jack Jefferson is a CBS correspondent in Korea—and a part-time aviation writer who has written some top war stories for FLYING. Several weeks ago Jefferson was sitting in a press camp just back of the UN lines when he heard about the narrow escape of Capt. William R. Yoakley, a jet pilot attached to the 8th Fighter-Bomber Wing in Korea.

Jefferson couldn't locate Yoakley in the Korean melee, but a few days later he found something just as good. He got hold of a tape recording made aboard the U.S.S. Manchester after Yoakley was rescued by the Navy. Yoakley's brief and dramatic story, as he told it in the cruiser's wardroom, was recorded so that it could be played back later to all the ship's crew.

Here is Yoakley's story in his own words.—ED.

MY EXPERIENCES really weren't too much in a way, kind of like a bad dream when I look back on it. But it wasn't bad at all the way it worked out—thanks to the Navy.

I was strafing Communist troops down in a mountain pass. I was leading my flight and it didn't look too good. We have quite a bit of difficulty with the jets in very rugged terrain such as we were in at this particular time. So I instructed my flight to stay up, and

I'd go down and see how it was, which I'm glad I did, or else there probably would have been four of us out there for the Navy to pick up. Maybe—if the four of us could have made it the way I did.

I went down in this ravine. It was quite deep, about 4,000 feet below the tops of the mountains. I took a good look at the Communist troops on the way down, and strafed them good. Clobbered them all. At least I got that much out of the pass because they were all on one road there.

As I pulled out, I had my fingers crossed, hoping and thinking that I could make it all right. But I hadn't taken into account one thing. I had a considerable load on board, still quite a few rockets, a lot of fuel, and a combination of things. So I didn't quite make it over the mountain.

I flew into the side of it instead of over it. I bumped about as hard as anyone can bump a mountain, I guess. I really believe that they're going to have to revise their maps, because I'm sure I changed the geography a bit. I hit hard enough to daze me and tear the airplane up considerably. I don't know what happened after that. I guess the good Lord took hold of me. Next thing I knew the plane was back in the air again after a terrific jolt and loud crash. I was heading almost straight up. (Continued on page 59)

'I HIT THE TRIGGER'

CAPTAIN Yoakley describes the escape mechanism of the F-80 *Shooting Star:*

"Bailing out of the jet is really quite simple. The seat ejection is nothing less than a 37-mm. shell mounted in a tube which in turn is mounted to the seat. The seat is on a track. Also, our canopy is loaded with a shell the equivalent of a 20-mm., and there are two handles to pull to get rid of everything. The first handle is the canopy handle. It blows the canopy off.

"They used to have just a canopy release, but the canopy had a bad habit of scooping in and knocking out the pilot. So they devised this canopy ejection which blows the canopy off and gets rid of it safely.

"The seat ejection has two arm rests and two stirrups for the pilot's feet. You put your feet in the stirrups and pull up both arm rests. The trigger is on the right arm rest. You pull the trigger and the rest of it is up to you and the parachute."
[Photo shows ejection test in a T-33, two-place version of the F-80.]

13

ESCAPE FROM A
SHOOTING STAR

by Timothy J. Mulvey*

His right wing was shattered, the engine hung by a single bolt and his F-80 was on fire—
Bill Yoakley staked his life on the short end of million-to-one odds and came out on top

CAPTAIN BILL YOAKLEY, WHO CHEATED FLAMING DEATH

THE BITING breeze of March that stings the orchards of Taegu is whipping the cold mists off the mountaintops. The atmosphere is brilliant where the sun soaks through. Great blasts of exhaust, pouring from the tails of jets that taxi to the runway, roar across the valley floor and shudder in the sound pockets of the hills. It is a day for flying.

Capt. Bill Yoakley of Yukon, Florida, snaps the button of his crash helmet, adjusts his lip microphone, and is set to go. Leader of this flight of F-80s out of the 8th Fighter Bomber Wing, this is just another armed reconnaissance job for Yoakley. Lt. Willy Wall is the element leader this morning. There are four planes in all. Weather to the north around Wonsan is reported not too good. At a signal from the tower, the sleek planes nose into the wind, gather speed, and leap to the air with quivering, rocket-laden wings.

Armed reconnaissance is all that the mission implies.

*From his book "These Are Your Sons," McGraw-Hill Book Co., Inc., New York. Copyright 1952 by Timothy J. Mulvey.

72

See page 98

ABOVE AND OPPOSITE PAGE: From *Real* magazine's reprint of a chapter on Bill's bailout, "Escape from a Shooting Star," in Timothy J. Mulvey's 1952 book, *These Are Your Sons.*

The pilot relaxes over friendly areas, recognizing the curvature of terrain already won. It is only when he soars beyond the hair lines of his map—those critical sections that lie in altitude tint legends—it is then that reconnaissance takes on the significance of the hunt. His jet has become a bird of war, seeking and being sought.

Bill Yoakley, as yet, has time to admire the weather and to feel the joy of being alive. Up here where the sun dances along the silver spread of the wings, he is conscious of the power that hums around him. There are those who said, with no end of ridicule from the lads who handle the flying Turkey, that jet pilots are *different*.

A Plane To Be Proud Of

Bill is not ready to go on record about being different. He has mixed with too many Mustang admirers and Corsair crusaders to be able to say that the cockpit of a jet has anything to do with the making a man. But this he knows. This glass dome above his head that juts like a bubble on a silver cigar, houses one of the finest pieces of workmanship that has ever knifed the air. Streamlining was the word that dictated every inch, fore and aft. Streamlining was the performance pattern that had been written into the blueprints. To attach any exterior equipment to the sleek contour of the ship was, theoretically, to knock the bolts out of it—as her designers had declared.

This F-80 was first and foremost a fighter-intercepter. Yet, though it was cleanly cut for the tricky business of interception, the jet that Bill Yoakley rode, that morning, had been harnessed, comparatively speaking, with a load bigger than a B-36's. The hum that trailed behind him was the war song of aviation's first improvised jet bomber. There is pardonable pride that runs in the blood of the man who sits at the controls of an F-80. Bill Yoakley was hitched to a Shooting Star.

The weather was a smudge about Wonsan. Like ducks avoiding scud, the four jets banked low to get under it. The bearing was westward, but when the clouds got darker and heavier, they twisted off at 180 degrees and whistled upward to Hamhung. The arc took them more than 80 miles above the coastal city. Clearer and colder up here, the terrain spread out in sunned and shadow-blue valleys. Snow in white splotches gleamed in the lowlands. This was the time for scrutinizing every paddy and road for telltale marks. The pace, clocked to the last gallon of fuel consumption, was the quick eye-raking of the area to spot human, animal, and vehicular movement.

At about 12:30 P.M. the four jets were sweeping over a valley. Like all Korean valleys, it spread wide and then was instantly choked in a funnel-pinch of mountains. Traveling at jet speed, it is easy to miss the mound that is really a camouflaged tank. But this morning there was no mistaking the trail of the enemy. He was abroad on trucks and in ox carts. His supply dumps were evident scars in the snow.

"Gas Mask Baker Lead," Yoakley spoke into the microphone. "I've got something."

The message was an instant alert. From the weaving, searching lines of reconnaissance, the four jets stiffened into the spaced slots of hungry falcons that have found their pitch and are getting set for the stoop.

Yoakley ordered the flight to hold off while he went in

SCREAMING DOWN in his F-80 to strafe Red vehicles in North Korea, Yoakley was trapped in a mountain-formed bowl.

for the first run. Overshooting the valley intentionally, he sped back in a hill-skirting sweep and ranged his jet for the direct dip into the target area. The accompanying team, with ordnance switches checked and tank tips poking at the sky, circled watchfully, ready to dart in as soon as Yoakley should speak.

In this split instant, as the lead F-80 climbs for the diving altitude, there is the quick juggling of target value in the back of Yoakley's head: What is the lay of the land? It is clearer now. There is the valley below him. There also is the mountain road. The road is what Yoakley wants to reach. It is a twisting line carved into the shoulder of the mountain, about 1,000 feet above valley level. The road bristles with men and material. But above the road rises 2,000 feet of bare, hard rock.

Target value is a quantum that involves the calculated

"My right shoulder." I rotated my right arm, giving myself another jolt of pain.

"Gotta get rid of that jacket," the crewman yelled.

We tried to unzip it, but the zipper was frozen shut—literally covered with ice, it had been that cold.

"Mind if I cut if off?" he asked, producing an impressive commando knife.

"Be my guest," I said, and he did.

"You want this back?" he asked when it was off, apparently impressed by the Flying Tiger-style "blood chit" sewn on the back.

"No, it's yours," I was just glad to be out of the water. Hells bells, if I'd had my checkbook, I'd have given him my life savings! He glanced at my shoulder but seemed more concerned with the pupils of my eyes and the color of my skin, which was becoming a lovely shade of blue. Teeth chattering, I got wrapped in a blanket as the helicopter peeled away.

A few minutes later we landed on the chopper pad of a big LST anchored just outside the line of warships. The medics helped me out and rushed me into the showers, where they kept me under hot water for almost an hour to stave off hypothermia. When they finally turned off the tap, they asked how I was feeling and I told them my right shoulder still hurt. The medic in charge said, "The helo pilot says you're fine. Tomorrow he'll take you to the *Manchester*." I asked them to send a message to my unit, to let them know I was okay, and they said fine, they'd to it, but didn't say when. I then had a hot meal and a nice long sleep in the infirmary.

The next morning I boarded the chopper again. It's pilot was Lt. Don Whittaker, the same fellow who had rescued me the day before. Fling-wing flying was like a black art to me then, but Whittaker made it look easy. We talked about the rescue and he said the 30- or 40-knot winds on the surface had given him fits. It took all the chopper's power to pull me up against the "sea anchor" of that big, wet canopy: re-inflating every time it left the water. Every flier does his job, but saving people is probably a lot more rewarding than blowing them up. Thank God for guys like Don and Bill whose guts and brainwork in Korea wrote the book on helicopter rescues: techniques our forces would use so successfully in Vietnam and later conflicts.

After a short flight, we landed on the aft deck of the heavy cruiser *U.S.S. Manchester.* I stayed there a few days because they were in the middle of shore bombardment operations and couldn't spare a bird to take me back to the mainland. In a way, it was a welcome vacation. That afternoon I got to watch the *U.S.S. Missouri* steam into the harbor and drop anchor. Hearing the Navy had an errant flyboy as their guest, the captain invited me to dinner, which I was happy to accept. I got a quick tour of the ship—one impressive piece of equipment, I'll tell you—and saw the brass plaque on deck commemorating the exact spot where the Japanese surrendered. A little later, the "Big Mo" fired a few practice salvos. Those big 16-inch guns, along with broadsides from the other ships in the task force, made our F-80's weapons seem like pea-shooters. I then heloed back to the *Manchester*, and two days later, a different helicopter arrived from the mainland with a case of Johnny Walker for her crew: the Air Force "ransoming" me for the return flight.

Pete greeted me on my return to Kimpo with a handshake and big slap on my sore shoulder. He asked how much the government was going to charge me for my plane. I said not much; it was in pretty bad shape the last time I saw it. I then told him I wanted to see Willie Wall as soon as possible so I could thank him for sticking with me. The smile faded on Pete's face.

"Willie didn't make it," he said. "He went down the day after you bailed out."

The way Pete said *didn't make it* said everything. Willie wasn't missing, wasn't captured, wasn't having dinner with the Captain on some battleship. He was gone. Forever. And I never got to thank him.

I went back into combat the next day. I missed Willie, but I missed Castellani and a dozen other guys, too. You don't get over losing your friends, but you get through it. My right shoulder continued to bother me, but it never affected my flying. Eventually, after a flight physical months later, I was told it had been broken but was healing nicely on its own. Compared to Willie, I got off easy.

✪ ✪ ✪

PJW: I wasn't flying the day Bill crashed or rather, *almost* crashed. But I knew Bill had a mission so I rushed over to 80th Squadron ops as soon as I heard a Headhunter was down. They said the flight leader—that was Yoakley—bent his airplane and bailed out over the Sea of Japan.

"That's all we've got," the ops officer said. "Lt. Wall, his element leader, just landed. If you want more information, go ask him."

I located Wall right after his debriefing. I told him who I was and asked what he knew about Bill.

"He hit that mountain hard," Wall said. "I don't know how the airplane stayed together. I got on his wing right after it happened and told him about his ship. It was real messed up—stuff falling off while I watched. The tailpipe was almost crushed," he joined his thumbs and forefingers together to make a very flat oval. "Flames coming out everywhere. Hell, half his left wing was gone! I don't know how it stayed in the air."

"But he got out okay?"

"I notified Monte Carlo and followed him to Wonsan Harbor. He was going pretty fast when he punched out, but he got a good chute, I saw that much. I was bingo fuel and had to get back. I didn't see any choppers, but there were a bunch of ships in the area. I'm sure somebody picked him up."

So I spent the rest of the day wondering if Bill was injured or drowned or got eaten by sharks or got picked up and was high and dry—nobody knew. I had lost wingmen before but not a best friend. Just thinking about it made me sick. I hung around squadron ops—*both* squadron ops—trying to get somebody to call the Navy, but they said there were channels for that and to just relax. For them it was all in a day's work. Barely a day went by without them having to confirm a loss or track down a missing plane and its pilot. Sometimes the guy had made a forced landing or put down at a different base because of battle damage or had been picked up by ROKs or the Brits or by another branch of the service like the Army or Marines and it took forever, sometimes, to get confirmation from them. But this was different. This was Bill.

First thing the next morning I went over to 80th operations again. I didn't have to tell them why.

Lt. Willie Wall (middle) with two other Headhunters. Willie, Bill's element leader, stuck with him until his bailout but was shot down and killed the following day.

"Oh, hey, Pete, Yoakley's okay," the captain said with a grin. "Got picked up as soon as he hit the water. Navy's going to keep him a few days because they're in the middle of an exercise, but we'll get him back right after that."

I wondered if Willie had heard the good news and asked where I could find him.

"Oh, Wall," the captain said, glancing at the status board. "He's on a mission near Inchon. Should be back about 0900."

I had to fly that morning, so I didn't get back to the "low rent" (Headhunter) section of the field until later in the day. When I asked where I could find Willie, they said he'd been shot down that morning and killed: no distress call, no chance to eject, no nothing—the airplane just broke up and augered in. I felt terrible about Wall, but I also felt bad for Bill. I knew they were pretty good friends, and no matter how tough you get, no matter how good you get at pretending to shrug things off, you appreciate a wingman who sticks with you even when your airplane's in trouble, and Bill's bird was as sick as they got. Somebody had to tell Bill when he got back. I made up my mind it was going to be me.

W*e finished our tours at about the same time. Actually, Bill got his hundred missions a few weeks before Pete due to that unfortunate volley-ball injury that kept him grounded for two weeks. During that time Bill worked in the operations office, so with all those radios and teletypes going all the time, he knew pretty much what everyone in the 8th FBW was doing, and where they were doing it. Sometimes, too much knowledge can be a bad thing.*

PJW: My last mission was a dive-bombing attack. I can't remember the target, but it was well-defended as most of them were. My wingman, Dick Heyde, was half-way through his tour; he was a good pilot and a nice guy who was very anxious to do a good job. He followed me into the target. We started our dive, as usual, at about 15,000 feet. We briefed for a simultaneous bomb release—also SOP—at about 5,000 feet. He would watch my airplane, see the bomb detach, then immediately drop his own. He was surprised, therefore, when he saw me pickle my bomb just as the "barber pole" came out on the altimeter, indicating that we were just passing through 10,000 feet. He hesitated slightly, thinking perhaps he had misunderstood the briefing or that I had seen something over the target that called for an early release, but the delay was only a second and his bomb fell pretty much where it was supposed to go.

When we got back to base, Dick ran up to my aircraft as I unstrapped and asked, with a very earnest and worried face, "Pete, why did you drop your bomb so soon?"

I just shook my head and grinned at him. "Dick, wait until it's *your* hundreth mission and see how low *you* are willing to go!"

WRY: I spent the last two weeks before stateside rotation working in 80th Squadron ops. I'd put in my hundred missions and knew Pete was getting close to his, so I tried to keep tabs on where he was and how he was doing. The day of his last mission, I was thinking of ways to celebrate when a call came in over the radio that a "red-tailed" F-80 had been shot down trying to skip-bomb a railroad tunnel. Naturally, my ears perked up and my underwear started to pucker. I got on the horn to *Mellow*, which often had better and more recent information than the squadrons did. The guy at the other end was really sympathetic and didn't know much more than we did, but what he added almost made my hair turn white.

"All we know is that it was an airplane from the 36th and the pilot was killed. They said he was a Guard guy from one of the southern states and was on his last mission. That's all we have. Sorry. I'm sure we'll know more later."

My stomach did a couple of snap rolls then split-S'd into my shoes. *Jesus Christ, Pete got it on his last mission!* Unbelievable!

I ran over to 36th operations, a few tents down, shaking like a leaf. I asked if they had any details about their lost bird.

"Yeah," the Pup's operations officer said. "The pilot's name was Flournoy—from the Alabama Air Guard. Hell of a nice guy, too. Aren't they all?"

My sigh of relief briefly inflated the wind sock by the runway. After Bud Haefel was killed, I didn't even know there were more Guard guys in the group besides me and Pete. Losing any pilot is bad, but God only issues so many best friends in a lifetime.

TOP: The crew chief guards Dick Heyde's "red-tail" at Suwon. Dick and the *Tucson Terror* flew Pete's wing on his last mission.

BOTTOM: Pete grins after "cheating death" on his last mission.

TOP: Bill's plane, "Little Dottie," Yellow Tail number 677, in better days.

BOTTOM: "Little Dottie" on her way to the scrap heap: a new lieutenant washed her out in a crash landing just before Bill rotated home.

Bill, a captain on arrival, helps Pete celebrate his promotion to that rank by the Officer's Club at Suwon.

Here are the Japanese "angels" who serenaded us leaving Japan after our tour. Recalling their songs still brings tears to our eyes.

"Pete Wurts is out flying, too," I said, "Different flight. When's he due back?"

"Should be landing about now."

I got into *Hobo* and headed out to the flight line. Pete was still in his cockpit, canopy back, and had just finished talking to another pilot when I pulled up. He threw back his shoulder harness, took off his helmet, and gave me a big grin under that handlebar moustache.

"Hi," he said, as if we'd just met for a beer at the O-Club.

"It's about time you got on the ground!" I snapped like a wet mother hen. I didn't know whether to kiss him or give him a slap on the side of the head.

The crew chief put the ladder up by the cockpit and Pete climbed down. Pete shook his hand and thanked him for taking good care of his airplane for all these months. I don't think the guy knew it had been Pete's last mission—that's the kind of thing a lot of people didn't talk about until it was over.

I gave Pete a ride back to debriefing and told him what had happened. Losing another Guardsman took the edge off our celebratory mood. Pete knew the pilot, John Flournoy, pretty well and had flown with him a number of times, but fretting over it wouldn't bring John back. Referring to his own scare after my Wonsan bail out, Pete said, "Well, I guess you know now how it feels!" What I *knew* was that we had done our job the best we could and it was now time to get back to "the world" and see what would happen with the rest of our lives. We could hardly wait.

I had flown most of my missions after the bailout in the same aircraft, tail number 677, which I called "Little Dottie." The crew chief painted the name on the nose, just behind the machine guns, against a yellow background. That was a fine little bird. Of course, any warhorse that takes you into battle and brings you back earns a special place in your heart. But "Little Dottie" was my airplane and after my last mission, I was reluctant to see her go to another pilot, especially the second lieutenant who got her, who was new to both flying and combat—not a good combination. While I was still on the base waiting for transfer orders, he and "my plane" got shot up on a mission and had to make a crash landing. He got away with minor injuries, but the ship was a total loss and wound up on the scrap heap. That was a sad way for the old girl to end, but hey—better the plane than me, or the new lieutenant.

I had better luck with my faithful houseboy, Lim. When I told him I was moving out, his eyes teared up but he hung around to help me pack. Before I left, he gave me a handwritten farewell letter, all in English, he had laboriously composed with the help of an English-Korean dictionary. I read it, gave him a hug and he hugged me back—not a typical gesture between men in Korean culture, but our friendship was something special. After that he just turned and walked away. I never saw him again. I don't know if he went back to Seoul or got another job on the base, but wherever he went, and whoever he worked for, I hope they appreciated what a fine young man they got.

Not long after our last mission, we both got orders to report to Luke AFB in Arizona—the field from which we graduated during WWII—to train "retreads" (previously discharged Air Corps pilots recalled for Korea) in air-to-ground gunnery. In addition to our DFCs, awarded for specific actions, we were presented with three Air Medals apiece in acknowledgment of our continuous service in combat: one medal for every thirty missions logged. It was nice to get that recognition, but what we really wanted to see were those rotation orders which, when we finally got them, looked like million-dollar bills.

In November of '51, we left Suwon together in an old C-46 twin-engine cargo plane. Man, we never heard engines backfire so badly as the powerplants on that creaky old bird, so we both put on our parachutes and wore them the whole way to Itazuke. The loadmaster and pilots must've thought we were nuts, or big chickens, but we weren't about to risk our necks in an old crate that probably spent most of the 1940s bouncing over the Himalayas.

After arriving at Itazuke, we were told to report immediately to a another facility for out-processing. You'd think the prospect of a long, bumpy drive and more red-tape would be a snap after almost a year in combat, but we were impatient to get home and both of us were in a pretty bad mood when we climbed into the back of the G.I. truck. To our surprise, the truck—just an old deuce-and-a-half with bench seats facing each other over the tires—was filled with Japanese women: housekeepers who worked on the base. Needless to say, this brightened our mood. As the truck pulled out, we asked if any of them spoke English and several did. We told them we just finished our tours in Korea and were on our way home. To our even greater surprise, the women thanked us for our service and asked if they might repay us a little by singing some folk tunes, including a Japanese "farewell song," to make the cold drive more pleasant. We said sure, and settled back on the bench. What we heard next can only be called miraculous. Their voices were beautiful as they sang the haunting, traditional songs in perfect harmony. Sure, we were bone tired from a lot of stress and impatient to get on with our lives, but hearing those wonderful songs, performed in a theater of war where love and compassion were rare commodities—and by former enemies to boot!—was like putting a compress on a weeping wound. Nobody gets over their wartime experiences overnight, and some sights and sounds you just never forget. But that strange and wonderful truck ride did more to put our heads on straight—and our hearts back where they belonged—than a hundred official booklets or speeches by some general.

We caught a C-54 transport out of Tachi and began the long, long journey to Travis via Wake Island and Hawaii. We had exchanged several telegrams with Maxine and Dottie over the last few weeks and they knew more or less when we'd be home. They left Crestline and came up to the Bay Area so they'd be on hand to greet us. However, our plane got into Travis quite late so instead of phoning them, we just piled our bags into a taxi and had the driver take us to their motor lodge.

We knocked on their door about two in the morning. The lights came on inside and Dottie—hair in curlers, eyes puffed from sleeping, chenille bathrobe wrapped tight against the cold—opened the door. Before we could say anything her doe eyes got big as saucers and she slammed the door. We heard from the inside, "Omigod—they're here!"

We heard more squeals and gawping and the sound of drawers being frantically opened and closed, then the door opened again. They weren't exactly dressed for a night on the town, but we guess they thought anything would be better than greeting us in pajamas. Boy were they wrong.

5

HOT SEATS IN THE COLD WAR

(L to R), Bill, Dottie, Pete, and Max celebrate the end of "their" Korean War in San Francisco, 1951.

*T*he reunion with our wives continued for a few glorious days in San Francisco—since the beginning of WWII, a favorite spot for returning GI's to rekindle a romance after a too-long stay in a war zone.

One of our first stops was the famous "Top of the Mark," the penthouse restaurant of the Mark Hopkins Hotel on Nob Hill. Like many other military and naval units, the 8th FBW had an "official bottle" of whiskey stored in the bar's legendary overhead rack. Any member of the wing passing through town could drink free from it, provided he replaced the bottle (at his own expense) if it went dry. That first celebratory "on the house" drink was generous, as was the second, but the portions got a little smaller after that. We won't say we chiseled the next guys by drinking it down to the last two fingers, but we can't guarantee that our replacement bottle was a single-malt scotch or Napoleon brandy. We didn't want any Flying Fiends or Headhunters chasing us around the U.S. after cheating the war gods in Korea.

After a little sightseeing and taking in a couple of plays, we went our separate ways, though we knew we'd meet again at Luke Field (now called "Luke Air Force Base") in Arizona to begin our post-combat assignment as F-51 gunnery instructors. Pete and Maxine grabbed their kids and went straight back to Phoenix. Bill and Dottie took their time, extending their vacation with a stopover in Palm Springs. As it turned out, that dally in the desert took a little longer than expected.

WRY: I'd put my new Hudson, the beautiful red convertible Pete had sold me in Florida, into storage at a dealership in San Francisco. The owner assured me the car would be well cared for and, on my way into a war zone, I assumed I'd at least get a patriotic fair shake. You can imagine my shock, then, when I picked up a vehicle that looked like it, too, had been in combat. The once-new tires had mysteriously gone bald and the trunk was cleaned out, costing me a small fortune in tools as well as my spare. When I complained to the front office, I was told the dealership had changed hands while I was gone. The new owner apologized and said the old owner must've ripped me off. All he'd been told was that a GI had put the vehicle in long-term storage and nobody was authorized to touch the car.

Well, I hadn't expected a homecoming parade, but this particular welcome was a low blow. I wrote a scathing letter to the Hudson Company and got a nice letter back, saying in effect that each dealer ran his own business and the auto maker was only responsible for the functioning of the car. So we fixed it up out-of-pocket, packed our things, and spent a few days exploring Los Angeles—a part of California Dottie and I would become *very* familiar with over the next twenty-five years—then had a pleasant stay in Palm Springs before heading out across the desert. We were half-way up that intimidating grade east of Indio when the engine on my "new" vehicle began to overheat. Spouting steam like a tea kettle, I nursed the sick buggy to Desert Center and the only gas station between Blythe and Indio, where the motor promptly seized. A quick inspection showed the engine block was cracked, so we got a tow back to Indio and waited several days in that somewhat less than picture-postcard setting for a new one to arrive from the LA basin. When we were finally good to go, I thought about writing the Hudson Company again, but decided against it. Fate was obviously trying to tell me something; either forget the old days and get on with life or "see the U.S.A. in your Chevrolet"—I could never figure out which.

PJW: From September of '51 through July of '52, Bill and I were back in P-51s—and back in the IP's seat, though the Mustang had now become the "F-51" (*F* for "fighter" while *P* was the pre-WWII designation for "pursuit") and that instructor's chair was at a briefing table or in our own cockpit. A two-seat version of the Mustang was available; they had twelve at Luke but they were used for instrument training and we didn't do much of that. Besides, most of our students were "retreads," the USAF's term for former P-51 pilots who'd been recalled for Korea, and were old friends with the Mustang.

Our F-51 "re-familiarization" program consisted of a few trips around Luke's pattern, mostly to remember how to manage those four big paddles. On one of these early missions, Bill and I were flying with several other experienced IP's, and I was one of the last to land. Bill was already on the ground and taxiing back as an F-51 from our flight flew "initial" over the runway (an upwind pass in the landing direction at pattern altitude, about a thousand feet above the ground), "pitched out" into a tight, descending spiral, dropping landing gear and flaps as he slowed, then touched down in a three-point attitude just past the lip of the runway. This was the way real tigers flew the plane and was very reminiscent of Bill's own "max performance" landing in the Mustang that used to wow the crowds at airshows.

By the time Bill got out of his airplane, I was just getting parked as were the other two IP's behind me. Bill walked up to my plane.

"Boy, you sure got proficient in the old bird in a hurry, didn't you!" He said, clearly impressed.

"What are you talking about?" I asked, climbing down from the wing.

"That pitch-out and landing. Wow! You haven't forgotten a thing!" His flattened right hand swooped down and gave his left palm a satisfying *smack*.

I glanced over to the ship pulling up next to mine. The pilot who flew it was an old WWII vet with some German kills to his credit. I knew at once Bill had mistaken his landing for mine; an easy mistake to make, since I always landed on three points, too, though it sometimes took me a lot of runway to do it.

"Uh, yeah—" I said. "Piece of cake. I guess that means you owe me a beer."

I could've told him the truth, but it was hot and I wanted that beer. Besides, why spoil his illusions?

Tactical gunnery school instruction was different from basic or even advanced flight training. All our "students" were well-qualified military pilots, many with hundreds of combat hours. If they were former P-51 drivers, they just needed a refresher course in low altitude bombing and strafing. If they'd flown other types of fighters (and a few even came from medium or heavy bombers) they needed additional time with the airplane, which they usually got on their own. All of them, though, needed to know the threats they'd face in Korea, from ground fire to MiGs, and tips on how to complete "their hundred" and get back to their families in one piece.

Typically, an instructor (us) would brief a practice mission then lead a flight of four to the Gila Bend Gunnery Range, a big stretch of open desert southwest of Luke, where we would attack a variety of simulated targets, including concrete bunkers, old vehicles, phoney gun emplacements, you name it. The IP would roll in first and show them how it was done, then the rest of the flight would follow. We didn't drop live ordnance, just 25-pound "blue bombs" (painted that way to distinguish them from the real thing) that had a small detonator, like a shotgun shell, in the nose that exploded on impact. The resulting cloud of dust gave the student and instructor some indication of where the practice bomb had hit. Strafing, of course, was done with real .50 rounds; there just wasn't any low-cost, safer way to simulate that, and it was always a high-point of the mission. After a few practice sorties to familiarize the pilots with the ship's weapons, we'd begin to simulate real missions, which included ingress and egress tactics with a variety of external stores from different altitudes and under various visual conditions. Unfortunately, the weather in the "Valley of the Sun" was usually just that, clear and a million; there wasn't even any smog in those days to reduce visibility, so newcomers to ground attack could count on a few surprises once they got to Korea. Occasionally, we had them at Gila Bend.

Once, I was leading a flight onto the range at dusk. The plan was to hit the pretend target at a very low sun angle, then fly the return leg as a night cross country. As we approached the target, a "convoy" of rusted-out old cars, delivery vans, and pickup trucks that had been shot-up hundreds of times, I noticed a glint of sunlight from what appeared to be an unshattered windshield. This was pretty amazing, since those old vehicles had been hit with everything but the kitchen sink over the last few years and were full of holes; there wasn't an unbroken headlight or window among them—or so we *thought*.

Things just didn't look right, so I ordered the rest of the flight to orbit while I dove down to check it out. I dropped the gear and flaps and as I drew closer, I saw that this particular car not only had an undamaged windshield, it was a late-model Cadillac with four white-wall tires and the lid to the trunk was wide open. A second later, four people ran from the line of rusty vehicles, threw some burlap bags into the trunk, then piled into the car. The driver started the engine and peeled out in a cloud of dust, bumping over the desert, trunk lid banging as he went.

I had been a Phoenix patrolman long enough to recognize a "211" in progress. These were obviously civilians out scavenging the .50 caliber brass casings ejected by the F-51s as we made our strafing passes. They probably thought the range was closed at sunset, so our arrival gave them quite a shock. I raised the gear and gunned the engine and made low pass over the car to let them know that they'd been seen, then rejoined the flight and continued the mission. After we landed, I told the C.O. about civilians on the range. There wasn't much he could do about it. Of necessity, the gunnery range covered a pretty big area and more "Government Property" or "Keep Out" signs added to those already there wasn't going to stop determined scavengers—or poachers, or prospectors. The final score was windshield 1, Wurts, 0, but at least it broke up the routine.

*I*n July 1952, we were released from active duty. Well—at least one of us was. The Arizona Air Guard had been around since 1946, when it operated that pair of old AT-6s from Luke, but after an upgrade to F-51s and federal activation for Korea, it returned to a new home at Sky Harbor Airport in Phoenix; and in May of '53, it received its first batch of F-86As, America's newest front-line fighter, the "MiG killer" that had hogged the headlines in Korea. Pete was still itching to make his first million (understanding now that it would not be as an auto salesman or gas jockey) and with two growing kids and an armistice in Korea, he saw no reason to keep wearing a blue suit—not when he could become a part-timer and fly jets like we did in Florida. He was discharged as a captain and immediately applied for a pilot's slot with the 197th Fighter Interceptor Squadron, as the Phoenix unit was called.

Bill, on the other hand, looked pretty good in blue and the Air Force had an important project in the works—an all-weather, radar-guided version of the F-86, called the F-86D—and needed experienced combat pilots to work on it. Once again Bill raised his hand and said, "Count me in."

PJW: The 197th was deployed at Nellis AFB in Nevada, still on federal status, when I asked about joining the unit. The Guard isn't like the active-duty service. You don't just walk down to the nearest recruiting office and enlist. Even experienced servicemen have to interview for a position in their specialty which is strictly governed by the Unit Manning Document, or UMD, which states how many pilots, crew chiefs, air policemen, avionics technicians, engine mechanics, and so on the organization is authorized to have. Like any other organizational pyramid, there is more room at the bottom than at the top, so units typically take more lieutenants and captains than colonels. And because each Guard unit is composed mostly of civilian "weekend warriors," its commanders take extra care to ensure that new personnel are responsible members of the local community with a true commitment to serve.

As a result, I interviewed extensively with two 197th pilots one hot afternoon in the Air Guard hangar at Sky Harbor. One of the screeners was Major Roy Jacobson, the squadron commander—a fine officer who would later make general—and Don Morris, a captain, who also made general and would turn out to be one of the best all-around pilots I ever knew. With me were three other applicants, Ted Crane, Hal Carney, and Bill Kemp. Kemp, who had a civilian job with the phone company, was a P-51 veteran—an ace from WWII, in fact—and a real "hot stick." From a flying standpoint, he was perhaps the most talented and aggressive, natural-born aviator I'd fly with, but he also seemed a little nuts. Maybe those things go together, I don't know; but we all became good friends over the years.

Anyway, we must've said the right things, because "Jake" and Don voted us into their club. I checked out in the F-51Ds and -Hs the unit was getting rid of, then got qualified in the F-86A, which was a real treat. If the F-80 seemed like a sports car, the F-86 was a formula racer. Its mission was interception, to stop Soviet bombers from reaching American targets, and we had no doubts that it could do the job in style. A lot of this burden, the mission of the Air Defense Command, or ADC, fell to the Guard. The reason for this was obvious. Guard units were scattered around the country, many near major population centers and their jet interceptors could be airborne in moments, climb to altitude quickly, and engage enemy bombers before they got too close to their targets. Throw in some surface-to-air missiles strategically placed around the borders and you had a pretty effective network that helped keep the peace for forty years. Until the early-1960s, the 197ᵗʰ would be part of that impressive shield.

Everyone who flew the F-86A loved it. The cockpit fit you like a glove, and placed well forward of the sweptback wing, gave you a tremendous view through its bubble canopy. Its automatic leading-edge slats drooped to grab more air in tight turns and at low speeds, and as one of the first American fighters with swept wings, it was one of the fastest, capable of supersonic speed at full throttle in a shallow dive.

Our main activity in the F-86 was doing what we seldom got to do in Korea—rat-race with other fighters and fire our guns at aerial targets. For practice, we shot at a long banner strung out a healthy distance behind a tow plane. Each pilot's ammunition left a different color on the banner, kind of like a game of paint-ball, so you could see whose rounds hit where. This sport got pretty competitive, not only within our unit, but between other fighter squadrons in the Guard and regular Air Force. Each summer, the whole unit deployed for two weeks in Boise, Idaho; and while the support troops conducted their training on the ground, we pilots honed our skills by flying as much as we could, often against other Guard units.

One of our distinguished visitors at camp was Barry Goldwater, a veteran pilot, founding member of the Phoenix unit, and a ranking officer in the Air Force Reserve. I helped check him out in the F-86 at Boise and had occasion to fly him around on government business in our C-47. A lot of people remember Goldwater as the Senator with a craggy smile who gave fiery conservative speeches, and that's true as far as it goes. It was certainly enough to win him the Republican nomination for President in 1964, though he took a real drubbing in the election from Democrat

Lyndon Johnson. Personally, I found him to be a very serious man who never joked about anything. He really hated Richard Nixon ("that crook," he used to call him) almost as much as he disliked liberals. We ran into each other socially from time to time, since he was a member of the Arizona Country Club, as I was, and he was friends with Danco Gurovich, my business partner. My daughter, Barbara, went to school with his daughter, Peggy, so I had occasion to see him and his wife (also named Peggy) when I picked the girls up or dropped them off at his spacious hilltop house in northeast Phoenix. I didn't have too many chances to assess his skills as a pilot, but I recall he was conscientious and competent, though not exceptional. Of course, pilot-politicians, like aviator doctors, have a lot of other things on their mind, even when they're flying—usually not a good thing.

Unfortunately, as a Cold War interceptor, the F-86A wasn't perfect. Its six .50 caliber machine guns, such as those we had on the F-80, were fine at close range, but Soviet bombers were made to fly high and fast, and most carried awesome defensive firepower, like quads or canons, that could knock us out of the sky before we closed in for the kill. Great as it was to fly, the A model was already becoming obsolete. We needed something better, right now. Fortunately, Yoakley was on the case.

WRY: My new assignment took me from Luke to Valdosta, Georgia, where the Air Force put me through all-weather interceptor school. This was a TDY (temporary duty) assignment, so Dottie went to stay with her parents while I figured out what this high-altitude, all-weather interception racket was all about—a big change from our ground-hugging chores in tactical fighters like the F-51 and F-80.

Essentially, our task was to meet enemy bombers head on, or at an angle, rather than chase them from the rear, like you do in a dogfight. We also had to do this day or night, in the clear or in the clouds, which meant both the ship and the pilot—not to mention a lot of equipment on the ground, such as advanced radars—had to be top notch and function flawlessly, or one day America might wake up missing a few of its favorite cities. It was a tall order and a whole different

The Arizona Air Guard's F-86A squadron was called the "Copperheads." The snake on the fuselage wrapped its tongue around the gun ports. The cactus on the tail was drawn by famed *Arizona Republic* cartoonist, Reg Manning. His son, Dave, later became the squadron's commander.

kind of flying, but the idea of helping to perfect a system that had never been tried was a challenge and an adventure I couldn't resist.

After boning up on the theory and practice of all-weather combat, I was transferred to Tyndall AFB in Florida where I met the F-86D. This was essentially an A-model '86 with a radome fitted above the air intake at the front of the plane. It was heavier than the A and not quite as responsive on the controls—but then again, it carried more gear and its mission was different. Instead of machine guns, the D fired unguided rockets that spread out like shotgun pellets into the path of an enemy bomber. It was a clever idea, but the system needed fine-tuning, as well as tactics to match the technology. That's where I came in.

The place selected for this latter work was Perrin AFB in Texas, a former A-26 school. The problem was, the facility didn't really exist yet, at least that part of it needed for '86D flight tests and crew training. As a captain with both advance detail and operations experience, they made me Ops Officer and said, essentially, go make it happen, so I did.

Dottie, now pregnant with our first child, joined me and we got a nice little house in Sherman, Texas, not too far from the base. After my second son (and first with Dottie), Donald William Yoakley, was born at the end of February '53, her mother came up from Jacksonville to give us a hand. Coming from Florida, we were no strangers to bad weather, but parts of Texas and Oklahoma were called "tornado alley"—and for good reason. One night as one of these storm systems approached, we were relaxing in the living room, listening to the radio, when they announced a tornado warning. We all stared blankly at each other. The house had no storm cellar and while we all knew what to do in a hurricane, no one had briefed us on anti-tornado defenses. Those walls and windows started to look pretty flimsy, flexing and rattling in the wind, so I told the girls, "If things get tough, we'll go out to the carport and pile into the Hudson," which had four doors and was built like a tank. I figured we could lie down on the floor in front of the seats and survive a few cartwheels and curlicues and still have enough car left to crawl out of.

Well, the night wore on and the storm got worse. We had dinner and tried to look calm, but the lights flickered as wind and rain buffeted the house. Finally, we heard the unmistakable sound of "an approaching freight train" which locals said was the tale-tell signature of an honest-to-God tornado, the last sound some people in Tornado Alley ever heard.

I told the women to get up from the table—just leave everything—and follow me to the car. Lightening flashed outside the window and we felt the whole house rumble. I opened the door to the carport and the roar was deafening. I ran behind the car to get in the driver's side and got hit in the face with the high-beam headlights of a huge semi-truck roaring by on the street outside our house. He must've been going 60 mph—way too fast for his size and the weather conditions—and his spray gave the back of the car, and me, a good wash. But you know, the roar died as he passed and the rumbling went away and all we could hear was the rain going pitter-pat. I just stared at the girls over the roof of that old Hudson and we all burst into laughter.

That night, it seemed, we had nothing to fear but fear itself; but over the next week or so we got a lot smarter about life in Tornado Alley. One thing we learned was to stay out of the car near a twister, to jump into a ditch or culvert or, if we were at home, to climb into the bathtub and hold a mattress over the top. Well, live and learn.

One of the key tests in the F-86D program was validating the concept of lead-collision rocket fire as a means of bringing down bombers. Ultimately, the only way to do this was to shoot down an actual plane, a test which was conducted at Eglin AFB in Florida.

The idea was simple and had been used for several experimental programs during and after WWII. Since B-17s were obsolete and plentiful, a number of them had been rigged with remote controls, operated by a pilot in another aircraft. In the war, a remotely piloted B-17 packed with explosives had been used as the first "cruise missile." A pilot and copilot took the plane off, then after reaching a safe altitude and putting it on course, bailed out, giving control to a following plane. The unmanned bomber was then guided into a fortified, high-risk target, such as a submarine pen. In addition to being risky and expensive, the system wasn't very effective, so the Air Corps abandoned it. For the '86D, though, all the Air Force needed was a stable, realistic target to destroy, so a remotely piloted bomber was just the ticket. The target drone was controlled by a second B-17 flying a mile or so ahead instead of behind the target. Unfortunately, early tests by North American ran into serious problems and the program suffered several setbacks before the D was declared operational and the Air Force was ready to train crews.

At that point, Perrin became a pretty busy place. NAA delivered new planes and the Air Force assigned new pilots about as fast as we could take them. My job as Operations Officer was to make sure we had enough planes for all the instructors and pilots. My biggest problem didn't come from the equipment, but from the maintenance organization, which wanted the last say on how many planes should be available for duty, and when, and for what missions. They even went so far as to try to match specific aircraft to particular pilots, and that's where I drew the line. Our schedules began to slip and we had several administrative "shoot outs" before the unit commander came down on my side and our very ambitious training program finally got back on course.

Now, this may sound like typical bureaucratic wrangling, but you have to understand, this was not a business-as-usual training facility. We had to familiarize pilots with new aircraft and new intercept subsystems, teach them to work with radar ground controllers (who were often in training themselves), and help them become proficient with some very unusual and tricky air-to-air combat maneuvers, while at the same time evaluating and installing upgraded equipment provided by the contractor and the Air Force. One of my biggest allies in this effort was NAA's chief production acceptance test pilot, Jack Bryan. I made numerous trips to the NAA plant in El Segundo, California, located on the south side of Los Angeles International Airport (LAX), to pick up new D models and ferry them back to Perrin. Although the company had given them a quality control flight check first, each trip was still a shake-down cruise and we usually had more work to do on most birds and their systems before they were ready for service. As a result, I got to know Jack pretty well and we watched each other's back when disputes arose with the company or Air Force brass. Our relationship worked so well, in fact, that one day Jack took me aside and asked a fateful question.

"Hey, Bill, why don't you leave the service and come to work for me?"

"I dunno," I joked. "How much does it pay?" I had no intention of leaving the Air Force now that I was just getting plugged into military R&D, which I found both worthwhile and exciting.

"A lot more than you're making now," he said, then he mentioned a number and he wasn't joking. Basically, the job he described was pretty much what I was currently doing but without the military bureaucracy. I had to admit, it was tempting. I told him I'd talk it over with my wife and give him an answer in a couple of days.

Well, the prospect of more money, better living conditions, better schools, nine-to-five work days, and a California lifestyle—with both surfing and skiing within an hour's drive from our house—appealed to us both; and, oh yes, I'd still be flying state-of-the-art Air Force fighters and helping to develop cutting-edge weapons systems. I asked Jack when he wanted me to start and he said, "Last week."

Of course, I already had an employer, so I paid a visit to my CO and told him I had decided to leave the service. He was sympathetic but tried hard to talk me out of it, which I considered quite a compliment, but my mind was made up. I put my paperwork through channels. A short time later the buck was kicked back downstairs: *Resignation Denied.* The reason given was that I was in a "critical MOS," meaning they just didn't have enough people with my set of skills to fend off the Ruskies for the foreseeable future. That was flattering, too, but I knew better than anyone how well and how fast our air defense program was coming along. We had trained a good cadre of pilots in lead-collision tactics—any one of which could fill my boots in the cockpit or behind the operations desk, and it wasn't as if I was quitting aviation and going into real estate. I'd still be working for the prime contractor on the same program and, hopefully, be around to pitch in on the development of new and better Cold War weapons systems for a long time to come. Still, the Air Force said *no*.

Frustrated, I moved Dottie and my son Don back to Jacksonville and, as a good Floridian and charter member of our local Air National Guard, contacted our Congressional Representative and asked for help. I don't recall if I mentioned Bill

Haviland's name, but within two weeks I had my Honorable Discharge and a Letter of Commendation for my "outstanding performance...and devotion to duty" from the Group Commander, Colonel Eugene Fletcher, endorsed in writing by every senior officer on the base. I didn't exactly leave the Air Force with a brass band and a *Thunderbirds* fly-by, but it was a mighty satisfying end to demanding, challenging, and ultimately rewarding phase of my flying career.

*T*he mid-1950s were busy for both of us. While Bill wrapped up his active-duty Air Force career and prepared to move to Los Angeles (adding a second child with Dottie, a daughter named Trisa Lynn Yoakley, born in Jacksonville in June, 1954), Pete set out to make his fortune in—of all things—the motel business. He continued to fly with the Arizona Air Guard, which in 1957 transitioned to an upgraded version of the F-86D, the bigger and more potent F-86L.

PJW: After my discharge at Luke, I was again in the market for a new career. This time I at least knew what I *didn't* want to try, which included peace officer, bus driver, commercial pilot, and anything to do with sales. I could scratch my flying itch with great planes at the Guard. Now all I needed was the "scratch" to fund a growing family and the joys of peacetime life that had for too long been on hold.

My opportunity came from an unexpected source. My brother Burke had been working as a desk clerk at the Frontier Village Motel on Grand Avenue in Phoenix—near "motel row" on Van Buren Street, the major highway coming into the Valley from the east. His boss, Ray Wilson, was a good guy and after hanging around with them for awhile, I began to see a future for myself in the lodging industry. Borrowing seed money from our Dad, Burke and I bought a small motel on Van Buren called the Seabreeze. It had been owned by a successful, local motelier, Bob Seebree, who became my mentor in the business. Over the next few years, we operated the Seabreeze profitably and I became General Manager for five other properties owned by Bob and his partner, Joe Sheldon, another Phoenix entrepreneur. These guys were not only sharp businessmen, but good marketers and understood that every successful enterprise needed roots in the community; in our case, Best Western. At that time, BW was a modest referral group of independent motel owner-operators cooperating under the iron rules—and iron fist—of its founder, M.K. Guertin. Although his methods annoyed a lot of people, they brought customers through the door and in those days, it was hard for a motel to succeed without a chain affiliation and endorsements by consumer organizations like AAA (the American Automobile Association) or travel gurus like Duncan Hines. I tried my hand at a couple of other ventures during this period, from an ill-fated uranium mine in Utah to building a pair of duplexes and a gas station in Buckeye, finally settling on a new motel, the Buckeye Motel, on the highway between Phoenix and Yuma. My biggest break came in 1957, when I formed a core partnership of friends and investors who would work with me in and around the lodging industry for the next thirty years. Our first project was the Copper Hills Motel in Globe, Arizona: a beautiful, modern facility that included a fine restaurant run by Danco Gurovich, an irascible character who became a great friend and seemed to know everyone worth knowing in Arizona and California—including actor John Wayne, who became another friend and investor.

Through Danco, I met Scott King, the founder of Travel Lodge, a highly successful national chain and pioneer in the art of franchising. Scott, a private pilot, was thrilled when I invited him to come out to Sky Harbor for a ride in our T-33, the two-seat version of the old F-80 that had by now become the USAF's advanced trainer. Today, it's unusual (to say the least!) for civilians to go joy-riding in fighter-type military aircraft. Back then, the Guard was pretty loose about who its pilots could take up on "goodwill orientation flights," and we made the most of it. At one time or another I think I took most of my business partners, potential investors, news reporters—even my barber, who was an aviation fan—up for a spin in the "T-bird." We never had any problems or complaints, though a bad accident with a local big shot or somebody's girlfriend on board would've undoubtedly stopped the practice and caused a few heads to roll. Anyway, King taught me a lot about profitable franchising, lessons that, in one form or another, helped craft my approach to business, especially when I became President of Best Western, Inc., almost 20-years later and took that organization international.

Pete, now a major in the Arizona Air Guard, in the cockpit of the North American F-86L, "big brother" to the F-86D interceptor Bill had tested for the Air Force.

But apart from these occasional jaunts, the Guard's ADC mission was anything but a joyride. As part of America's strategic air defense network, we kept two aircraft on "strip alert" 24-hours a day, seven days a week. That meant the planes were parked outside the hanger in a special revetment (with a barrier protecting the airport from our guns), fueled and armed and ready to launch at a moment's notice. Our alert pilots hung around a "ready room," a converted fire station which had a couple of bunks, table and chairs, and an old TV. If and when the klaxon went off, we had five minutes to get both ships airborne and pointed in the direction of trouble. Our 'chutes and helmets were kept in the cockpit with a ground crew standing by to help us start the engines and pull the chocks. We got "scrambled" periodically but—thank goodness—only for drills. Most Guard pilots hated strip alert, but a few of us volunteered for the job. You got paid for the hours on duty (all of which accrued toward Air Force retirement) and you could spend your ready-room time any way you wanted. This was great for pilots taking college courses, or budding entrepreneurs like me, since it gave us time to read books or study contracts and blueprints, and get paid for it in the process. All in all, it was really a pretty good deal.

Our warhorse during this period was North American's F-86L, "big brother" to the somewhat smaller and less sophisticated F-86D which it replaced. It's main armament was a rack of about twenty 2.5-inch unguided rockets launched from a pod, or tray, that dropped down from a compartment below the cockpit. The plane used attack patterns basically worked out by Bill and his colleagues during D-model development, augmented by a more complex airborne radar linked to ground controllers at various strategic points. Altogether, the system was called Semi-Automatic Ground Environment, or SAGE, and it worked well enough to discourage aggressors during a critical time in the Cold War when ICBMs (Inter-Continental Ballistic Missiles) had yet to be deployed in large numbers and manned bombers still posed the biggest security threat.

A lot of pilots disliked the L-model; and although I was not one of them, I could understand why. It was bigger and heavier than the nimble '86A, and was good only for shooting down big, high-flying bombers, not dogfighting with MiGs (or friendly jets). It wasn't even useful for ground attack missions; the day of the "multi-role" fighter had yet to dawn. But the so-called lead-collision aerial attack pattern—basically a 90-degree suicide run that you broke off at the last minute after firing your pod—was challenging, as was working with SAGE controllers. And, of course, had our practice attacks ever become the real thing, we would've been true Minutemen, our nation's first line of defense. The "L" also had one heck of an afterburner, which made it the fastest climbing jet in the inventory until the advent of the Century series fighters—those with a designation of "100" or higher, like the F-100, F-101, and so on. On one occasion, however, that afterburner's big "kick in the pants" almost drop-kicked me into the middle of downtown Phoenix.

I was making a single-ship takeoff from Sky Harbor, heading west, which took me over the city. For an F-86L on takeoff, the afterburner (called AB for short) was not only a good idea, it was a necessity; the "lead sled" just wouldn't get off the ground without it, especially on a hot day. To understand the predicament I was about to face, though, you need to know a little about jet engines. All jets work like a garden hose; they simply take a "fluid," hot air in this case, and squirt it behind the airplane. This thrust pushes the airplane forward. Now, we all know you can make a garden hose squirt more powerfully by putting your finger partially into the flow. This simply gives the same amount of water a smaller "hole" from which to escape, so it speeds up. As it speeds up, thrust increases, so all jet engines, afterburning or not, have nozzles, like the nozzle on a garden hose, that closes down a bit when you advance the throttle to max power. However, when an afterburner is engaged, a lot of raw fuel is dumped into the tailpipe, making the exhaust gas even hotter and expanding it much more rapidly than usual. In this case, a nozzle "necking down" is not only unnecessary, it's deadly, because the sudden super-hot, expanding gases get trapped inside the tail pipe and can explode or set the plane on fire, neither one of which is good.

So, on that particular takeoff, at about 300 feet above the ground just as I was raising the gear but still in afterburner, the engine started to surge and the nozzle began to close. Normally, this malfunction is cured by simply coming out of AB. Unfortunately, my "lead sled" was still too low and slow and heavy to continue the takeoff without it. I needed that AB for at least another ten or fifteen seconds to get sufficient flying speed and altitude.

I immediately hit the manual switch, which was supposed to open the nozzle, but it didn't. With one eye on the Exhaust Gas Temperature (EGT), which was rapidly rising, and the other on downtown Phoenix, which was getting closer, I began wondering just which local business I hated enough to put a F-86-sized hole through the roof, when the plane achieved the magic airspeed needed to continue a climb at "military" (non-AB) power and was able to come out of afterburner. Heavy with fuel and wallowing like a sick goose, I nursed my little bruiser around the pattern and made a normal landing; which was good, because without an afterburner, a go-around at that weight would've been impossible. As I taxied back to the ramp, I began mentally composing a strongly worded letter to the Chairman of North American Aviation. I would've sent the letter to Bill, but as it turns out, he was ahead of me in line at the NAA complaint department.

WRY: In July 1953, I left the USAF for a job as Inspection Test Pilot at North American Aviation. While Dottie was in Jacksonville, I did my "advance detail" bit and came to California, finding a nice little house in Westchester, just north of LAX, where she and the kids would join me later. I also joined the California Air Guard (which flew out of the Van Nuys airport), mostly out of habit and to get that last bit of wear out of my old blue suits, but I didn't stay long. They flew '86As, which sounded fun, but the work at NAA turned out to be pretty focused and I was just getting stretched too thin. Because we had two types of fighters in production at that time—the F-86D and F-100A—and they were among the most advanced planes in the inventory, you could count on something going wrong on just about every flight, though most of our problems were minor. The average production test flight took about 45-minutes. We flew out of LAX, where the plant was located, and conducted our tests over the ocean, but occasionally inland when weather was a factor, and we were busy every second.

Pete's new unit, the 197th in Phoenix, still had some F-51s, but eventually flew F-86As and Ls, so he made occasional trips in them to LAX and I was always glad to see him. He usually parked at the NAA ramp and we made sure his plane was refueled and checked over and all the bugs were cleaned off the windshield by the time he was ready to go. He wasn't the only Guard pilot to visit us, and we were always pleased to play host to good North American "customers." Not all of the arrivals at LAX were so cordial.

On October 27, 1954, I had the dubious distinction of becoming the first pilot to successfully make a dead-stick landing in an F-100—the first of the Century series fighters and the first American production fighter to go supersonic in level flight. We were delivering the "short tailed" version of the plane to the Air Force; so-called because the vertical stabilizer would be enlarged on later versions to minimize a "Dutch roll" problem that could be fatal if it occurred at the wrong time and the pilot didn't catch it. The Dutch Roll phenomenon was pretty common among early, swept-wing aircraft. It would begin if the airplane yawed excessively during high-speed flight, making one wing generate a tad more lift, and therefore a tad more drag, than the other. That made the nose pitch up slightly and the wing that was slightly forward fall back, giving the other wing a chance to do the same thing. This "inertia coupling" would continue, making the nose inscribe a Figure 8 on the horizon, until the pilot corrected it or it got so bad that the airplane began to tumble, which led to structural failure. Thus many swept-wing aircraft were eventually equipped with "yaw dampers" (and some with bigger vertical stabilizers), which counteracted this tendency before it got destructive. But in those days, a little Dutch roll went with the territory. At minimum, it was annoying, and at worst it could sneak up on you when you least expected it and cause real problems. Accidents involving inertia coupling claimed the life of several test pilots before the problem was pinned down and resolved.

Anyway, on this particular flight, Dutch roll would be the least of my worries, although the yaw damper designed to counteract it would turn out to be more of a hindrance than a help. I'd had flameouts or engine failure in the F-86 a couple of times, always in the pattern or near an airport, and was able to make a dead-stick, or power-off gliding landing without a problem; the controls were all mechanically linked and the Sabre Jet handled equally well with or without engine power, although the flight path inevitably was down. The F-100, on the

The North American F-100 Super Sabre—America's first supersonic fighter. On October 27, 1954, Bill was the first pilot to make a successful dead-stick landing in the bird.

other hand, had hydraulically boosted controls, since the forces on the stick were excessive at supersonic speeds. The problem was, the hydraulic system needed power, and when the engine quit, there went the power required by the hydraulic pump. Many Century Series fighters (as well as jet airliners) have something called a RAT, or ram-air turbine, that pops out into the airstream like a little windmill to give the aircraft limited power to run essential functions in case the engine fails. But those little windmills slow down as the airspeed drops, as it must in order to land. That means its power output drops, too, and the aircraft eventually loses hydraulic pressure and, in a bird like the F-100, control of the airplane. As a result, the F-100 flight manual forbade pilots to even *think* about making a dead-stick landing. But I was in flight test now, and our motto was to save the bird whenever we could, if for no other reason than to have enough shiny parts left over to analyze what went wrong.

In any event, it was about 2 PM and I was at 22,000 feet over Fullerton, California about half an hour into a routine acceptance flight. I had just finished checking the ship's gunsight when I reduced throttle for a descent into LAX, about 25 miles away, when the engine flamed out—just quit. Now, a pilot doesn't hear much in a jet: between the helmet and earphones and the pressurized cockpit and the engine way in back, you're mostly aware of high-speed air hissing by. But all airplanes have a rhythm, a little buzz in the airframe like an animal's nervous system, call it what you will, and when that changes, you sense it real fast, although you may not know exactly what happened or why. A flamout (literally, a loss of combustion in the engine's burner cans) can be caused by lots of things and, although it's not always serious, it always gets your attention. Most of the time, you simply re-start the engine go your merry way, which is usually straight to the airport to get things checked out. This time, though, the *hisssss* of my healthy bird slipping through the air suddenly dropped and I felt the tug of deceleration on my shoulder harness. I glanced down at the engine instruments and, yup, fuel flow was zero and both EGT and RPM were winding down. We had no annunciator panel in those days, like they do on modern aircraft, to tell you exactly what was wrong and what systems were off-line, but other warning lights began to flash around the cockpit and it was pretty clear what had to be done. I tried normal air-start procedures, to no avail. I selected the emergency fuel system and tried again—still no luck.

By now I had the nose pinned on LAX, so my long, high glide was at least taking me toward the runway and the ocean. I called NAA ops on our company frequency and told them what was happening, asking them to notify air traffic control and the tower as I would be pretty busy for the next few minutes. My boss, Jack Bryan, assumed I would bail out if I couldn't get the engine started—that was SOP—but I always thought the Super Sabre, as it was called, could be dead-sticked safely if the pilot used the right technique. Now it was my chance to find out. If I was right, it might save the lives of many pilots over the service life of the aircraft, not to mention spare potential crash victims on the ground and enhance NAA's reputation for building very dependable, survivable aircraft.

So I deployed the RAT and decided to keep control inputs to a minimum, especially on final approach when that little turbine would slow down, controls would get stiff, and there wasn't much margin for error. I lined myself up for a long, slow descent toward the airport, determined to stay as high as I could for as long as I could in case bailout became a necessity, but mostly to ensure I'd have enough time and space to set up an adequate dead-stick pattern.

This was when I got my next surprise. Due to a design peculiarity in the yaw damper system, when power gets too low, the air start switch is on, and the RAT is deployed, the rudder goes "hard over" to the right. I immediately mashed the left rudder pedal, avoiding a Dutch Roll problem, but the system kept trying to push the rudder in the opposite direction so I knew I'd have to finish the flight with a stiff left leg and fly final in a mild left skid, an unwelcome complication to what was already going to be a hairy enough landing. As I wrote later in my incident report, that particular problem might have gone away if I'd just turned off the electrically powered yaw-damper, but that wasn't in the flame-out/air-start checklist and, frankly, I was more concerned about making it safely to the ground than troubleshooting yet another curious technical problem.

I arrived over LAX at about 12,000 feet and 300 knots, "high key" for a dead-stick approach. Such landings always followed a similar pattern, with specific altitudes and airpseeds suggested for each type of fighter. *High key* and *low key* were handy reference points where the pilot could adjust his rate of descent and distance from the touchdown point according to surface winds and the condition of his plane. Dead-stick landings took a bit of nerve and good judgment; you couldn't go around, after all, but it wasn't entirely a game of craps. By now I'd turned all unessential systems off and radioed my intentions to the company, keeping them informed of my progress, since there was no guarantee I'd be around later to debrief them. Control was good—that little RAT was doing its job, despite my rudder problem, and I completed a descending, 360-degree turn and rolled out on runway heading at 250 knots passing through 8,000 feet. At 6,000 feet I turned downwind and opened the speed brake. This used more valuable hydraulic pressure, but the Super Sabre slipped through air like a greased pig, even without thrust, and I'd need all the drag I could get to slow down on the runway. At 225 knots and 3,500 feet, I dropped the landing gear using the emergency release system; no sense pressing my luck with the hydraulics. With "three in the green," all wheels down and locked, I turned onto base leg at 2,500 feet and 200 knots.

The turn to final approach for runway 25L came up real fast, and the tight bank cost me more altitude and airspeed. It looked like I might be landing short, so I raised the speed brake using the hydraulic dump valve, an ace-in-the-hole that gave me one last shot of pressure. The "Battery Low" warning light now came on; that little RAT was starting to die on me.

I "crossed the fence", the threshold of the runway, at 160 knots, a bit faster than normal, but I needed the extra speed to ensure control down to the flare. The stick was now getting very heavy so I gave up any idea of a grease job and decided to just fly the bird onto the runway, holding a steady 100 feet per minute rate of descent and let the landing gear absorb the shock.

The main gear touched the concrete about 300 feet down the runway, which was great because the flight controls instantly froze; the stick wouldn't budge an inch. I touched the brakes and noticed some effect, but without nosewheel steering and differential braking questionable, I was afraid I might lose control on the runway so I left the brakes alone. Fortunately, the drag chute, a small parachute rigged to the tail that is used routinely on every landing, was mechanically actuated, so I popped that sucker after 500 feet and became a passenger for the ride to the end of the runway, a stone's throw from the ocean. The emergency vehicles on either side of the runway peeled out to follow me, lights flashing. As the ship rolled to a stop, the battery, which had taken the load when the little RAT gave up, went dead.

Jack met me in a jeep and as they hooked a tow bar to the airplane, I rode with him back to operations. A big meeting was called later, attended by NAA's senior engineers. This was the first time I'd been surrounded by so many "rocket scientists" and it felt a little like the Spanish Inquisition, though I'd brought their bird back without a scratch. I admit, some of their questions baffled me.

"How many times did you move the stick?" the hydraulic engineer asked.

Jack and I could only grin. "Beats me," I said, "I wasn't counting."

Most of the debriefing was useful, though, because engineers in one area sometimes overlook how decisions made for good reasons about one system can adversely affect another, or the performance of the entire ship. I said there was no reason to continue the ban on dead-stick landings for the F-100, provided the pilot keeps his pattern close to the field, flight control hydraulics are improved, and battery life is extended. The only real danger I faced, I said, was the rudder hard-over caused by that damned yaw damper, and none of the experts seemed surprised about that. After all, with a dead engine that failed to restart, the aircraft was expected to crash. The meeting ended with a consensus that a successful dead-stick landing would be possible for line pilots if the yaw damper was disabled when the air-start switch was activated, the RAT beefed up so that hydraulic pressure could be maintained below 200 knots, and a longer-life battery was installed. Instead of being burned at the stake, I got a nice commendation from the Chief Test Pilot for the "coolness and dispatch" with which I handled the problem and saved the plane.

Still, nothing remarkable came from the incident. The company didn't want to sink more money into changing something the customer had already accepted—namely bailing out after a failure to restart; and if a couple of planes were lost each year due to flame-outs, well, NAA would be happy to sell the government replacements. As a result, the Air Force never lifted their restriction and a few more birds did, indeed, leave smoking holes in the ground. But we test pilots are a hearty, optimistic crew, and even a little bull-headed. A few months later, famed stunt pilot Bob Hoover, then an NAA test pilot, tried a similar dead stick landing in an F-100 at Rogers Dry Lake up at Edwards AFB in the high desert. Despite freedom from the confines of a runway—or maybe because of it—Bob tried to fly the plane into a normal flare for a soft touchdown and the controls froze about fifteen feet above the ground. The bird dropped like a rock, but nobody builds 'em like North American, and both pilot and plane came away unscathed. Bob echoed my call to modify the electrical and hydraulic systems and recommended that a small electrical pump be added to augment the RAT at low airspeeds—again, to no avail. I guess the government just likes buying new airplanes and our job, after all, was to make them.

Hoover and I weren't the only test pilots to run into potentially fatal problems, of course, just two of the luckier ones.

NAA's chief engineering test pilot when I joined the company was a fine airman who had quite a history even before he got involved in flight test. He was one of only two Army Air Corps fighter pilots to get their P-40s airborne during the Japanese attack at Pearl Harbor, and went on to become an ace in the Pacific. He was a nice guy but pretty independent, and not everybody appreciated his style or his methods. A project pilot on the first F-86, he actually took an A-model supersonic—albeit in a shallow dive—a few weeks before Chuck Yeager broke the sound barrier in the rocket-powered X-1: a feat described in Al Blackburn's fine book, *Aces Wild*. The company naturally wanted to trumpet this accomplishment; a number of pilots in the U.S. and Britain, including famed aviator Jeffery de Havilland, had been killed trying to do the same thing in those early, post-war jets, but the Air Force said not only "No," but "Hell, no!" It seems that Bell Aircraft, maker of the X-1, was an influential contractor with their fingers in lots of pies, including a variety of "X-planes" in the pipeline, and the Air Force didn't want to do anything that might tarnish their image, such as giving the world news that a conventional jet by another manufacturer had pretty much done the same thing.

It was not the first time a prime contractor had been asked to keep its mouth shut and it would not be the last. (NAA took most of the blame for NASA's failure after the fatal fire in the Apollo program, but that's the nature of the business.) Anyway, the poor guy was killed a few years later investigating the Dutch Roll problem in the F-100. He was conducting a test at Mach 1.5—really screaming for that bird— when inertia coupling set in. They figured the plane hit at least 20 G's—*laterally* and *instantaneously*—just before it broke up and the pilot was probably dead in the cockpit before the first rivet popped.

A somewhat luckier colleague actually took a bullet that, in retrospect, was probably meant for me. His story was written up in gory detail in *Life* Magazine, as well as most newspapers at the time, and in a couple of books. Fortunately for me, the pilot's name was George Smith, but it came close to being Yoakley.

The saga began during a relatively rare spate of bad weather that had socked in the LA basin. NAA was cranking out lots of airplanes then, F-86Ls and F-100Ds, and our flight line was getting backlogged with birds that needed testing. But the weather wouldn't cooperate, so Jack put several of us pilots on telephone standby so at least we could wait at home instead of at the plant. One morning during this period, the weather looked like it would break and I got a call from the dispatcher. "We've got an airplane ready. Do you want to take the flight?" I said sure, and since I only lived about 15 minutes from the airport, I put on my flight suit and jumped in the car.

As I entered the dispatcher's office, I saw an F-100 taxiing out. I asked, "Who's going up in my airplane?"

"Oh," he replied, "That's George. He walked in just a couple of minutes after I called. He said he had nothing else to do, so I gave him your bird. But don't worry. We've got another one right behind it, just about ready to go."

"Okay, great."

George took off and after hanging around our lounge for a few minutes, I went up to the little NAA "tower" that overlooked the ramp. It had a couple of radios and a good view of the runway and was always manned when we had birds in the air. Ted Coberly, the Air Force rep, was on the radio and from the worried look on his face, I could tell something was wrong—*really* wrong.

"How is it now?" Ted asked anxiously.

"Still jammed," I recognized George's voice. "Can't get it to budge."

Apparently George had leveled off at 40,000 feet to begin his test card when the horizontal stabilizer, which was all once piece (as opposed to a conventional tail, which had a fixed horizontal stabilizer with movable elevators attached) had jammed in the down position, sending the F-100 earthward. He immediately pulled back the throttle, but at that altitude and Mach number, he went supersonic before you could spit, and the plane continued to pick up speed.

"For God's sake, George, get out!" Ted shouted. "Get out now! George? Do you read? Bail out!"

We wouldn't know for sure until later, but George had already pulled the handles on his ejection seat, becoming the first pilot to bail out at supersonic speed. Nobody knows exactly how fast he was going, but witnesses put the bailout altitude at about 7,000 feet, pretty thick air for a high-speed ejection, let alone one above Mach 1. They said his parachute deployed automatically and brought him—or his body—down in the water off Laguna Beach, a pretty little seaside community in Orange County. The airplane crashed at sea and George was picked up at once by a sport fishing boat that just happened to be nearby—great luck, since bad weather had kept most small boats in their marinas most of the week. The fishing boat skipper radioed the Newport Harbor Patrol immediately, reporting the pilot "looked pretty beat up," so they were sending a speed boat to pick him up and take him by ambulance directly to Hoge Memorial Hospital, the nearest emergency medical facility.

Ted was pretty upset. I was, too, but Ted had double concerns. First and foremost, he was worried about our pilot, but as the Air Force rep, he also had responsibility for the plane and the program. If some glitch in the design was beginning to show up, he needed to get on top of it. He was also concerned about the effects of a supersonic bailout; nobody had done that before. Given the circumstances, there was no guarantee that George would be, or remain, in a condition to tell us what happened, so Ted wanted to interview him as soon as possible.

"Can we get a company airplane?" Ted asked me.

The NAA ramp at LAX where newly minted F-100s await production acceptance flight test. Bill's colleague, George Smith, became the first pilot to survive a supersonic bailout when a test—originally scheduled for Bill—went terribly wrong.

"Sure," I replied. "We've usually got a Navion all ready to go."

"Great," Ted said. "I'll call Orange County airport and see if we can get a sheriff's car to take us to the hospital. See you down stairs." I dashed out of the tower and began pre-flighting one of the company's Navions, a great little single-engine private plane (the only small bird ever made by North American, though it was out of production by this time), which meant we could zip down the coast and get over to the hospital in less than an hour. In fact, we arrived about 15 minutes ahead of George's ambulance, which we met at the ER. Unfortunately, George couldn't talk—he was still unconscious—and the physician on duty said he didn't have any experience with "aviation medicine," particularly the trauma of a high-speed bailout. He asked us to accompany him into the examination room to give him the benefit of our experience. We weren't doctors but we were sure concerned about George, so we agreed. In fact, it would've taken that deputy sheriff to haul us out before we knew if George was going to make it.

George was wrapped in blankets to ward off shock, so we didn't get a good look at him until they had him on the table. What we saw was enough to make us retch. He had gone flying in slacks and a sports jacket, not that unusual for a production flight test, but I don't think there was a piece of flying gear on earth that would've done him much good. We helped the doctor and nurses cut away what was left of his clothing. George's face was badly bloated from the wind-blast; every cavity on his body had suddenly been force-fed with air. His eyes may have been torn briefly from their sockets, but were now back in place and looked like two shriveled apples. He undoubtedly had internal injuries, too, but couldn't tell us where he hurt. The sport-boat captain said he was unconscious when they fished him out and unconscious he remained—probably a blessing in disguise. So we just told the doctor what we knew about the possible sources of injury, from the lap belt and shoulder harness digging into his torso, the parachute straps and risers catching his limbs and neck, the opening shock of the canopy (which must've been colossal—it's amazing his legs weren't torn off), to possible contact with the seat, broken bones from hitting the water—a whole list of things I remembered from Korea but would just as soon forget.

They wheeled poor George off, still breathing, and that was the last we saw of him for a week, though every pilot in the organization made a pilgrimage to visit him at least a few times over the coming months. Gradually, his color and faculties returned, but he faced a long, hard road of surgery and rehab before he left the hospital. Believe it or not, six months later he was checked over by the NAA flight surgeon and given a green light to return to flying.

Of course, nobody can go through an ordeal like that without it having some affect on him, and nobody wanted to see George harm himself (or anyone else) by getting back in the cockpit too soon or at all, if any lasting psychological damage was done. But the company took care of its own, at least in those days, and Jack said George was welcome to have his old job back if he could hack it. His flight check was pretty simple. Jack asked me to "escort" George as his wingman while we ferried two F-86s from the plant at LAX to Edwards AFB near Lancaster, about 120 miles to the northeast. George did fine, as he said he would, and Jack returned him to flying status. I couldn't help thinking, though, if I had just arrived at the flight line ten minutes earlier, or if George had decided to kill the afternoon some other way than dropping by the plant, both our futures might've changed forever. Would I have bailed out sooner, sparing myself those horrible injuries? Or would I have ridden the sick bird even longer, like I did in Korea, or over Fullerton, trying to figure out a way to save us both? Those questions are usually academic, but as it turned out, I would face them again—and soon—only this time, I would be on the hot seat.

On May 26, 1958, I took off from LAX for a routine acceptance test on an F-86L, the same model interceptor flown by Pete's Guard unit in Phoenix. The climb to 45,000 feet took only minutes, that big afterburner really moved that bird, even with a full load of fuel. The weather was "CAVU" (ceiling and visibility unlimited), conditions every pilot loves. We already had two other '86s in the area wrapping up their own test flights. I was looking forward to a productive and enjoyable hour in the bright California sunshine.

The initial high-altitude checks went well, so I rolled into a high Mach dive and briefly went supersonic, then leveled off at about 25,000 feet for some medium altitude tests. Again, every check was "A-OK," as the astronauts would soon be saying, so I was quickly becoming satisfied that the plant had cranked out another bird with "zero defects."

The next test was to verify handling qualities at what was known as "Max Q," short for *maximum quantitative aerodynamic pressure*. That's a fancy way of saying that because air is denser at low altitudes, a jet or rocket flying at high speed will experience more stress at low-to-medium altitudes than at higher ones. This test, technically at the "edge of the envelope," was to ensure that no line pilot would encounter unusual flight characteristics or structural problems at high-speeds in this particular airplane due to manufacturing errors or faulty materials.

So I advanced the throttle and rolled the bird again into a max-performance dive. Almost at once, as it bit into heavier air, the engine began to surge. RPM and fuel-pressure dropped then *poof*—no more combustion. The engine had flamed out.

I had plenty of energy from the dive, so I immediately zoomed up to buy some time and altitude as I tried for an air start. I switched on the emergency fuel pumps and made sure that the appropriate circuit breakers and switches were in the right place then made several attempts at a normal air-start. None of them worked.

I was still on company frequency, so I notified the NAA tower of the situation. The airplane had soared from 10,000 back up to about 15,000 feet, but airspeed was bleeding off and although it was still fully under control, I had to starting thinking about other options. I pointed the nose toward Catalina Island which, although 26 miles from the mainland, was the closest land and began a glide at maximum "lift over drag," that airspeed that yields the farthest distance for the least loss of altitude. But an '86L isn't exactly a sailplane, and the vertical velocity indicator was showing an alarming rate of descent. Catalina had a small runway, but it was way too short for a dead-stick landing. Ditching was out of the question. Low wing, swept wing airplanes had a tendency to cartwheel when they hit the water; and as a veteran of a previous bailout, I had confidence in the ejection system, which was much improved over the one in the old F-80. I switched to guard frequency and told everyone in the area—including the two other NAA test birds, that I was preparing to punch out.

By the time I reached Catalina, I'd been joined on both wings by our two NAA '86s, one flown by Harry Hoch, an excellent pilot, and one by none other than George Smith, the same man who had survived that supersonic bailout a couple of years before.

"When are you leaving the bird?" George asked, noting we were now below 8,000 feet.

I said, "I'll eject after passing Avalon," which was the only town on Catalina. I wanted to come down reasonably close to shore to improve my odds of a quick pickup, but not so close that the inevitable crash would endanger people on the ground. I figured two miles or so off shore would do the job.

"George, I'll stick with Bill and mark his chute for the rescue boats," Harry said.

"Roger," George replied. "I'll follow the bird so they'll know where to dive for the pieces."

It was very reassuring to have a couple of old pros like that on my suddenly very wobbly wings.

I passed Avalon at about 4,500 feet. As the island slid behind me, I slowed to 180 knots and jettisoned the canopy, getting that *deja vu* feeling all over again. Without further thought, I reached down and pulled the ejection handles on either side of the seat.

The kick in the pants was just as I remembered it, only a whole lot warmer this time. Seat separation was automatic; the Air Force now had a "butt kicker," a nylon strap folded against the seat cushion and backrest that snapped taut, literally "kicking" you out after you cleared the plane. I pulled the familiar D-ring and the parachute deployed with a brisk but comforting tug. I took a couple of swings like a pendulum then settled down for the short ride to the sea. Harry circled me a couple of times, waved at me, and I waved back, indicating that I was okay. I hit the water feet first, no harder than a kid jumping into a pool from a diving board, and was happy I wasn't weighed down this time with a winter flight jacket, side arm, and all the other gear I'd carried as a combat pilot. I was equally pleased that, this time at least, I'd be rescued with my pants on. I inflated the one-man raft that came with the chute and climbed aboard.

Needless to say, on a sparkling Southern California day, the Catalina channel was filled with pleasure boats and I had just given them a pretty exciting show. A dozen were on top of me almost as soon as I hit the raft—so many, in fact, that I was a little concerned there'd be a collision or somebody would whack me with a propeller or something like that, so I tried to wave them away. An Avalon Airways shuttle plane, a little amphibian used to run tourists back and forth between the island and the mainland, even taxied through the armada and offered to fly me back to LA, but I yelled "No, thanks," since I had just noticed a blue Navy helicopter about a half-mile away closing fast on our position.

The small craft pulled back and Uncle Sam's chopper got down to business—another "blast from the past." As it turned out, the mighty aircraft carrier, *U.S.S. Kearsarge* was on maneuvers nearby and picked up my distress call. I wondered if my bosses at NAA would pony up a case of scotch to buy me back from the Navy.

The helo dropped a sling and I grabbed it. With no problems releasing my chute this time, they hauled me up without incident. The crewman on the winch checked me over real quick and asked me how I felt and I said, "Just dandy." I made my way to the cockpit and gave the chopper pilot, a Lt. J.G. named Dan McKinnon, a clap on the shoulder and said, "Thanks a million!" He was grinning from ear to ear, even happier than I was. It seems he had just finished Navy Search-and-Rescue (SAR) training and I was his first operational pickup. We chatted on the way to his ship, where I would be checked by the Navy flight surgeon and spend the night. Dan gave me a quick tour of the ship and returned me to LAX the next day. Because it had been such a big day for both of us, our cordial visit turned into a lasting friendship. A week later, NAA's President, Ray Rice, invited Dan to LA and gave him a tour of the plant, along with a certificate of appreciation. Everybody treated him like royalty, which he richly deserved. The afternoon of his visit, I took him up in a two-seat version of the F-100, flew low over the Sierras and buzzed Kern River Canyon before climbing to 50,000 feet for a supersonic run—pretty high and pretty fast for a fling-wing pilot—and Dan enjoyed every minute of it. I can't take all the credit for broadening his horizons beyond helicopters, but Dan went on to fly just about every high-performance jet in the Navy inventory and wrote several books with aviation themes, including one of my favorites: *Bullseye One Reactor*, the story of Israel's surprise attack on Iraq's nuclear bomb facility in the 1980s. President Reagan thought so highly of Dan that, after a distinguished Naval career, he picked him to dismantle the Civil Aeronautics Board, streamlining the way our government polices aviation safety. Dan later started North American Airlines, a small but successful outfit that flew out of New York. Frankly, I don't think there was a thing old Dan McKinnon couldn't do if he put his mind to it, and I was just happy that he was there, doing his thing, when I needed him most.

Oh yes, as a footnote to this whole adventure, the troubled F-86L that put these events in motion wound up circling back and crashing on Catalina, in an uninhabited area, fortunately, where it started a minor brush fire. This made recovering and analyzing the failed components much easier. It seems a wiring problem closed the main fuel valve and, because of other peculiarities with the electrical system, prevented it from re-opening. Thus what amounted to a short-circuit in the main canon plug began a series of failures that eventually cost the taxpayers one fairly expensive airplane. I was just glad the story had a happy ending, and that it was me and not some green second lieutenant who discovered the problem.

A s the Sixties began, we had no inkling of the changes we'd see in American society, in the military, and in aerospace, where NAA became a star player for the team that put a man on the moon. The road from Lucky Lindy to Neil Armstrong was a long one, technologically, though surprisingly quick as the scale of human progress is normally measured. Between the pair of us, we'd met these two cornerstones of achievement in the conquest of the air and the exploration of space and would come to know many more. Yet even then, our adventure was far from over.

While Bill (when he wasn't flying) enjoyed the good life in Southern California, boating and fishing and camping with his growing family (his second son with Dottie, David Calvin Yoakley, was born in Inglewood in 1956), Pete continued building his business "empire" while defending American skies in the latest Air Force interceptor, the Mach 2, F-104A Starfighter, Lockheed's famous "missile with a man in it."

TOP: Bill (far right) looks on as Navy helicopter pilot, Lt. Dan McKinnon (center left), accepts a certificate of appreciation from NAA President Ray Rice for rescuing Bill after his bailout from an F-86L over Catalina Island.

OPPOSITE PAGE: A nuclear family for the nuclear age—Dottie's and Bill's fine brood (stair-stepping L to R) Dave, Trisa, and Don.

Bill and several other NAA test pilots hoped to build a resort at Site 6, Lake Havasu, but construction delays and personnel problems led them to sell it to another developer, who turned it into Lake Havasu City—a retirement gold mine.

Our paths crossed regularly during this period, mostly quick stop-overs on military flights or the occasional family vacation (Dottie's southern "chicken and dumplings" were an instant hit with Pete's kids), but such visits were all too rare and over too quickly. Finally, Pete invited Bill to come back to Arizona and join him in a new venture: not a flight school or a service station this time, but a grand motel he was planning to build in Glendale, Arizona, a stone's throw from Luke AFB, where so many of our past adventures took place. Despite the challenges and rewards of flying for NAA, Bill was sorely tempted.

WRY: We civilian test pilots were paid pretty well in those days, and even with the expense of raising a family in a LA, I squirreled away a few dollars from each paycheck and looked for a way to put them to work. Some of us started an investment club, but we were a lot better at picking good planes than good stocks, and after giving it a whirl, we were lucky to break even. An attorney we knew suggested we start buying second mortgages that were in default. It sounded like a bad idea at first, and the California real estate boom hadn't really started yet, but we picked up some pretty good houses in good locations—seaside cities like Redondo Beach and Santa Monica—for a song, then fixed them up and sold them for a tidy profit. If I'd been a sharp businessman like Pete, I probably would've made that my profession and gone back to flying jets part-time with the Guard, but I was still addicted to flight test so that's where I hung my hat, or helmet, while I tried to learn more about this game called business.

One of my first solo ventures was as an inventor. I was always pretty good with tools—seems to run in the family—and, because Dottie was so short and always asking me to get cans down for her in our kitchen, I created a gizmo with little mechanical fingers at the end of a rod, actuated by a lever on the handle. It allowed short people like her (or kids, or elderly people, or disabled people in wheelchairs, or whatever) to securely grab small items from a distance; kind of like the soil samplers used by Apollo astronauts to grab moon rocks. (Heck, maybe those geniuses at NASA stole my idea!) Anyway, I patented the dang thing (#2,869,914 if you really want to know) and had it manufactured by a tool-and-die company in Hawthorne, California. We sold quite a few units, mostly through catalogs, but I enjoyed the tinkering, not the marketing, and eventually turned the product over to a more capable businessman, John Gavin, in exchange for royalties. Well, John got sick and his partner wasn't nearly as scrupulous about business. When the royalty checks stopped and the company wouldn't answer my letters and phone calls, I consulted a lawyer who concluded it would cost me more to enforce the contract than I'd make with 100% of the profits, so I chalked the whole thing up to experience and went hunting for different game.

I found it (along with four other guys from the investment club) in the form of some undeveloped land, called Site 6, around Lake Havasu in Arizona, 600 acres of prime, lakefront property with options to buy more. We thought it had great potential, but none of us wanted to quit flying, go to Northern Arizona, and develop the darn place, so we hired a manager; actually, we hired a whole series of managers to supervise the work for us, which was a big mistake. Those managers that were honest weren't very smart, and those that were smart were in it only for themselves—couldn't keep their hands out of the cookie jar. We thought we'd found a "white knight" to save us in the person of Jim Dillon, an executive with NARCO, the aviation radio company, who bought some shares and became a partner. Jim was a good businessman and the project showed real progress. He was also a private pilot who often flew himself up to the site. One night, we agreed to meet him there and parked our cars along the edge of its dirt landing strip, illuminating it with headlights. Jim's plane arrived on schedule, made one low pass, then flew straight into the ground. Jim was killed.

That tragedy was the last straw; somehow we just weren't fated to develop that property. After protracted negotiations, we finally made a deal with Bob McCullough of the McCullough Corporation (the chainsaw people) who was buying property in the area like mad. Well, I guess it pays to know what you're doing. Before long, Lake Havasu City was born, becoming a vacation spa that evolved into a huge retirement community. If you want to see the London Bridge, that's where you'll find it; McCullough brought it over from England, stone-by-stone, as a promotional gimmick to lure visitors, and it worked. But don't ask Bob to land an F-100. He may be superman, but he can't fly.

✪ ✪ ✪

PJW: Bill and some friends bought Site 6 at Lake Havasu with the idea of developing it. I thought it was a good idea, but they had all kinds of trouble getting their act together: management problems, contractor problems, you name it. He and his buddies spent a lot of time there, at least initially, so during one of their visits, I thought I'd surprise them. I had gone to LAX to pick up one of our F-86Ls that had just come out of IRAN—not the country; *IRAN* is Air Force jargon for "inspection and repair as needed" for work on a plane that could only be done at a major overhaul facility, or at the factory.

Anyway, I knew Bill was at Site 6 and because it was pretty much on the way back to Phoenix, I dropped down from cruising altitude to give him a buzz. I lowered the nose, picked up speed, and went supersonic, pulling up just over the site. I did a slow roll then went on my way, unsure if anybody had seen me, although that sonic boom undoubtedly woke up the rattlesnakes, as well as any contractors asleep in the trailers and sheds that dotted the property.

After I landed in Phoenix, I got a phone call from Bill.

"Hey Pete," he said. "One of your birds buzzed our crew up at Site 6 today. Was that you?"

He sounded kind of excited, but not the good kind of excited. "I don't know," I said cautiously. "Maybe it was and maybe it wasn't."

"I *knew* it was you! You scared me half to death. I was out in the shed with a flashlight looking for a gas leak, taking meter readings on a clipboard. I thought a propane tank had exploded! That clipboard looks like an earthquake hit it!"

I saw the paper in question later and it's true. In the middle of Bill's meticulous notes and numbers is a big jagged line that looks like, well, an earthquake hit it. He still has the piece of paper to prove it. They say that in comedy, timing is everything. I guess they're right.

WRY: After Site 6 folded, at least for me, I was still interested in making some money from my nest egg and so was very receptive when Pete came to LA and, over a couple of beers on my boat, asked if I wanted to become a partner in a new motel he was building in Arizona in a town just east of Luke. He was going to call it the "Sage Inn," a name inspired partly by its western connotations (sage brush, cactus, and all of that) but it was also the acronym for the Air Force's air defense system, SAGE, which employed a lot of people at Luke. He was sure a nice new motel with flight-friendly name would snag a lot of business from the base.

Since production of the F-86 and F-100 was winding down, those fine ships being replaced by even newer Century Series fighters made by other companies, it seemed like a good time to make a change, so I told Pete, "Hell, yes, let's give it a try."

I told my boss at flight test about my plan to move to Arizona and he said he understood completely and that there would always be a job for me at North American if I wanted to come back. "Consider it a leave of absence, not a termination," Jack said, which I much appreciated. Of course, you don't get anywhere in life or going fishing if you keep one foot on the dock while the other's in the boat, so I had already begun to make the shift, psychologically, from aerospace to another kind of life. Dottie liked flying and knew it was a big part of my life, but I think she felt a little better about me leaving for work each day knowing I'd be supervising a construction site, or driving a desk, instead of tooling around in the stratosphere with a parachute on my back. For her, two bailouts in one lifetime was enough.

So we packed up the kids and relocated to Scottsdale, a nice little upscale town where Pete and Max had been living for several years and I began to re-experience the joys and sorrows of entrepreneurship, which at this point meant raising money for our project. There was a core of investors who liked and trusted Pete, but they didn't have much spare cash and we just couldn't swing the minimum funds needed to start construction. I still had a family to feed, so to make ends meet while we tried to raise money for Sage, I got a job at Anderson Aviation, a Piper distributor at Sky Harbor airport, teaching civilians how to fly, demonstrating aircraft to potential buyers, making occasional charter flights, the usual FBO thing. It was a good outfit and I enjoyed the work, though the big pay cut from what I made at NAA took some getting used to. I admit, I sometimes felt a pang of regret when I looked to the south across the runway and saw all those shiny fighters parked on the Air Guard ramp.

By 1962, I was losing the race between funding the Sage and preserving my savings so when Bob Hoover and Warren Swanson, now president of NAA, called one day to invite me back into the fold, I was all ears. NAA was getting out of the fighter business, they said, but other even more exciting, cutting-edge projects were either underway or in the works. The North American X-15 rocket plane was setting speed and altitude records virtually every month at Edwards AFB and the company had a contract to develop the first supersonic strategic bomber, the truly stupendous and awe-inspiring B-70 Valkyrie. They wanted me to be a part of it. How could I say no?

By the end of the year, my family was back in Southern California, this time in the Antelope Valley north of LA. I once again put on my NAA flight suit and drew that very satisfying test pilot's pay check. As frosting on the cake, Warren said I was rehired with no loss in seniority; my little excursion to Arizona wouldn't affect my pay grade or pension. When you look at it that way, my three year visit with Pete was one of the best vacations I ever had.

PJW: We ran into problems getting money for Sage. Eventually, I found the right partners and the property got built in 1963, and it was as successful as we hoped, but by then Bill was back at North American and I felt bad that, on the strength of my suggestion, he'd made the commitment to come to Arizona only to leave after a couple of years. Fortunately, the hiatus proved a blessing in disguise for us both.

In 1960, the 197th transitioned out of the aging F-86L into the new and dramatically more powerful F-104 Starfighter, the product of Lockheed "Skunk Works," which had specialized in quick development of astoundingly innovative and effective military aircraft since before WWII. This change of aircraft brought with it a change of mission. Our group left ADC (which still relied heavily on ground-controlled intercepts, or GCIs, with the delta-winged F-102 and F-106) and joined TAC, the Tactical Air Command, which was responsible for just about everything else a fighter could do, from air superiority to ground attack.

In any department, the F-104 clearly outclassed the "L"—except, perhaps, in forgiveness of pilot mistakes. Where the L was subsonic in level flight, the '104 could make limited dashes past Mach 2, over twice the speed of sound, which greatly enhanced its ability to catch a target. Where the L fired salvos of unguided rockets, like shotgun pellets, the '104 carried two heat-seeking, Sidewinder AIMs

Plywood highway patrol cars located beneath the Best Western Sage Motor Hotel's billboards in Arizona are one way to get motorists to slow down to see the message.

LEFT: In the early '60s, we tried to raise money for a new motel, the "Sage," near Luke AFB, but this billboard was about as far as we got. The fake Highway Patrol car—a two-dimensional cut-out—made a lot of travelers slow down and take notice.

BOTTOM: The Sage Motel was finally built, but not until Bill had returned to North American.

A flight of four F-104As in echelon over Phoenix. The Mach 2 "missile with a man in it" was one of Pete's favorite airplanes, but it was a handful to fly.

(air intercept missiles) that homed-in on the hot exhaust of an enemy aircraft, literally flying up its tail pipe. Even the ejection systems were different, at least initially. Early Starfighters featured a downward firing seat because engineers feared the high "T-tail," made necessary for stability and control at supersonic flight, would snag a pilot in a conventional bailout. Because of this, we '104 drivers were given a set of "spurs" to wear on our flying boots, very similar to spurs used on horseback. Each spur ended in a slotted knob to which we attached a steel wire linked to the seat. During ejection, the wire snapped our feet back from the rudder pedals and locked them against the seat, preventing them from flying up (or staying in the cockpit!) during a downward ejection. Later versions of the Starfighter had a ventral fin attached to the aft fuselage under the tail, improving stability, though the downward-firing seat was phased out before that for obvious reasons; to eject at low altitude (such as shortly after takeoff) a pilot with the downward seat first had to roll inverted, which wasn't always possible. The system retained the spurs, though, which distinguished Starfighter pilots from other, lesser mortals who flew less flashy and exciting planes.

For all its foibles, though, the '104 was a surprisingly stable fighter, a good platform for the Sidewinder missile and just the ticket for climbing quickly and catching high-flying, high-Mach intruders. (A specially modified '104, in fact, flown by Chuck Yeager, would capture the world time-to-climb record from brake release to well past 100,000 feet.) Unfortunately, the ship still had teeth that could bite an unwary pilot. One was a by-product of that high, T-tail. While it enhanced pitch control during normal flight, in a stall it could be "blanked out" by turbulent air from the wing, rendering the elevators useless and the airplane unrecoverable. As a result, the '104 was the first airplane I'd seen with a stick-shaker and stick-pusher, basically a device that made the control column vibrate unmistakably when the airplane approached a stall, then if you continued to ignore it, pushed the nose down for you, getting you out of that deadly corner of the envelope. Another limitation came with those stubby wings—great for supersonic flight, but at low airspeed and low altitude, look out.

One example of this came during an F-104 "dollar ride" given by our Air Force advisor to one of our best pilots, Lyle Peterson, in the two-place "B" model we used for transition and proficiency training. (A "dollar ride" is flying jargon for any initial orientation flight. It was coined when barnstormers gave civilians their first ride in an airplane from a cow pasture, promising them a bird's-eye view of their hometown "for only one dollar.") After returning from F-104 ground school at George AFB in California, Lyle climbed in the back seat of the '104B for a quick demonstration of the bird's handling characteristics and a couple of sample landings. On their first approach to Sky Harbor, however, landing from east to west on Runway 27L, the Air Force instructor undershot the runway and snagged a chain-link fence near the threshold, completely tearing off the left main landing gear strut. Even worse, part of the fence wound around the right main strut, making it impossible to raise the gear for a go-around, which the IP immediately and wisely initiated.

The pilots were now left with a terrible dilemma. Because of the long, narrow fuselage and short, stubby wings, a belly landing or landing with only one main gear extended was strictly forbidden in the F-104. It had been tried once or twice in previous incidents and the aircraft inevitably tumbled as soon as it touched down. According to the book, the only solution was to punch out, but neither Lyle nor our advisor was in the mood to walk home that day, so they diverted to Luke AFB, about ten minutes flying time away, and asked the Air Force to foam the runway.

I said Lyle was one of our best pilots, and that's true; but he was also one of the luckiest—a great combination. Although the instructor made the approach, the stricken '104—still dragging that section of fence!—came in for a partial-gear landing. Final approach speed in the Starfighter was always pretty high, but between perfect technique, deployment of the drag chute at just the right time, and the extra stability provided by that fence dragging along the runway, the bird remained upright and came to a rest on its two good gear and left wingtip. That was Lyle's dollar ride in an F-104, and already he was re-writing the flight manual!

In the summer of 1961, just as we were getting proficient in our sexy new airplane, the Soviets cracked down on refugees fleeing from Communist East Germany by building the notorious "Berlin Wall," precipitating a world crisis and an American response on par with the Berlin Airlift of 1948 and the Cuban missile crisis that would follow a year later. President Kennedy reinforced American units in Europe by mobilizing several Air Guard units, including ours. On October 9th, we got our orders to deploy to Germany; the USAF said we were to be fully operational at our new base by November 1ˢᵗ. That gave us a lot to do in less than a month, and I was one of the guys they tagged to do it.

By this time I had been promoted to Major, having set some kind of record as the longest-serving Captain in Air Force history—or at least it seemed like it. After all, I'd made that rank in Korea and even won the Evans Trophy for "Most Outstanding Officer" in the Arizona Air Guard for 1957, though I'd rather have had the gold leaves and bigger paycheck. I still believe that Major is the ideal rank for an Air Force pilot. Below that (as captain or lieutenant) you get tagged for a lot of extra duties, most of which are bothersome and don't involve flying. At Lt. Col. and beyond, they threaten you with command, which means administrative and personnel headaches; and while those are important, they take a lot of time and energy and don't leave you much of either for flying. So once I'd made Major, I thought I'd have it swacked for at least a few years, doing my bit as a flight leader while those poor guys above and below me actually did most of the work. The Berlin Wall crisis proved me wrong.

I was picked, along with another part-timer (our intelligence officer, Curt Williams, a great guy who later became a good friend, business associate, and general) and two senior enlisted men to go as an advanced detachment to make arrangements for our unit's move to Ramstein AFB in Germany, one of America's biggest Cold War installations and now, being close to East Germany, one of its most important.

In those days, the active-duty Air Force was generally indifferent to Air Guard personnel. At best, they regarded us as weekend warriors who unfairly got to play with military "toys" while earning a civilian paycheck and avoiding the hassle of frequent transfers. At worst, their attitude was contemptuous, assuming part-timers couldn't possibly stay proficient with increasingly sophisticated, high-performance planes and systems. In truth, we won their respect (at least the respect of the active-duty pilots) by simply flying the pants off them during informal rat-races and at periodic Air Force-Air Guard gunnery meets. This shouldn't have surprised them. Most Guard pilots had seen one or two active-duty tours, many of them in combat, and stuck with military flying because they liked it and were good at it. Thus most of us were more experienced than our active duty contemporaries in similar assignments; and we were usually more flexible and resourceful, having to juggle both military and civilian careers.

At any rate, our advance team got more cooperation than we expected (I think the local, permanent party was happy for all the help they could get) and by the end of November all our aircraft, equipment, pilots, and support personal had left Sky Harbor and were in position at Ramstein or other duty stations in Europe.

As I said, Ramstein was a big base, one we shared with another '104 Squadron as well as a variety of other TAC and MAC (Military Airlift Command) units. But not even one of the biggest, best-equipped bases could compensate us for one of the worst problems we immediately ran into, the horrible German winter. Although many of us had operated in bad weather during WWII or Korea, German winter storms arrived fast and seemed to stay forever. And when it wasn't snowing or covering everything with freezing rain, heavy fog took over. We were used to flying high-altitude interceptors out of Phoenix, where even if storms moved through the area, the Valley of the Sun was usually clear or at least well above instrument minimums, as if covered by a big glass dome. Here, we had to adapt to poor or marginal conditions for weeks on end. This was one reason the F-104G and J-models, purchased and operated by the Luftwaffe, suffered such a high accident rate. Because of the way they rationed training hours, their pilots didn't get much stick time, let alone actual weather flying, so as their old joke went, if you live in Germany and want your own F-104, just wait a few weeks and one will fall on your property. Our weather-related incidents weren't nearly that bad (we didn't have to stand strip alert in Germany, with its periodic scrambles, and we seldom flew at night), but it was just another factor that made a touchy airplane and a tough mission a little harder to fly.

All in all, we remained in Germany just under a year, enough time to get to know the place and begin to miss what we had back home. I, for one, had a new daughter, Terry (Theresa) Anne Wurts, born in March 1960, who was cute as a button, but I was out the door almost as soon as she came home from the hospital.

TOP: *Wilkommen* to Ramstein AFB, Germany, 1961, where they took the "cold war" literally.

BOTTOM: The F-104 flight line at Ramstein. Pete was one of four 197th flight commanders who saved the free world from communists and Canadians in 1961-62.

Pete's youngest daughter, Theresa, was born on the eve of his deployment to Germany.

The first XB-70 rolled out on May 11, 1964 at Palmdale, CA to a stunned and awestruck crowd. The 186-foot long bomber weighed half-a-million pounds and had a wingspan of 105 feet.

The B-70 Valkyrie in all its glory landing at Edwards AFB. Test pilot Al White, left, narrowly escaped death in the tragic aerial collision that claimed two lives and effectively ended the program.

Bill (center), now a member of the Society of Experimental Test Pilots (SETP), is flanked (L to R) by flight-test legends Joe Walker, former chief pilot for NASA (killed when his F-104 collided with the XB-70); Jack McKay and Milt Thompson, both NASA test pilots; Joe Engle, who became a Space Shuttle commander; Neil Armstrong, the first man on the moon–then testing the X-15; and Bob Rushworth, former commanding officer of Edwards AFB.

Still, we Guardsmen considered ourselves modern Minutemen and the national emergency was real. We had no idea how long our deployment would last or where it would ultimately lead, but if the past was any indication, even a few months would be enough time to rack up some adventures we could never have in the states.

WRY: I knew the activation of Pete's Guard unit was pretty disruptive to his family and business life, just as my own short detour back to Arizona had been a bit disorienting for Dottie and the kids. To be truthful, part of me was a little jealous. That F-104 was a beautiful bird and could be a handful to fly, so they didn't hand them out to just anyone. And flying back into harm's way, in a potential theater of combat, was enough to give me goose bumps. If the cause is important enough—as this one surely was—part of me wanted to get into the fight.

At the moment, though, my battle was at NAA, helping to fill a brand-new niche in the warplane industry that had become increasingly dominated by heavy science and hardball politics. We had a big plant at Palmdale, California (adjacent to the flight test center at Edwards AFB), which would be my new base of operations. The F-86 and F-100 production lines had closed a couple of years before, so I was asked to head customer relations, which meant government relations, for the B-70 project, now less than two years from its first flight.

Despite its enormous potential, the fantastic, futuristic plane had trouble getting off the ground, at least administratively. Originally, the Air Force wanted a Mach 3 jet bomber that could fly higher and faster than any defensive fighter or missile, yet still carry an enormous nuclear payload. Essentially, they wanted a "B-52 with the speed of a B-58," a tall order, even with today's technology. Back then, there was even some talk about making the B-70 nuclear-powered itself, giving it unlimited range and endurance limited only by the frailty of the crew. That was a pipe dream, of course. No politician was about to tell his constituents that there's a chance, however small, that a tiny nuclear reactor might one day fall on their house.

But the plane they came up with was still a marvel of engineering. The Air Force originally wanted the plane to make a conventional, subsonic cruise to enemy territory, then dash supersonically to the target. Optimizing a design for these two basically incompatible traits, though, eventually proved less practical than sizing the aircraft for supersonic flight the whole way. This was a decision North American liked, because it meant the same design might find a commercial market, say, for a supersonic airliner that could cross the Atlantic or Pacific in a couple of hours. It was an exciting time to be in aerospace, and my seat—if not in the cockpit—was at least near the leading edge.

My job had two major components: setting up publicity and promotional events for the program, then making sure they happened the way we planned. Part of that meant transporting VIPs (politicians, senior military officers, media figures, foreign dignitaries and the like) from Los Angeles to Palmdale and back, often wining and dining them in the process. Whenever I could, I flew the company plane myself, a Beechcraft Baron, a lovely little six-passenger twin with a comfortable cabin. Pete would own one just like it twenty years later to commute between his motel properties. During those few years I escorted such dignitaries as Charles Lindbergh, Jimmy Doolittle and his wife, Roscoe Turner (a famous racing pilot from aviation's "golden age" in the 1930s), Senator Hubert Humphrey (later Vice President under Lyndon Johnson and a presidential candidate himself), the Shah of Iran (before he lost his job to the Ayatollah), and former members of the Flying Tigers—even the last four surviving WWI pilots. I also squired around my share of Hollywood celebrities, from Bob Hope (a real military booster) and Jimmy Stewart (a decorated B-24 combat pilot and general in the Air Force Reserves—every bit as nice in person as he is on the screen), to network TV newsmen. I also got to know quite a few experimental test pilots who either had, or would shortly make, aviation history: great guys like Chuck Yeager (the real deal, though his later, greater fame, a result of *The Right Stuff* book and film, would cause him problems), Scott Crossfield (a little aloof to some people, but sharp as they come), and Neil Armstrong, the first man on the moon, though at the time I met him, he was testing our X-15. Neil was a brilliant and thoughtful young pilot, but tough as nails under that quiet, self-effacing exterior. If he'd been ten years older, he might very well have been our first man in space. As it turned out, his "one small step" into world history would come a few years later.

Of all these notables, I have to admit my favorite was Lindbergh, the man who first kindled my interest in aviation. He was a delightful person—quiet, thoughtful, and considerate—though he had no use for the photographers who dogged him everywhere. My least favorite, perhaps, was an icon in American broadcasting whose name I will not mention who, despite his later role as "America's conscience" during the Vietnam and Watergate eras, seemed a bit too impressed with himself to get our story really right.

Needless to say, I learned a lot about handling talented and sometimes temperamental people during those years, and although I had my share of frustrations (and would have much rather been up in the nose of that Valkyrie than down in the hangar shmoozing bigwigs), I tried to carry my end of the log. Unfortunately, that marvelous bird was just too far ahead of her time—politically, economically, and technically—to get the future she deserved. From its startling "goose neck" and forward canards, to the revolutionary "honey-comb" skin and variable, drooping wing-tips (a stroke of engineering genius that improved high-Mach stability without upsizing the tail, increasing weight and drag, like we did on the F-100) it was an aircraft that inspired instant awe in everyone who beheld it. In fact, the ever-present security guards began referring to it as "the Savior" rather than the Valkyrie because everyone seeing the prototype for the first time—dramatically lit in its top-secret hangar—inevitably addressed the Deity, saying something like, "Jesus Christ!" or "Oh my God!" Sadly, it would've taken divine intervention to resurrect the program after the death blow it was about to receive.

PJW: We crammed a lot of flying into a German deployment that lasted about nine months. That was as long as it took for the Kremlin to get the message that Communism had gone about as far as it would go in Europe, and their influence stopped abruptly at the wall they built to imprison their own people.

One my earliest adventures took place at the end of one of our rare night flights. I was leading a two-ship formation and we landed about ten or eleven. I had just touched down when my landing light revealed a blur at the edge of the runway, followed immediately by a slight jolt to the airplane, like hitting a speed bump on a highway. I immediately called the tower.

"I think I just hit something on the runway. You got any vehicles or people out this late?"

"Negative," the controller replied, "but we'll send somebody out from mobile control to take a look."

Well, they didn't find a busted jeep or an injured airman, but they did find enough venison parts to stock a large refrigerator. Like most airports, Ramstein had a grassy clear zone between the runway and the boundary fence. They had occasional problems with wild deer jumping into the area to eat the grass, and in this case one of them seemed to have concluded that the grass was greener on the other side of the concrete. Unfortunately, the poor critter made his move just as my plane was touching down. The aircraft was inspected but undamaged and when I went out to fly the plane again, I notice that a fine pair of antlers had been painted by the cockpit under the canopy. As far as I know, I was the only Air Guard pilot to score a kill—one six-pointer, confirmed—while we were in Europe.

While we flew many missions patrolling the Rhine and the aerial corridor into Berlin, occasionally spotting Red aircraft, our mere presence discouraged them and there were no real incidents. Our greatest rivals, it turned out, were our allies to the north: the Canadians.

The RCAF operated out of Zweibrucken (German for "two bridges") on the border of Switzerland and Austria. They flew Canadair F-86s—Sabre Jets built in Canada under license from North American; so when the opportunity presented itself, a flight of our guys would bounce a flight of their guys, or vice versa, and we'd rat-race until fuel got low or somebody in German ATC or the NATO command post asked what was going on. The Canadians were good pilots, and although the '104 could engage and disengage at will because of its greater speed and altitude capabilities, the F-86 by comparison could turn on a dime, so these engagements became good practice for those all-too-possible instances when allied aircraft might have to take on fast and maneuverable second- and third-generation Soviet fighters, like the MiG 17 and MiG-21. For now, our dogfights were strictly for training and fun, though unit and personal pride were at stake in each engagement.

After a few months of friendly jousting, the RCAF thought they'd host a party for we ungovernable colonials: a formal "Dining In" which is a soup-to-nuts, dress-uniform party very much in the tradition of regimental dinners going back to the age of Wellington and George Washington and whoever the heck the Canadian military national hero might be. Our squadron commander, Tom Barnard, one of the early members of the 197th, accepted on our behalf and, although a fun-loving guy at heart, took his command responsibilities very seriously. He said we could participate only if we all took a bus to the Canadian base and returned in one group—no individual cars and therefore (he assumed) no troubles with the German police.

Well, we put on our dress uniforms, got on Tom's bus, and arrived at the appointed hour. I have to admit, the Canuks had done everything right from the formal china and crystal stem-ware, wonderful French and German wine with every course, and impeccable table service, to the inevitable round of complimentary, reciprocal toasts saluting various Queens and Presidents and famous aircraft everyone loved. By the time desert was removed and the after-dinner brandy and cigars were finished, however, the real agenda was revealed, namely a contest to see which set of fighter pilots could drink the other under the table.

To facilitate this challenge, our hosts had devised a series of imaginative games, a "special Olympics" for participants who were rapidly losing the ability to remember their own names, let alone a set of complicated rules like "stand up" and "face this direction" and "try not to fall down."

The first event (or maybe it was the third) involved rolling up the carpet—a fine, oriental rug—and setting lit candles in two rows along the floor about three feet apart. At one end was a stein full of beer. At the other was a contestant who had to slide down the floor between the candles on his belly, like a wheels-up landing on a runway, then snag the beer and drink it. Everybody had to do this once, and repeat if necessary. Another event was to hurtle over a couch placed in the center of the room (this was a freestyle event—you could jump or roll on your back or do whatever seemed best) while carrying said stein of beer and not spilling a drop; for to do so meant you had to drain the stein, refill it, then start again.

These and other tests of motor coordination and good judgment went on until well past midnight, when our bus was supposed to return to Ramstein. A quick tally showed more Americans still standing at that point than Canadians, so we agreed to get out while the getting was good. Our re-boarding procedure resembled a baggage drill, with half the guys lifting the other half on board, although I'm sure some American in authority remembered to say thank you for the lovely evening and sorry for all the broken dishes.

The drive to our base was probably pleasant, though nobody seemed to remember it. Roll call at the other end revealed that an important member of our team (the pilot who was also our Engineering Officer, Don Owens, who years later would become a Major General and commander of all Guard units in Arizona) was missing. In fact, he was so missing that even the select few who could remember getting on the bus didn't remember him boarding. So we called the Canadians and contritely asked if they had seen our Engineering Officer, perhaps behind the couch when they slid it back.

"Yes, as a matter of fact," one Canadian pilot blustered, "we *have* seen your man. In fact, we've got him right here, and it's going to cost you plenty to get him back!"

We said, "Nuts to that. You can keep him!" and hung up.

Later that day, Don was delivered to Ramstein in an official Canadian staff car, dressed in an ill-fitting RCAF uniform. He never found out what happened to his Air Force uniform and had to buy another suit, poor guy, which nobody helped him pay for. So, if I got credit for our only "kill" in Germany, Don got the honor of being our only POW.

Now don't get me wrong, deployment wasn't all fun and games. Another flight leader, Jack Brasher (also slated to eventually become State Adjutant General—is there a pattern forming here?) and I were the first to take our flights from Ramstein to Wheelus AFB in Libya, North Africa, for a live-fire exercise with our GAR-8 Sidewinders, the Starfighter's primary (and only) weapon. At this point in the Cold War arms race, heat-seeking missile technology was new and expensive, so like the real Minutemen of old, we were allowed only one shot apiece with our high-tech "musket," and the Air Force wasn't about to waste an expensive, maneuverable drone just to give us better target practice. The Sidewinder was mounted on our right wing and a standard HVAR was mounted on the left. The idea was to launch the HVAR first, then after hurriedly going through the intercept procedure (listen for "missile tone" in our headsets, indicating target acquisition, and so on), launch the Sidewinder and shoot the rocket down before its little motor burned out. In other words, we not only had to shoot our musket at tin cans, we had to bring our own tin cans.

This is as good a point as any to recall how unpopular Uncle Sam was, even then, in those parts of the world we had so recently liberated from the Nazi scourge. The flight to Wheelus was a lot longer than necessary, since the French didn't belong to NATO and refused to let its warplanes fly over their country. As a result, we had to land in Pisa, Italy, refuel, and enter Libya literally through the side door. Upon arrival at the heavily guarded base, we were given a quick "theater briefing" by the local intelligence officer, which was essentially, "The Arabs don't like you, so while you're here, don't go into town." He was right, of course; America backed Israel, which the Arabs also hated, and most Arab states received their military equipment from the Soviet Union, not the west, so they didn't even want our foreign aid. As it turned out, the U.S. Government would soon be expelled from Libyan territory, but at the time, Jack and I figured we were guests in an exotic country we were unlikely to visit again, so why not do a little sightseeing? This was not a wise idea and may be one reason most USAF intelligence officers aren't pilots.

We had no trouble getting a pass to Tripoli, the capital city. We stopped by Leptis Magna, an old Roman coastal city whose ruins are magnificent, then found ourselves shopping at a colorful Arab bazaar in the old quarter of town. We were in our civies, but between our GI haircuts, low-quarter shoes, and near proximity to a big American air base, a local would have to be pretty stupid to conclude we weren't Americans. I have to admit, the vendors were enthusiastic, if not particularly courteous, and we thought we'd give "dollar diplomacy" a try. One dealer showed me a stack of sheepskins, which actually looked pretty nice, I could see one as a rug in my office or saddle pad for the horses I'd recently bought for the kids following our move from Phoenix to rural Scottsdale.

"How much do you want for it?" I asked, fingering the top skin, which was fleeciest.

"Five dollah! For you, five dollah!" He held five fingers aloft.

"No, no. Too much!" I started to move away.

"Okay, Joe, three dollah! That's it. Three dollah! Good quality. You take a look. You like, you buy!"

I felt the sheepskin again. Heck, I might buy the same thing in the states for ten times that much and not think twice about it, but I felt I had to play the game. When in Rome...

"Okay, *one* dollar. But that's all!" I held up one finger, then reached for my wallet and paused for his reaction.

He threw up his hands. "Okay, Joe. *One* dollah! You get good deal!"

I fished out the bill and gave it to him. He flipped through the stack and eventually pulled out a moth-eaten sheepskin about half the size of the one on top.

"No, no!" I said, grabbing the one on top, "*This* one. I buy *this* one!"

He then jabbered something in Arabic which I obviously couldn't understand, but it didn't sound complimentary. I remained unmoved.

"No, no. This one." I took the one on top and began walking away.

"Hey, Joe—bastard Joe! You steal sheep! Give back sheep!"

I stopped and turned, "Okay, give back dollar!"

By this time we were drawing a crowd and even Jack, a pretty big guy, was starting to look uncomfortable. "Jeez, Pete," he said, "are you sure?"

"Give skin!" the Arab shouted, then reached under his shirt. "I have knife! You want me to stab you?"

Stupidly, I got in his face and put my hand under my jacket, "I have a gun!" I lied. "You want me to shoot you?"

The vendor paused a moment and I could see a flicker of doubt pass over his eyes. His hand slowly came out from under his shirt. It contained the dollar.

"Okay Joe. You take dollah."

"Okay, you take sheepskin," I snatched the bill and tossed the skin back on the stack.

"Are we finished now?" Jack asked nervously over my shoulder. He obviously wanted to do more shopping and see more sights before it got dark.

Now, some people may wonder why I made such a big deal about something I didn't really need and an amount of money that meant a lot more to that poor, if dishonest, street vendor than it did to me. I could say it was a matter of principle, or that I had spent too long as a cop to look the other way when somebody tries to rip off somebody else, but that wouldn't be exactly true. What irked me at the moment was the fact that I was giving—and had given—a substantial chunk of my life to keeping poor, ignorant guys like that from having to call each other "comrade" or say "Heil Hitler" as they passed some jackbooted jerk in the street, and a lot of other Americans had sacrificed, and would sacrifice, a whole lot more than me to ensure that this guy's little piece of free enterprise would survive another generation.

"Well, Pete," Jack laughed as we drove back to the base, "you make one hell of a diplomat!"

"Yeah," I replied. "Good thing we got other guys for jobs like that."

One "other job" I temporarily held, along with another flight leader, Bob Kanaga, was that of acting squadron commander. When our real squadron CO, Lt. Col. Tom Barnard, deployed with two flights for his turn at Wheelus, he left Bob and me "in charge" of our operation at Ramstein. This was like letting the inmates run the asylum. Bob was a born fighter pilot and one-time member of the Air Force *Thunderbirds*, and I had a reputation for not always adhering strictly to the rules, or even knowing, precisely, what those rules might be. So when Tom went TDY to Africa, we felt a little like teenagers who had been left home alone for the weekend *with* the family car.

Our first official act was to contact all the rated officers at Air Division and Group who had said repeatedly that they admired our '104s and wished they could fly them. We told them to come down the flight line and take a dollar ride in one of the two-seat B models we used for training. Bob and I figured that giving a few joy rides to some highly placed desk-jockeys might go a long way toward atoning for any sins our squadron may have committed, or would commit, during our deployment.

Well, the flu must've been going around headquarters that week, because without exception every officer we called replied that he was DNIF (limited by the Flight Surgeon to "Duty Not Including Flying"), or had an important staff meeting on the day we suggested, or had to take a sudden trip to Bonn or Brussels. The Starfighter's reputation as a widow-maker had apparently preceded it, especially in Germany. When Tom got back, our offer of free "orientation rides" for the upper echelon was understandably rescinded. Then again, maybe the mere thought of going aloft with Bob or me was enough to scare off the honchos. Discretion, after all, is the better part of valor—and longevity.

More impressed with us, and more receptive to a demo, were the crew members of the massive radar site that directed most of our operations in Germany. One day when I was up with another member of my flight, a fine flyer and airline pilot named Gil Lopez, we got a call from "Moonglow" (as our radar control was known), asking for a flyby of their mountaintop facility. I said, "Fine, we're always happy to show off our new bird," so Gil and I rolled down from altitude and lined up on the site. Now, Gil was a great wingman and tucked that stubby wing in tight, so I had no qualms about making our "high-speed, low altitude pass" *really* fast and *really* low. We zoomed within a stone's throw of the domed structures, whose exterior catwalks were jammed with people, at just below Mach 1 (a sonic boom at that level would've cracked concrete and broken ear drums—not a good idea). We pulled up, made a high-G turn, then roared by a second time to an even bigger crowd, all cheering and waving.

About then I noticed that our fuel level—already low when we got the call from *Moonglow*—was now bordering on critical. We could've made it back to Ramstein using our planned reserves, but it would've been cutting things close, so I decided to divert to nearby Munich to "refuel and have lunch," as I told our squadron ops. This wasn't that unusual. Our birds often made unscheduled landings at other bases after rat-racing with other units. But we had just improvised an air show for a pretty big group and you could've measured our proximity to the buildings with a dime-store tape measure. We landed without incident and had a quick bite at the flight-line snack bar, during which I half expected to get called to the phone, or to Base Operations, but nobody had complained so Gil and I finished eating and returned to the home 'drome as if nothing had happened, which technically, it hadn't. Another impromptu air show didn't end quite so pleasantly.

In late spring or early summer, somebody at the 86th Air Division decided to celebrate some now-forgotten event with a massed flyover of four to six fighter squadrons. This would've been an awesome display of some sixty to a hundred planes, but it would've been a real bear to organize. After the initial announcement, we waited days, then weeks, for some sort of briefing or ops plan showing coordinated takeoff times, rendezvous points, flyby sequences, and recovery schedules; you just didn't throw that huge a gaggle into the air all at once and hope things turned out well. As the appointed date loomed, the pilots and squadron commanders all became rightfully nervous; although the poor maintenance guys kept working around the clock to make sure all our birds would be in the air.

Finally, common sense prevailed. At the last minute, Air Division cancelled the gaggle. Bob Sowers, our Operations Officer, and Tom Barnard called a meeting of our squadron's four flight commanders (me, with A Flight; John Koerner, B Flight; Lyle Peterson, C Flight; and Bob Kanaga, D Flight) to tell us the show was off. Our birds were ready to go, however, so Tom told us to take each of our four-ship flights to a different sector of sky, run some training maneuvers, then recover one flight at a time. "But," Tom said, "I repeat—I don't want to see more than four ships over the base at any one time. Has everybody got that?"

We all nodded obediently and went out to fly. My call sign that day was *Scorpion* and, since I was first off, I headed immediately for Zweibrucken in hopes of catching some unsuspecting Canadians in the air, bouncing them, and adding to our squadron's glorious list of allied aircraft "destroyed" in mock dogfights.

About ten minutes into the mission, I got a call on the radio. It was John Koerner leading B Flight a few minutes behind me.

"Scorpion One, where are you?" he asked.

I figured he was headed in the same direction with the same idea, and was making sure he had open sky.

"Over Zweibrucken," I replied, "looking for bandits."

It then occurred to me that John's flight just might try to bounce us themselves. We did that from time to time when we couldn't find dissimilar aircraft to "fight," so I told everyone in A Flight to "check their six" and keep our eyes peeled for bogies. Well, we saw some airplanes behind us all right, and it was John's flight, although not in combat spread or paired up in two elements the way we'd attack, but in picture-perfect fingertip formation. Without another word on the radio, John's people slid into close trail just behind and below us.

I now started a gentle turn back toward Ramstein, trying to figure out what to do with two flights, when Lyle Peterson's C Flight, also in perfect, close fingertip formation—appeared inside our turn and joined up behind and below John Koerner. As the turn was nearly complete, Bob Kanaga's D Flight appeared miraculously behind all of us and joined below Lyle Peterson. Other than John's first call to find out where I was, this had all been accomplished with complete radio silence.

I now found myself in command of a sixteen ship formation—as far as I know, the biggest formation of F-104s to have flown in Europe at that time. Obviously, our airshow hormones had kicked in and we weren't about to land without giving somebody a performance.

I called Ramstein tower.

"Scorpion One with sixteen, request permission to fly by."

"Roger, Scorpion, at what altitude?"

Um... "Pattern altitude."

Hey, if you're going to put on a show, make sure everyone sees it.

I lined up over the active runway at about a thousand feet above the ground, knowing that the fourth and last flight, "Thunderbird" Kanaga, would have five or six hundred feet clearance.

"Okay Scorpion," Bob said on the radio. "Everybody's in and tight. We look great."

We flew initial at just above pattern airspeed. I saw from the corner of my eye that a ton of people had run out from the buildings, left their desks and work benches, and gathered on the ramp. Auto traffic on the base and nearby highways had stopped or slowed to a crawl; four flights take up a lot of sky, and sixteen J-79s, even at reduced power, really make the ground rumble. At the departure end of the runway, I began a slow turn to the left and signaled all flights to go right echelon, which they did. We then turned back onto initial and each plane pitched out in turn with crisp precision and landed with a squeak of the tires so regular that you could set your watch by them.

I was the first to park and as soon as my canopy was open, a yellow ladder appeared on the cockpit rail. The crew chief said, "Major Wurts, Colonel Barnard wants to see you immediately."

I couldn't imagine why, so I unbuckled and signed off the airplane with no discrepancies (except possible pilot malfunction) and climbed down. Everybody I passed said how great we looked and thanked us for the show—really made them feel proud to be on the team. Tom was in his office pretending he hadn't run outside like everyone else to watch our show, which of course he had. I saluted in a military manner. He returned the salute but remained in his chair.

"Okay, Pete," he said, "would you mind telling me what the hell that was all about? What part of 'only four planes over the field at one time' didn't you understand?"

I told him that the fly-by kind of happened by itself (which sounded pretty lame even then) but that the flight leaders all volunteered and everything went well and it seems to have been a big morale booster for everyone on the base.

Tom tried unsuccessfully to suppress his smile while he continued a perfunctory chewing out, but he knew as well as anyone that this was just the kind of gesture that ground personnel appreciated, a thank-you from the flying unit for doing a good job tightening bolts and shuffling papers and keeping aspirin in the dispensary. It also validated another old military adage: it's always easier to get forgiveness than permission.

6

INTO AND OUT OF VIETNAM

*T*he Phoenix Air Guard was released from active duty and returned to the U.S. in August, 1962, having saved the free world from the Warsaw Pact, greedy Arab street vendors, and the Canadians. We already knew the aviation community—despite its globe-girdling reach and huge budgets—was surprisingly small, especially among flyers, where many veteran pilots knew each other. Pete wasn't completely surprised, therefore, when he ran into our old squadron commander and Florida Rockets leader, Bill Haviland, while on duty at Ramstein. Haviland's current career was as tech rep for Bill Lear, whose snazzy new biz-jet was revolutionizing corporate air travel. Europe was his turf and he operated out of Weisbaden, so it was a good opportunity to get re-acquainted and get caught up.

But the Air Force had ulterior motives for pulling the 197th back to Phoenix. The world was changing, and the threat originally posed by Russian bombers was quickly being supplanted by ICBMs, for which, when it came to cities, there was simply no defense. Both countries maintained strategic bomber fleets, but in reduced numbers; and fewer bombers meant fewer interceptors. The future, we learned, belonged to the multi-role tactical fighter—planes that could dogfight at medium altitudes and attack targets on the ground. These planes, in turn, had to be supported by aerial tankers and transports that could haul troops and equipment to trouble spots all over the globe. This new emphasis on rapid deployment to regional, "brush fire" wars meant the Air Guard, or at least the 197th and units like it, would receive a new mission, and new aircraft. In Pete's case, that "new" bird would be the venerable C-97G Stratofreighter, a four-engine, double-decked cargo plane powered by the largest reciprocating engine ever put into production. It was the military version of the Boeing 377 Stratocruiser, the "747" of its day, which commercial airlines used for long-haul, international flights from the late 1940s through the middle 1950s. For old fighter pilots, though, this change was a bitter pill.

Back in Palmdale, between the reduced need for bombers and skyrocketing costs, the XB-70 program had gradually been reduced from a projected purchase of 210 aircraft to a meager three: two flying prototypes and a third that never made it into the air due to Congressional budget cuts. The two research birds were aimed mostly at developing an American SST (supersonic transport) and technology that would eventually be used, along with X-15 data, for the Space Shuttle. The death knell for the B-70 rang on June 8, 1966, when General Electric, maker of the B-70's engines, requested a "photo flight" to publicize its aircraft powerplants, a six-ship formation in which the second B-70 prototype would be surrounded by five smaller jets all powered by GE engines. One of the planes, a late model F-104 like Pete flew, was moving under the B-70 from right to left, when its high vertical tail struck the down-turned wingtip of the big bomber. The '104 immediately went out of control, rolling over the B-70 and shearing off its vertical stabilizers. The F-104 pilot, Joe Walker, a NASA civilian with experience in the X-15—was killed instantly, although the crew of the B-70, pilot Al White and co-pilot Carl Cross, managed to maintain control long enough to activate one of the plane's unique capsule ejection seats. White, a veteran of over 60 Valkyrie missions, mangled an arm as the "clamshell" closed around him, but he survived an estimated 44-G impact when his capsule hit the ground. Cross wasn't so lucky. He was trapped in the cockpit by the tremendous transverse Gs of the spinning plane and rode the bird down, dying in the crash. It was a dark day for aviation and a real tragedy for all concerned, including Bill, who had poured so much sweat and energy into making such an unimaginable bird a reality. NASA flew 34 more missions with the original prototype, then retired it to the Air Force museum at Wright-Patterson AFB, Ohio, where it stands today, mute testimony to one hell-of-a plane that advanced aerospace technology in countless ways, and without which such later miracles as the supersonic Concorde and STS (the Space Transportation System, or Space Shuttle) simply wouldn't have existed.

This sad accident was especially poignant for us, since we'd had our share of close calls in the air, some inescapable, like combat in Korea and various in-flight emergencies; some like the occasional tight squeeze brought about by our own inexperience, high spirits and bad judgment, completely avoidable. But by now we both occupied positions of responsibility and the lives of other pilots seemed a little dearer. Pete was promoted to Lt. Colonel in 1963 and would later become squadron commander. Bill became an NAA marketing executive and shortly returned to the cockpit as Chief Pilot of its Sabreliner

Division. We realized more than ever that over the last twenty-five years flying had become as much about "managing" a complex web of people, machines, and systems as it was about skills with stick and rudder. That reality became even clearer as we and the nation entered a period known as "the Vietnam era," a time when a lot of attitudes about ourselves, our mission, and our country would be sorely tested.

WRY: In addition to costing the lives of two fine pilots, the crash of "Proto One" B-70 destroyed a lot of hopes and nearly demolished many careers, including mine. When the program was finally cancelled, I was re-assigned to the main plant at LAX and continued to coordinate VIP visits, though the luster of that job now felt a little tarnished. Bob Hoover and I continued to squire people around in the company Navion and Aero Commander, a fine little twin-prop business plane whose original manufacturer had been purchased by NAA, though Bob spent much of his time as the company's "aerial goodwill ambassador," giving astonishing airshows in a bright-yellow P-51D and the Aero Commander "Shrike," including a dazzling dead-stick landing with the Shrike's two propellers feathered.

In 1969, I was promoted to Director of Subcontracts Marketing, reporting directly to the company president. To the uninitiated, this may sound like a boring job, but in those days, before the B-1 contract, it was an important way to keep the plant's doors open. You see, while prime contractors (airframe manufacturers like NAA, Lockheed, Boeing, MacDonald-Douglas, and others) got famous putting their names on aircraft and systems they designed and assembled, a lot of the fabrication work was farmed out to subcontractors, many of which were prime contractors themselves on other programs. Thus a big company that lost a major contract, like the B-70 (Boeing and Convair were our hot competitors in that one), might still participate by making subassemblies and components for the prime, who performs final assembly and checkout of the finished aircraft. It's an old system that goes way back in aviation, and without it unsuccessful bidders would have to lay off their most experienced workers or simply go out of business. My job was to travel to all the major airframers—hat in hand, sometimes—and show how good-old NAA, makers of some of America's premium aircraft, could help make *their* new airplane even better.

This brought me into contact with a lot of companies and a lot of people I would never have known otherwise, but I still hankered to get back in the cockpit of something a bit faster than our company bug-smashers. Fortunately or unfortunately, the Cold War was heating up in another little-known corner of the world (at least to most Americans) in Vietnam. The Air Force was getting spread pretty thin, and one small but critical component in their network was a little plane called the T-39 Sabreliner, the first small, twin-jet passenger plane, designed and built by North American. It was operated with great success by the Air Force and the Navy, partly as a high-priority transport (whisking generals and admirals around the country and overseas) but also for specialized missions, like navigator training and as a test bed for new systems. The design, based on a modification of the legendary F-86, was so successful that NAA, despite its preference for military programs, marketed a civilian version of the T-39 designated the NA-265-40, or Model 40. The civilian bird was considered the Cadillac of corporate jets, despite the longer range of our more expensive competitor, the four-engine Lockheed Jetstar, and the cheaper price tag of the Lear Jet, which was a kind of tinker-toy by comparison. All in all, the Sabreliner was a moneymaker for the company in those pre-B-1, pre-Space Shuttle days, so the company looked for ways to keep a good thing going.

One way to do that was to "sell" the same plane twice. Here's how we did it. Most T-39s were built and delivered in the late 1950s and early '60s and had seen a lot of hard use. Though they were tough little birds, designed to strict military specifications, they were beginning to wear out, particularly with all the flying they had done during the Cold War and all the flying they would have to do in Southeast Asia now that a shooting war had started. The main culprit was stress put on the fuselage by thousands of pressurization cycles, and the threat of corrosion from operations in some pretty inhospitable places. The Air Force decided to rehab their inventory of several hundred planes through a factory "re-manufacturing" program at the LAX plant. This was a real boon to the company and a Godsend for me. In 1970, North American *Rockwell* (NAR, as it was now known after its merger with Pittsburgh-based Rockwell Standard Corporation) asked me to put on my flight suit again and take over the job of Chief Production Acceptance Test Pilot for the Sabreliner Division. They didn't have to ask me twice.

✪ ✪ ✪

Bill, seen here receiving his 25-year service pin from NAA executive Jim Edwards, returned to the cockpit as Chief Production Acceptance Test Pilot for Sabreliner, shown between them in Marine Corps colors.

Arriving in 1962, the Boeing C-97G Stratofreighter changed the 197th's mission from air interception to world-wide air transport.

PJW: Our first C-97s arrived in September of 1962 and we officially became the 197th Air Transport Squadron, assigned to MAC, the Military Airlift Command. This was bad news for a lot of pilots, who had flown nothing but fighters for their whole careers. About half our guys dropped out; but I'd been on a many-motor crew before, so flying the big plane—though one more complicated than the B-24—was no particular hardship, or mystery. In fact, the Stratofreigher was one of the most comfortable planes I'd ever flown. It had a roomy cockpit, great visibility through that big greenhouse nose, and pilot's seats that felt like easy chairs. With a nice galley and a couple of airline-style bathrooms, plus a few sleeping berths in the lower compartment, you could eat a full meal and stretch your legs (or stretch out) on a long flight and almost forget it was a military plane. Besides, unlike the giant C-124 Globe Master, its nearest heavy-lift competitor, it was pressurized, allowing us to cruise above a lot of (but certainly not all) bad weather. It wasn't particularly heavy on the controls, and those four big paddles on those four big R-4360s delivered a lot of power when we needed it. The worst thing about the plane (other than its speed—the fastest you could go anywhere was about 240 knots) was the complexity of its systems. It was basically a double-decker version of the Boeing B-50 (an up-sized derivative of the B-29), which was built at the end of the "vacuum tube" era. As a result, it had a Rube Goldberg system of interconnected electrical and mechanical devices that caused some of our pilots to dub it "Mr. Boeing's electric airplane." Still, I looked forward to a world-wide mission, a chance to travel and see new places without having to crate-up our airplanes. We also had quite a few airline pilots with the Guard and would acquire many more when our mission changed. A bigger problem was filling the other aircrew slots. We now needed navigators, flight engineers, and load masters—all of whom had to be trained from scratch or recruited from Air Force personnel leaving active duty.

By early 1963, we had enough qualified people to make up our first long-distance, over-water flight, to Tachikawa Air Base in Japan. By the spring of 1964, we were making monthly flights to both Japan and Germany, as well as a variety of routine missions moving men and material for other Guard units, as well as the active-duty Air Force, around the continental United States, including Alaska and Hawaii. As our military involvement in the Vietnam War deepened, we participated in Operation Guard Lift, which ran from 1966 through 1968, during which we averaged five Southeast Asia support missions each month, mostly into Saigon and Danang, but also to other destinations near the war zone, such as Thailand, the Philippines, and Okinawa, in addition to our other assignments within the MAC system.

Personally, I made four trips into Vietnam during this period: one to Ton Son Hut, South Vietnam's national airport and the biggest American installation of the war; two to Da Nang on the central coast, just south of the DMZ, the demilitarized zone between North and South Vietnam (not that it meant much to either side; a steady stream of communist troops infiltrated to the south from the beginning of the war; and after the Gulf of Tonkin incident, American warplanes bombed northern targets regularly); and one to Cam Ranh Bay, about half way in between.

As support rather than combat missions, these flights were pretty routine. The C-97 was a heavy cargo plane, not an assault transport like the C-7 or C-123 or even the C-130, all key movers inside Vietnam during the war, so our operations were confined to big airports that were always heavily guarded; although "Charlie" (the Viet Cong, or southern communist insurgents) or the North Vietnamese Army (NVA) sometimes shelled these bases from a distance with rockets, artillery, and mortars. Occasionally, our planes would take small arms fire during takeoff or landing, but the enemy never got the hang of "leading the target" (that is, aiming slightly ahead of a moving airplane so their bullets and our plane would meet at the same place) and the worst we ever suffered was a few bullet holes in the tail or lower fuselage, which didn't do much damage.

On the trip into Cam Ranh Bay, we had a problem with one of those big engines that we just couldn't fix, so we had to have a replacement flown in from the states. Of course, the flight crew had to wait to fly the airplane out, and none of us were too thrilled about hanging around for a week or so under the threat of hostile fire while the paper-pushers back home processed our requisition. Fortunately, the new engine arrived in two days and our highly motivated flight engineer and the mechanics we brought with us had it changed in record time. We did experience a mortar attack one night, and it brought back old memories of Bed-Check Charlie and Korea, but the base didn't suffer much damage and since the active-duty Air Force guys didn't seem too worried about it, neither was I.

I thought flying into Ton Son Nut would be a piece of cake, being the country's largest airbase and surrounded by more Union troops than Lincoln had at Gettysburg, but the Army guys we had on board, some of them Vietnam veterans, were pretty nervous about it. Part of our cargo that trip was a load of steel plate, 3 to 4 inches thick and 5 to 6 feet long, used to repair naval vessels. As always, the theater briefer at our staging area (usually Clark Field or Sabu NAS in the Philippines) warned us of possible enemy fire on final approach, so I came in extra steep. The Marines protecting the base did an excellent job suppressing heavy automatic weapons, but some of the enemy definitely cooked off a few rounds at us with AK-47s—again, to no effect. While we were on final approach, though, the loadmaster called me on the intercom and said, "Colonel Wurts, the Army passengers won't fasten their seat belts."

"Why not?" I asked.

"They're sitting on top of the steel plates and won't get down."

I glanced at the copilot and we both laughed. "Well, Sergeant," I replied, "that sounds like a good idea. Why don't you join them?"

The landing was uneventful and we taxiied to wherever it was we were supposed to drop our cargo and, I have to admit, I was more than happy to refuel and get out of there. Like most of our major bases, Ton Son Nut was one busy place, with servicemen and locals everywhere, running around like ants on an anthill; with all kinds of aircraft—USAF, Navy, South Vietnamese, and allied—parked everywhere, some of them showing considerable battle damage. I could only think about my own experiences at Kimpo and Suwon, where we fighter pilots, stuck there for our hundred missions, had to watch the transport pilots (flying for MATS—Military Air Transport Service—in those days) come and go. We imagined them spending their evenings in some well-appointed officer's club and sleeping in nice, comfortable beds in an air-conditioned BOQ. For that matter, Air Force fighter pilots in Korea were jealous of Navy flyers, too, although their reward for a harrowing combat mission was to make an even more harrowing landing on a pitching carrier deck; but at least they had good chow, decent quarters, and familiar, friendly faces around them. I wondered briefly if these poor guys on the Ton Son Nut flight line (enlisted men servicing our aircraft or pilots flying in and out) glanced at my big, old, piston-powered transport and felt the same way about me. I have to admit, it bothered me for a long time, in fact, all the way to the end of the runway.

WRY: The late 60's was another roller coaster ride for me, as it was for much of the country. In 1966, my first grandchild, Lisa, was born to Bill Jr. in Alaska. Tragically, she would die only three years later in a freak accident when a big branch from an oak tree fell on the camper in which she was sleeping. My stepmother, Hilda, passed away about this time, too. Both of these sad events gave me an unwelcome, but probably useful, opportunity to reflect on the decisions I'd made when I was younger, such as not being the world's best stepson or treating Marian the way I did at the end of our marriage. Time may never completely heal old wounds, but a little understanding and perspective sure can ease the pain. By now I'd become good friends with my adult son, Bill Jr., and treasured my occasional visits with him and his family, including his second daughter, Vicki, born in '71 in Alaska.

For about ten years, things were going gangbusters at Sabreliner. I hired two or three new production acceptance test pilots to keep up with T-39 re-manufacturing, and although the original commercial version of the Sabreliner, the Model 40, was out of production, it had been replaced by the longer, sleeker Model 60 and our own "wide body" business jet, the Model 70, which featured a roomer cabin. This last plane was kind of a bastard child conceived by the marketing and engineering departments. Operators loved the 40s and 60s. Who wouldn't? They were cousins to the F-86. But our competitors, chiefly Gulfstream, but also Dassault's Falcon Jet, were making bigger, more fuel-efficient corporate aircraft, and we were under pressure to do the same. The "big body" Sabreliner was originally designed for the Garret ATF-3 turbofan, a very compact, high-thrust, high-tech engine that was having the devil of a time getting certified by the FAA. So as an interim step, we kept the original Pratt & Whitneys (used on the Model 60) on the Model 70. While this bigger airplane gave customers more seats and head room, its performance with the old engines was mediocre. So, around 1970, NAR decided to retrofit the Model 70 with a new turbofan, the General Electric CF-700. This

Bill with Bill Jr. and Ann, the children from his first marriage. All grown up now, they enjoy their Dad's company, and vice versa.

wasn't quite the wonder-engine promised by the ATF-3, but it was FAA certified, reliable, and because it was the same engine used on the popular Fanjet Falcon, customers liked it. Still, the Model 80, as the new plane was called, wasn't exactly the super-plane we'd touted for so long in our brochures. That's probably the point where Sabreliner began its long, slow slide into obsolescence. There were just too many other companies out there willing to put big money into biz-jet development, a product line that our corporate bosses in LA and Pittsburgh, now more concerned about the B-1 and Space Shuttle programs than the Sabreliner, just couldn't get behind. Plus, Rockwell Standard, while a big name in heavy industry, didn't really understand the airplane business. By 1973, North American's assimilation into this new corporate culture was complete and the last vestige of one of America's classic names in aviation officially disappeared. A new company emerged as my new boss, Rockwell International (RI).

Of course, a company is more than a name, and lots of good NAA engineers, production people, and pilots were still employed, though that employer had now been reduced to the Los Angeles Aircraft Division, which absorbed the Sabreliner Division, and the B-1 Division, both co-located at LAX. After FAA certification of the Model 80 (for some reason, marketed as the "Sabre 75A"), we moved on to what would be the last bird in a long line of fine Sabre aircraft, the Sabre 65. The best part of the deal was that, although I had run production acceptance test flying for all Saberliners over the last ten years and had conducted numerous company tests and FAA certification flight tests in the Model 80, I was appointed to Chief Engineering Test Pilot for what would turn out to be the fastest, best performing, and most remarkable Sabreliner of them all, the Sabre 65 which finally had those new, high-tech engines and a revolutionary "supercritical" (meaning "almost supersonic") wing, an innovation that was, and still is, unique among corporate jets.

*T*he '60s and early '70s were busy for Pete as well Bill. In addition to seeing a lot of sky in the C-97, his lodging business was booming. In addition to completing the Sage Inn in Glendale in 1963, he built the Papago Inn in Scottsdale, a beautiful motel and restaurant, finished in 1965, that would expand over the years to become The Papago Inn and Resort—a local landmark to this day. Since both properties (along with several others Pete co-owned or managed) were Best Western affiliates, he got heavily involved with that organization, joining its Board of Directors in 1972. In 1974, he was elected its president and that same year led two initiatives that brought the somewhat stodgy, stagnant organization into the 21ˢᵗ Century by hiring Robert Hazard, a marketing dynamo from American Express, as its Executive Director, modernizing and energizing the headquarters staff and beginning the expansion of Best Western into foreign markets, such as Britain, Europe, Australia, and Mexico, turning it into the world's largest lodging chain while creating a new American icon still recognized around the globe.

During this time, we met and did business with numerous celebrities both in and out of aviation, some of whom became good friends. Hollywood legend John Wayne became one of Pete's investors and, along with several other prominent Arizonans, he spent time at "the Duke's" ranch and on his famous yacht: a converted Navy vessel. He also hired Vincent Price, a veteran character actor, whose soft-spoken good humor belied the villains he often played on screen. "Vince" was Best Western's spokesman for several years and remained friends with Pete until the actor's death. Pete also played host to General Omar Bradley, the "GI's General" who commanded American forces in Europe after D-Day, when the General visited the Valley, making the Papago Inn his temporary "headquarters." We both joined "Helmet and Goggles," a national association of flyers taking its name from America's Golden Age of aviation. At its many events, we got to know such luminaries as Jimmy Stewart, Jeanne Yeager (copilot with Dick Rutan for their record-breaking, non-stop around-the-world flight), and Joe Foss, America's leading WWII ace in the Pacific, who later worked with Bill at the Champlin Air Museum at Falcon Field.

Of course, every bed of roses contains a few thorns. Pete and Maxine divorced in 1975 and he was remarried the next year to Mary Lou Melville—the "soul mate" he had perhaps been seeking all his life. She became a private pilot herself, accompanying Pete on many adventures as they flew a steady succession of bigger and longer-ranging corporate and recreational aircraft, from a four-place, single engine Mooney to a twin engine, six-place Cessna Crusader. They may not have been F-86s, F-104s, or C-97s, but they were a whole lot cheaper to fill with gas.

PJW: Some of our biggest adventures in the C-97 happened on what we referred to as "off route" missions, flights to obscure parts of the U.S., or the world, not

TOP: Pete's flagship property, the Papago Inn and Resort in Scottsdale, Arizona, is still a local landmark.

BOTTOM: Film legend John Wayne was a friend and investor in several of Pete's business ventures.

Veteran character actor Vincent Price was hired by Pete as a spokesman for Best Western during its international expansion. A friend in subsequent years, Price's good humor and gentle manner belied the evil characters he often played on screen.

TOP AND BOTTOM: Pete and Mary Lou, Bill and NAA's Ruth Bantle, join famed actor and Air Force veteran, Jimmy Stewart, at a meeting of "Helmet and Goggles," whose roll-call includes some of aviation's best known names.

normally covered by the MAC system. Some of these flights were for some very strange reasons.

One of these memorable missions came in 1966 as an adjunct to a routine flight to Germany. Rhein-Main was a major hub for military air transportation throughout Europe and the Middle East, as it is today, and our unit stopped there frequently to deliver passengers, equipment, and materials. On one such Rhein-Main mission, we had discharged our cargo and were headed back to the states, stopping to refuel in Zaragosa, Spain. While there, we were notified that a fully armed B-52 had collided with a KC-135 aerial tanker over Palomares to the south, destroying both aircraft. Everyone on the tanker was killed, but a few crew members from the bomber survived. Even worse, four nuclear bombs were lost. Three were recovered in southern Spain after contaminating some of the surrounding fields with plutonium, but the fourth was lost at sea. The bodies of the dead crewmen had been found and were being transported to Zaragosa for return to the United States. Our plane, empty and available, was assigned to carry them home.

The bodies arrived at the base in aluminum coffins, and as I recall, there were almost a dozen of them. Our loadmaster secured them in the cargo compartment and we were just getting ready to go when we received word that *another* Air Force transport, a C-47, had hit a mountain in Greece, and that more human remains in similar coffins were on the way. There had been even greater loss of life in that accident, so by the time the coffins were loaded—stacked end-to-end, three deep, in the cargo bay—the plane looked more like a mortuary than a transport. This so unnerved the cabin crew, who usually spent our long transatlantic flights sleeping atop the cargo, that they all crowded onto the flight deck on one pretext or another. Nobody wanted to ride in back with our sad, unfortunate "passengers."

Our loadmaster on this mission, a Sergeant Inez, was a conscientious crewman, although he had the bad habit of starting his safety briefing for passengers (you know, the one where the flight attendant says, "in case of emergency...") with the phrase, "Now, *when* we crash..." as if an accident was inevitable. (We chided him about this all the time, but he'd never change his patter.) Today, Inez came up to the flight deck with a worried look on his face.

"What's the matter?" I asked sympathetically. "Has our cargo got you down?"

"Kind of," he answered. "I was just wondering, Colonel, according to Air Force regulations, we can't jettison human remains. What happens if we have engine trouble and I have to lighten the airplane?"

I thought for a minute—or at least pretended to think for a minute—then answered, "Well, Sergeant, I'll tell you. If we run into that kind of trouble, I'll personally come back into the cargo compartment, hold a brief service for these poor people, then you can give them a burial at sea."

That seemed to satisfy him; and fortunately, we never had to make that choice. Not all over-water crossings were so uneventful.

It seems like half our MAC missions were at night, and droning hour after hour over the ocean in the dark after a long, hard day, particularly homeward bound after a two-week deployment, people could get pretty sleepy on the flight deck, what with the subdued red cockpit lighting, infrequent radio transmissions, and maybe a full stomach from one of MAC's incomparable in-flight dinners.

On one of these marathon nighttime flights, we had a different loadmaster, a Sergeant Ballinger, who was a real gourmet with the airborne galley. Usually, MAC gave you a choice between a box lunch (usually a sandwich and apple and chips and a cookie—things like that) or a hot meal, which was basically an airline-style TV-dinner the loadmaster heated in the oven. But Ballinger always spiced things up with a few original ingredients, so it wasn't unusual to have the typical *eau d'C-97* (a mixture of avgas, oil, hot electronics, and B.O.) mixed with the aroma of fresh garlic, tomato sauce, or something else a little more appetizing.

It was about midnight, a few hours after one of these delightful meals, that we were halfway across the Atlantic. The weather was clear and the untroubled sea reflected a full moon and starry sky. My copilot was asleep at his station (not unusual and not a problem—provided everything's going fine he tells you first that he's zonking out) and I was watching the store from the left seat. Among their other amenities, such as cup holders and a jump seat for observers, the pilots' stations had a nice foot rail built onto the bottom of the instrument panel so a weary aviator could rest his flight-boots, which is just what I was doing. I wasn't exactly dozing, but with the sound of the droning engines and the flight engineer only occasionally flipping a switch, it was a pretty relaxing environment. Suddenly, Ballinger burst onto the flight deck.

"Colonel Wurts! Fire! Fire! We're on fire!"

Needless to say, this abruptly changed the mood in the cockpit. The copilot was instantly awake and ran his seat forward to take the controls. The flight engineer was scanning his huge instrument panel, checking circuit breakers and hitting "press to test" buttons to make sure some critical warning light hadn't burned out. I was out of my seat and following Ballinger into the cargo compartment, half-expecting to see a wisp of smoke coming from the oven where he'd done his cooking, perhaps burning, a bit of spilled lasagna.

Nope. As soon as I left the cockpit, I was enveloped by a stream of ominous black smoke pouring from the edges of the hatch that separated the main deck from the lower cargo compartment. It was a relatively small space that housed a few crew bunks, some electronic gear, and other odds and ends, including most of our luggage, that didn't fit anywhere else. There was clearly something going on down there, and that something wasn't good.

Immediately, I tried to clear the cobwebs from my brain and began silently rehearsing what I was all-too-afraid would happen next *if* we were lucky: have the navigator take an immediate fix and begin continuous position reports on the HF radio; make a distress call on VHF and UHF channels to any aircraft or surface ships that might be in the area; review ditching procedures and assess wave height, sea swells, and wind conditions on the surface; try and remember how the heck you inflate those big 20-man rafts and climb into them wearing a life jacket and boots; how long a C-97 would float once it hit the water, assuming it stayed in one piece; how long a quart of water per man per day would actually last, and what Ballinger could do to make a week's worth of survival rations more palatable. The list was endless.

"Open it up," I told Ballinger, and he lifted the hatch.

Immediately, more dark smoke billowed up—thick, ugly, sickening. Two crewmen were already beside us with hand-held fire extinguishers. The one with his rubber mask already on went down the ladder, blasting white foam as he went.

Miraculously, the smoke in the cabin began to clear. A few seconds later, the assistant loadmaster stuck his head back up, and pushed the mask back on his hair.

"No sweat, Colonel," he said. "The compressor on our AC froze up, but the shaft kept turning, so the belts got hot and started smoking. Nothing to it, though we won't have any air conditioning for the rest of the trip."

That was great news, though there'd be a little explaining to do to the Guard Bureau, and maybe the Air Force. You see, our "air conditioner", a Godsend for ground or low-altitude operations during summer in Arizona, was strictly a "unit modification"; that is, a piece of gear authorized by the local commander but installed only in his unit's aircraft. There was nothing about an air conditioner in the flight manual, the maintenance manual, or any other paperwork associated with the C-97G, even at Boeing, assuming they still had drawings and specifications on the old bird available in the basement of their Everett, Washington plant. Our "autopilot" was the same thing, a unit modification that held wings-level at a constant altitude, although we pilots had to manually input every heading change and turn it off to climb or descend. This was a nuisance, but it sure beat flying by hand all the way across the country, or the ocean. Still, if one of these home-grown "improvements" malfunctioned, we couldn't fix it until we returned to the home 'drome.

So that was the end of our cabin fire emergency and, I'm happy to say, the ditching drill that was bound to follow. Needless to say, my copilot and I had no problem staying awake for the rest of the flight.

Although the C-97 couldn't make dirt-field assault landings, we could deliver a lot of cargo in a lot of different ways through those big, aft-facing clamshell doors.

During one regional emergency, we dumped bales of hay from the aircraft at low altitude for starving cattle isolated in the pastures of Northern Arizona, New Mexico, and Utah after a severe blizzard. Every crew member participating in "Operation Hay Lift" received a nice certificate and, as far as I know, no cows were injured in the making of this miracle; none were bonked on the head or otherwise hurt by the wire-bound bales, which tended to break up anyway as soon as they hit the airstream.

A mercy mission of another sort occurred after the massive 1967 earthquake in Alaska. We were initially tasked to airlift food and water and other emergency supplies to the survivors, since most of the infrastructure on the ground—roads, railways, and bridges—had been knocked out. One of my last Alaska support missions, as I recall, was also one of my highest gross-weight takeoffs in the C-97, partly because of the fuel required (it's a long way from Phoenix to Anchorage, further, even than from San Francisco to Hawaii) but also because of our cargo, which included aluminum pipes for temporary water lines, and palate after palate of...toilet paper. (It must not have been fluffy and extra absorbent, but the thick, tightly wound industrial kind you find in crummy gas stations.) But it was nice to be helping people who really needed it, and I got a special kick out of thinking that one of those hearty souls we were assisting was Bill's son, Bill Jr., and his family who had made that rough country their home.

We had other missions that ranged from the scary to the sublime to the ridiculous. On one mission, we were dispatched again to Alaska to pick up some U.S. Geological Survey support equipment and transport it to Bogota, Columbia, of all places, stopping at Panama to refuel. What we hadn't really thought about, though, was our destination's altitude and the political attitude of our hosts. With a field elevation of 12,000 feet, our landing was basically a matter of dropping the landing gear and flaps at cruising altitude then pulling back on power. We had to RON (remain overnight), of course, so most of us wanted to do a little sight seeing. As it was in Libya, the local authorities advised us not to leave the base, and if we did, to be sure we wore civilian clothes. And if anybody asked us, we should probably say we were from Canada or Ireland as well, Americans didn't have a lot of friends, internationally, during the Vietnam era. Most of us went to town anyway, wearing the rumpled civies we usually carried on our trips. I had the wisdom, this time, not to shop for souvenirs, though a few of those llama skins were mighty tempting. When it came time to leave, we had to use the turbo-superchargers on our engines, normally employed only for high altitude cruise, to take off, the first and only time I remember having to do that, with any airplane.

A more pleasant task—and one that came to absolutely nothing—was our assignment to take a plane to Pago Pago, capital of the Society Islands, as a standby rescue bird for the Gemini astronauts, then currently in orbit. They weren't scheduled to land anywhere near us, but when you're hurtling down from space at 25,000 mph, even a small discrepancy in re-entry angle can put you thousands of miles off target, so America, with its global aerial reach, had to be ready for anything. Well, we were ready in Pago Pago and would've been happy to drop some para-divers and a raft to fish our astronauts out of the drink, but that never proved necessary. We enjoyed a few days in the tropical sun, then were told to pack our swimming trunks and go home.

A much more bizarre, and ultimately comical, mission (though one that left us scratching our heads as citizen-taxpayers) was the "great statue caper." With Jack Brasher as my copilot (yes, the same man who had watched my back as I bargained with that Arab street vendor), I was dispatched on a kind-of Mission Impossible to Springfield, Ohio where, I was told, I would receive further instructions. It seems a foundry that specialized in ornamental artwork had, among their commissions, been hired to create a commemorative statue of Harvey Firestone, founder of Firestone Tire & Rubber Company and, naturally, a big cheese in that part of the world. However, the same company had also been commissioned to make a statue of General George S. Patton for Belgium, who considered him a national hero for liberating them in WWII. Somehow, the two statues had been switched and the bigwigs in Brussels raised the ceremonial curtain on some geek in glasses with a slide-rule in his pocket, while the likeness of Old Blood and Guts, with his ivory-handled revolvers, had been shipped to Springfield where they were pining away, apparently, for their founding father. Our job, should we choose to accept it (well, we had to accept it) was to switch the statues before too many more people noticed the difference.

So we went to Springfield, picked up George, then flew to Brussels, where Harvey was waiting for us in his crate. I suppose the stencil read, "Return to Sender" but I can't read French so it could've said "Yankee Go Home." It was a civilian airport, not an Air Force base or a NATO installation, so although it was a RON assignment, we were on our own for a place to stay. Because I was the Aircraft Commander, or maybe because everyone knew I was in the lodging business, the crew looked to me to get them bed and board. So I led everyone to a tourist kiosk and talked to an English-speaking clerk, who referred us to a *pensione*, one of those low-cost, dormitory-type hotels catering to college students and budget travelers. It was a comfortable enough place, and when we emerged the next morning, we were pleased to see that breakfast was included in what was already a pretty low price. We went into the small dining room and, like good Americans, took the liberty of sliding a few tables and chairs together and talking louder than French-speaking people are used to hearing before noon. Somebody said that Belgium was famous for its pastries, so we gobbled down a basket of fresh rolls as soon as it was presented and, sure enough, they were delicious. As AC, I was concerned for my crew, so I held up the empty basked to the waiter and indicated as best I could that we needed a refill. He gave me a dirty look, but brought a new supply, but only half as many as before. Halfway through the rest of the "continental breakfast" Jack or somebody else asked again for more rolls and the waiter just ignored us. But it was time to go so we went upstairs and gathered our things then checked out at the front desk. The clerk spoke some English so I explained we'd had some problems with the service in their little restaurant; they just stopped bringing us rolls, no matter how many times we asked and, being in the hospitality business myself, I was sure the owner or manager or whoever ran the place would want to have an immediate talk with the staff.

"Oh, *Monsieur*," the clerk replied. "Your room rate is based on one roll per person. It is a very strict rule. We must ensure there is enough food for every guest!"

Can you say, *Ugly American?*

Well, even the Aircraft Commander can't know everything. I offered to pay the difference but the clerk was very kind and sweet and understanding and said that our immediate departure from their beautiful French-speaking country would be thanks enough, which was fine with us. After all, I don't think Harvey Firestone much liked the place either.

WRY: Appropriately enough, my most challenging and enjoyable flight test assignment came as the climax of my tenure at Sabreliner. In fact, it came near the end of Sabreliner history.

State-of-the-art business jets were popping up all over in the late '70s, and

Rockwell just didn't want to sink more corporate money into further upgrades to a basic airframe that was over 25 years old. In a way, the quality of that design was the Sabreliner's undoing. The T-39 had been designed to military specifications, which meant the civilian versions, beginning with the Model 40, were over-designed for the commercial market. To make matters worse, the T-39—and all subsequent Sabreliners—were built with a "safe life" structure instead of a "fail safe" structure, which was the way big airliners and other modern passenger jets, including our competitors' biz jets, had been built since the Boeing 707. Now, "fail safe" sounds like a good thing—and it is—but it's not really an improvement over the "safe life" philosophy. Safe Life means that the structure is built so solidly that it will survive years of abuse in the aircraft's expected operational environment, take a licking but keep on ticking. Fail Safe, on the other hand, is an attempt to save money on materials and get a lighter airplane (which translates to fuel savings) by making the structure a tad lighter than it should be, then building predictable "failure paths" into the structure so that they can be spotted and repaired during periodic inspections. All this assumes, of course, that the engineers know enough about the plane's future flight regimes to design those failure paths correctly, and that technicians spot them in time, and that the materials don't have flaws, and that any corrections or repairs are done properly, and that those repairs are done on time. That's a lot of "ifs," Personally, I'll take the Air Force's old "safe life" philosophy any day. The Sabreliner, after all, was the only business jet with a built-in belly skid, just like the F-86; you could make a gear-up landing, slide to a stop, then have a crane lift the airplane, lower the gear, and then taxi the plane away under its own power. Just try that in a Lear Jet or a Falcon!

Anyway, the Sabreliner's last hurrah took the form of the Sabre 65, a marvelous little airplane that took the popular Model 60 airframe, mated it to a new turbofan, the Garrett 731 (similar to the ATF-3 and an improvement over the CF-700 used on the Model 80) and installed a wing with a revolutionary new shape, called a "supercritical" airfoil. This new wing design allowed the plane to fly faster by delaying the formation of the transonic shock wave that increased aerodynamic drag dramatically—one component of the famous "sound barrier" that my friend Chuck Yeager had broken more than thirty years before. The new wing also allowed

First flight of the last of her kind: the Sabre 65 begins flight tests with Bill and copilot Evan Myers up front, flight test engineer, Don Byrnes, at the panel in back.

customers to use less fuel at a given cruising speed, increasing range and lowering overall operating costs. Although the concept of the supercitical wing was developed by NASA, its application to the Sabreliner was engineered by the Raisbeck company in Washington state over a period of several years. Although Raisbeck provided the wing modifications for the prototypes, production itself would be performed by Rockwell. Any way you looked at it, it was a good deal on a great airplane for a lot of customers, and would keep our factory doors open for at least a few more years. Our job in flight test was to make sure the new airplane did everything we promised.

Most people think flight test is the glamorous, dangerous business of "pushing back the envelope"; but as you've seen, there's a lot more to it than that. Experimental Flight Test,the kind of work done with the Bell X-1 and North American X-15 and dozens of other "X planes" the public seldom if ever hears about, is only one part of a long chain of flight testing that brings new technologies to aircraft and new aircraft to the public. Once an experimental concept has been demonstrated, it moves on to Engineering Flight Test (EFT), where all the data needed to employ the concept on a new or existing aircraft is generated and verified, usually at company expense. Some of this work is certainly exciting, if not glamorous, but much is tedious and repetitive, and all of it must be precise and well-documented. When the company is satisfied the concept works for a given design, a certifying agency is brought in to verify the findings. For military aircraft, that agency is the Air Force or the Navy—whatever branch of the service will be using the bird. For commercial aircraft, that agency is the FAA. After the agency certifies the plane is safe and does what it's supposed to do, it goes into production and a third type of test pilot is needed, production acceptance test pilots who make sure that each individual plane has been built to, and will operate in accordance with, its specifications.

At this point, though, we were just trying to get the Sabre 65 off the ground— literally. Like all EFT programs, this one would have its teething problems.

The first trouble we encountered was with the plane's stalling characteristics. Because the supercritical wing requires an unusual leading edge, the Model 65 could not have the leading edge slats that had been an integral part of the Sabre wing since the first F-86. These slats were simply sections of the leading edge that drooped down at high angles of attack, keeping air flowing smoothly over the wing during high-G maneuvers and at very low speeds. Also with a swept wing aircraft, airflow tends to run down along the span as well as horizontally across the wing, reducing lift and causing control problems—not a good thing.

So, to make a long story short, we fixed those handling problems by attaching a "stall fence" on the upper surface of the wing. This is a tried-and-true technique that you see on many high-performance, swept-wing aircraft. The fence acts like a little barrier to span-wise flow, re-directing air over the flaps and ailerons, where it belongs. Engineers hate to see these, since it is an admission that there was something wrong with the initial design, but flying is a practical profession. If the bird needs a stall fence to fly right, that's what it gets.

The next problem we ran into was a little tougher to solve. Exhaust gas temperature, or EGT, is an important measure of jet engine performance, and the new Garret engine had a tendency to run hot in certain regimes of flight. Actually, the temperature would spike dangerously high, requiring us to shut the engine down in flight on several occasions before it became damaged and failed. The solution, again, turned out to be an old one. Splitters were installed in the inlet at the front of each nacelle, ensuring a smooth flow of air at all angles of attack and power settings. We'd had similar problems with other engines on other Sabreliners, so the trouble wasn't entirely unexpected. However, like the stall fence, engineers hate to do anything that makes a design more complicated or expensive to build, but without these necessary fixes, our beautiful little bird would never pass FAA certification and would've become a very large and expensive lawn ornament.

The rest of company and FAA certification testing went off without a hitch. The Sabre 65 scored stellar numbers in all the right areas. Specific fuel consumption, or SFC, which is the main criteria a lot of customers used in those days—and still do—when selecting a jet transport, was just as advertised. And of course, many of our loyal customers liked the idea of flying one more generation of a plane they had grown to love, one with a lot of advanced features but which still had parts commonality with older airplanes in the fleet.

In a way, that's how I felt about things, too. By 1980, I'd spent 27 years with the company and was nearing the mandatory retirement age for test pilots. I didn't want to wind up another old "spare part" logging time behind a desk; so, although the company offered to keep me on after its move to St. Louis and Perryville, Missouri (LA had gotten too expensive for airplane production), I put in for retirement. The company gave me a great going away party—literally. Not only was I leaving the firm, but I intended to take my beloved sailboat, the *Silver Wind*, on an extended cruise, hoping to see if the world could be as exciting at 5 or 10 knots as it was at 500. Their going-away gift was a beautiful nautical sextant which I promised to put to good use.

W*ithin eight years of each other, we'd both retired from our "official" flying careers—Pete from the Air Force in 1972, stepping down as a full ("bird") Colonel; Bill from Rockwell as Sabreliner's last Chief Engineering Test Pilot. From then on, our flying would be for fun or for business—preferably both—and sometimes together. By that time, too, our families had grown up and some got into the act, becoming pilots themselves.*

PJW: Knowing I was nearing retirement from the Guard, I indulged myself in a pleasure I had gone for too long without, a plane of my own. Still, it was a shock to realize that I, rather than Uncle Sam, would have to pick up the tab for fuel and maintenance. Who'd have thought flying would become so expensive since I last owned that Ryan, or all those J-3s?

My first investment in life-after-the-military was in a Globe "Swift," a cute little single-engine tail-dragger with two seats designed in the 1940s with the rakish lines of, well, a plane designed in the 1940s. Although it had a small, four-cylinder engine that would become typical of virtually all light planes in the future, it was considered a handful by some private pilots, with a fairly high sink rate on final approach, low aspect-ratio wing (which made it quite maneuverable and light on the controls, but not much of a glider) complete with fixed slots in front of the ailerons to assure control well into a stall, and a short-coupled fuselage that sometimes made it hard to "keep the tailwheel behind you" when taking off and landing. In short, it looked like a little P-40 and flew like a little P-51, which made

Bill at the helm of his beloved sailboat, *Silver Wind:* a "retirement" that never quite happened.

it fun in the local area but pretty impractical for cross-country trips.

Within a couple of years I replaced the Swift with a single-engine, four-place, tricycle-gear Mooney, another classic of the post-war private aviation era, called the "Volkswagen of the sky." With space for three passengers and the pilot, plus a little luggage, Mary Lou and I had a chance to do some traveling without the hassles of scheduled airlines, and included trips to destinations off the beaten path.

One flight took us to Dolphin Island in the Gulf of Mexico. We arrived at its barren strip an hour or so before a storm front, so the winds were strong and gusty and about 90-degrees to the runway. I made a low approach and saw that landing was hopeless, so we diverted to a unicom-controlled field at Point Clear, Alabama, located at the end of a wooded peninsula. I radioed ahead and asked about accommodations, since we obviously had to land pretty quickly and wait out the storm. The FBO running the unicom replied that a place called the Grand Hotel was not too far away, and he would call ahead and have them send a car. We said, "Great!" and landed, just happy to have our wheels on the ground and a roof over our heads. To tell you the truth, we expected the worst, a cheap hotel in a small southern town. Between the bedbugs and the flashing neon light, we expected to be up all night.

We were pleasantly surprised, therefore, when a freshly washed limousine pulled up and whisked us to a perfectly preserved, and perfectly monumental, ante-bellum mansion. On the way, the chauffeur told us that the plantation had been used as a hospital during the Civil War but had been renovated and was now a prestigious resort, often used by corporations for special functions and retreats. Sure enough, the place was elegant beyond description and most accommodating, considering we didn't have a reservation and the house was full.

"Tell you what I can do," the desk clerk replied when we told him our predicament. "I can give you a double roll-away in the housekeeping room. There's a public restroom across the hall, and it's always open. Of course, you're welcome to use our dining room. It's right down the hall. If you don't have a tie for your jacket, I'll be happy to provide one."

Well, we "checked in" if that's the right word for it, and although Mary Lou can duck into a broom closet with her handbag and come out looking like a million bucks, I felt a little shabby in my borrowed tie and wrinkled sports coat. But they let us in the Grand Ballroom and gave us two enormous menus as we sat beneath a great chandelier. Their specialty was chicken, so I asked our waitress how the *specialite d'maison* was tonight, and she replied, "Honey, I ain't ripped off none o'that yet, but I'll lets y'all know." Suddenly, we felt right at home.

A year later we returned with another couple, Bob and Kay Cowie (Bob, a P-38 pilot during WWII, had been shot down over Italy and spent a brief time as a POW) but a hurricane had just passed and the Point Clear airport was closed. We made one low pass just to look at all the upended airplanes, and finished our vacation elsewhere.

With all this puttering around, we decided a light twin would suit us better, get us to places faster and more comfortably, so I reluctantly sold the old Mooney and invested in a Beech Baron, E-55. Mary Lou was getting interested in flying now, so she took lessons and got her private pilot's license. We added a Cessna 150 to the fleet, so we'd have a less expensive way to commute the short distance between Scottsdale, where most of our business interests were, and our other properties in Arizona, which now included a vacation house in Sedona.

After seven years with this combo, we decided to upgrade so I sold the '150, which Mary Lou had affectionately named "Woodstock," complete with a little drawing of Snoopy's favorite bird on the tail (hope "Sparky" Shultz didn't mind!) along with the Baron and put the proceeds into a Cessna Crusader 303, a fast, modern twin with a high, cruciform tail that, although still a six-seater like the Baron, had a lot more headroom and space for more luggage and gas. Our business and pleasure trips now included more destinations that were out of reach before, and our passengers accompanied us in a little higher style. Mary Lou also upgraded to a Cessna 172, the four-place big brother to the two-seat '150, which had gotten a little cramped for our weekly or bi-weekly business jaunts around the state.

One of our early trips in the Crusader was to La Paz, Mexico, with friends from Sedona—a local policeman, Jim Nemeth, and his wife who, like us, were avid scuba divers. We entered Mexico with an IFR flight plan, partly because of the weather and partly to keep things simple when crossing a national border,

Pete and Mary Lou flew friends to exotic locations in their Cessna Crusader, a stylish, turbo-charged twin.

especially one so popular with aerial drug smugglers. Nearing our destination, I cancelled the IFR flight plan and continued into the unicom-controlled field under VFR. We had just parked in the transient area and shut down the engines when the van we'd arranged to take us to the hotel (only a few hundred yards away, but we had a lot of gear) pulled up. The driver and bellman got out and glanced nervously into the low hills surrounding the airport. There, on their way down to us, were a half-dozen well-armed men in uniform. They arrived as we transferred our bags to the vehicle.

"Friends of yours?" I asked our driver.

"*Federales*." He didn't smile back.

A rather lengthy conversation ensued, in Spanish, which I understood, having learned a good bit of it when my oldest daughter, Barbara, was married to a Spanish citizen and lived in Madrid. When it was clear the officials weren't buying our driver's story, I jumped into the conversation. Maybe it helped that Jim was a peace officer, with an Arizona policeman's ID; and having been one myself, I had my BFOP and Interpol cards, as well as my Air Force retirement credential. All in all, we looked not only innocent and harmless, but people who ought not to be bothered, so they nodded and let us go without the customary request for some special "landing fee" or "parking permit" or "admission to see the ocean" which other American tourists often had to pay to local officials. Our main memory of the event was not the potential shakedown, or even that Mexico's federal officials actually seemed serious about catching drug offenders; it was the absolute terror in the eyes of our driver and bellman. We had the feeling they had seen these officers before, probably under different circumstances, and had no desire to see them again.

But that wasn't the end of our adventure. After a couple of days of diving, a hurricane forecast to pass harmlessly out to sea veered suddenly straight at La Paz. We didn't have time to fly out, so we lashed down the airplane and rode out the storm in the hotel. By the time it got to us, the winds were 70 to 80 mph, so while there was a lot of rain and damaged palm trees, the plane and the hotel came through in good condition, which was more than we could say for the airport. As we prepared to leave, we discovered the plane's battery was dead and, of course, there was no local facility to charge it and getting a replacement would take a week. Fortunately, Jim knew an old policeman's trick, and touched the battery terminals for a fraction of a second with a borrowed arc welder. I wouldn't have thought it possible, but not only did the battery charge immediately from the spark, it held that charge for several years—as long, in fact, as I owned the airplane.

Loaded, strapped in, and ready to go, we taxied to the end of the runway, only to be told by the unicom operator that the laborers hired to drain the saddleback in the middle of the sloping runway weren't quite finished, and we'd only have a narrow strip of dry ground about 20 feet wide in the middle of the field to use for our takeoff—with a deep trench on either side.

"Do you still want to give it a try, señor?"

Well, I sure didn't want to wait another couple of days for the "work" crew to finish its work, so I said, "Sure, no sweat," and made the takeoff flawlessly, although my passengers said later that, had the aircraft commander put the issue to a vote, a couple of people in our party might have opted for another margarita and an air conditioned hotel room instead.

I said some members of my family took up flying, and that's true. My oldest daughter, Barbara, got her private and commercial license in the 1970s, and flew all over the American west with husband number two, a real estate developer and rancher named Bill Long, who was an enthusiastic flyer himself. Sadly, Barbara was destined to pass on before her time in 1994 after a sudden illness. We light a candle for her on the mantle during family holidays, but her memory will always remain brighter to her Dad than any flame.

My son, Jay, joined the Phoenix Air Guard in 1966 and served as an airman until he was commissioned a second lieutenant (with two years of college and a private pilot's license, just like his Dad) in 1968 and sent to USAF pilot training in 1969. His training base was at Enid, Oklahoma, where Bill served briefly after WWII. Maxine and I attended his graduation, where he got a little surprise. While the other new pilots received their standard, USAF-issued wings, I secretly gave his CO the wings I'd received in 1942 and asked that they be presented to Jay during the ceremony. Jay was surprised and pleased when he found out about the switch, and it was obviously a satisfying moment for us both, although the Air Force later gave him the set the taxpayers had paid for. He then returned to Phoenix where he flew C-97s with the Guard, including a couple of trips as my copilot, setting an unusual unit record; we were the first father-son team to fly together in Arizona Air Guard history.

Of course, two such clever and resourceful "bus drivers" in one plane were destined to break other MAC records as well. Returning from Vietnam-era deployments in Europe, our unit's aircraft almost always refueled at Lajes, in the Azores, before continuing across the pond to a U.S. port of entry, usually McGuire AFB near Washington DC. On one particular trip, however, Jay and I were flying the second C-97 in a two-ship "formation" (actually, our takeoff times were just close together; both planes were from our unit and we were headed in the same direction). We left Torrejon in Spain, and arrived at Lajes just after a blustery frontal passage, with high winds blowing at the edge of our airplane's cross-wind limits. The C-97 ahead of us, flown by the Group commander, didn't even try a landing and instead diverted to Santa Maria, an island about 45 minutes away. We, however, thought we'd give it a try. After all, with two Wurts's in the cockpit—me in the left seat and Jay in the right—how could things go wrong? Well, one of our relief pilots (a C-97 Instructor Pilot and also the 197th's Flying Safety officer), Lt. Col. Dave Manning, a nice guy and very laid back, was sitting in the jumpseat and asked somewhat nervously if I would feel better if he took over the copilot's position just for this particular landing, which might be a hairy one. I replied, no, we had things under control. Jay's a qualified pilot and this is how you get experience; we all need our turn in the barrel.

Well, it took us a couple of tries, but we made it. As we taxied to the ramp, we watched a Navy P-3 Orion, a four-engine turboprop sub hunter, land behind us. He made a low- or no-flap approach, wing low, and just about scrapped off the left wing tip on touchdown. Immediately after that, the tower closed the runway; the winds were just too high.

Of course, we laughed our heads off that night at dinner, and planned to razz the flight crew of the other C-97 for taking the easy way out. (What postal workers we would've made: the mail must always get through!) But, as it turned out, the other crew had the last laugh. The high winds around Lajes lasted another two days, keeping us stranded, while the other plane departed Santa Maria and got home on schedule. Of course, Lajes is a pretty place, but three days is a long time to live off Mateus Rose and *carracouche*, the Portuguese word for *escargot*, which seemed a staple of islander diet.

"Let this be a lesson to you," I told Jay sternly as we finally boarded the plane.

"A lesson about what?" he reasonably asked.

"Well, I don't know. You're the college student. Think of something."

He did, and we agreed on it. Some adventures you just can't plan, and wouldn't if you could; but you're still glad they happened.

He graduated from my old college, now called Arizona State University, with a degree in aeronautics and got a job as a flight test engineer. It was 1972, at the height of an aerospace recession, so he was lucky to find work in his field, let alone with a premium airframe company: North American Rockwell. Then again, he got a good introduction from one of their most respected, senior pilots, Bill Yoakley.

WRY: I was tickled pink when Jay told me he wanted to work at North American. The B-1A was a year or so away from flight test, and Sabreliner Division was about to begin company flight tests on the Model 80 (our big-fuselage Model 70 re-fitted with GE's CF-700 turbofans), so for once there was plenty of work to go around. Jay went with Sabreliner and was one of two flight test engineers who flew regularly on that program right up through FAA Type Certification a couple of years later. During that time, I checked him out as a Sabreliner copilot, so he flew a few of those flights from the right seat, which had a much better view than his engineer's panel. He also helped us out from time to time as copilot on our production acceptance flight tests and ferrying "green" (just manufactured) airplanes to Perryville, Missouri, where the new aircraft were painted and had their custom interiors installed. I flew quite a few flight tests with Jay and, between our adventures in the air (including one electrical fire in flight, we landed ASAP and went out through the over-wing hatches) and "hangar flying" in the bar at the AVI (the Antelope Valley Inn in Lancaster, the official residence for company crews when we tested at Mojave, near Edwards AFB), it was the next best thing to having Pete around.

When the Model 80 was certified, Jay got promoted to Project Engineer and traded in his flight suit for a neck tie, so we didn't see too much of him on the flight line. It was about that time my son, Don, came to work for Rockwell's Los Angeles Aircraft Division as a draftsman. He had the flying bug, too, and Old Dad gave him some lessons, resulting in a private and then a commercial pilot's license. In 1979, he turned in his T-square for a control wheel and began flying copilot on our production acceptance flight tests, upgrading in no time to first pilot and getting his ATR (Air Transport Rating) in the Sabreliner. By this time, the Division had transferred most of its operations to St. Louis, so Don moved there to fly the corporation's Aero Commander, then to Perryville to fly the Sabreliner. By this time, too, he was obviously hooked on aviation as a way of life and got snapped up by Kerr-McGee, old Sabreliner customers who knew a good corporate pilot when they saw one. After a few years, Don was wooed away by CSX, where he is now their Chief Pilot, flying the Hawker XP and later, the Grumman Gulfstream II, the "Rolls Royce" of business jets with true intercontinental range. The hours for a corporate pilot can be long and squiring company executives, their wives, and the occasional celebrity means you sometimes have to be a diplomat as well as an ace, but he goes to work with a smile and in the long run, that's all that counts.

O*ur story might have ended here, with our sons taking over our seats in the cockpit, but nature has a way of keeping a good story going. Two of our grandsons got involved with aviation, in ways that made both us and their dads pretty proud. Jay's son, Mick, got his private pilot's license when he was in high school and wound up going to M.I.T. where he got a degree in Aeronautics and Astronautics—yep, he's a genuine rocket scientist. Don's son, Billy, earned an appointment to the U.S. Air Force Academy, graduated, and was commissioned a second lieutenant in 2004, and was accepted for pilot training. He won his wings in 2006 and, while hoping for a fighter, was assigned to teach other aspiring Americans to fly and fight as an Instructor Pilot at Randolph AFB in Texas. They say what goes around, comes around, and sometimes, that cycle turns out pretty darned good.*

7

OUR AMERICA:
THEN AND NOW

*O*ld soldiers may fade away, but old pilots have a way of sticking around and sticking together.

  With their kids grown and Bill's retirement from Rockwell, he and Dottie went their separate ways. She got the Silver Wind, so the resources aimed at a leisurely life at sea went mostly to the lawyers. In the mid-80s, Bill moved to Florida to help a friend who was having trouble with a pest control business, but when that was squared away, he got restless for new horizons, preferably those best seen from the air. That's when he got a phone call from Pete.

WRY: Apparently, I've always made a better dad than a husband—at least according to my ex-wives' lawyers—so when Dottie and I split after 30 years of marriage, I figured I'd best confine my future amorous interests to the sea and sky and enjoy, as often as they'd let me, the fine families my kids were raising. But you've got to stay busy, and what you do should mean something to yourself and the community, and killing bugs, for me, wasn't the long-term answer. I was therefore pretty thrilled, one day in 1989, when Pete called and said he was having trouble finding a General Manager for the Papago Inn—his flagship property in Scottsdale. Could I stop spraying termites for awhile and come to Arizona and run the store for him? I took about a second-and-a-half to mull it over, then said, "Yep!" and jumped in my almost-new Lincoln Continental and headed west.

  In a way, working with Pete at the Papago was the realization of the dream we'd conceived in the late '50s, when we first talked about building the Sage. That motel had come and gone, but I always admired Pete's ingenuity and persistence in getting business ventures off the ground (making that "quick buck" no matter how long it took!) and I was happy to be part of this one. Maybe fate had a hand in this adventure, too, since my years in Customer Relations and marketing at North American had better prepared me for the unique (and sometimes exasperating) demands of the hospitality industry, challenges that, in retrospect, I might not have been up to just out of a jet cockpit. For part of the time at the Papago, too, Pete's daughter, Theresa, who was learning the business and shared her Dad's love of fast machines—especially motorcycles—worked at the Papago with us, so it felt like a real family business.

Best of all, Pete now had his own "air force"—not quite another Skytel, but close enough—with the big twin Crusader and handy little Cessna 172, which we flew often, together and separately, between his properties and to various lodging industry events around the west. Later, Pete got a surplus T-34 Mentor; for years, it was the Navy's basic trainer, a single-engine, two-seater with a greenhouse canopy and retractable tricycle landing gear that was a real hoot to fly. Painted in camouflage Air Force markings, it resembled a little T-6 and was pretty useless for anything except aerobatics over the red rocks of Sedona and formation work with his other planes. Compared to some of the birds we'd flown, flying these little guys was like playing miniature golf after a grueling PGA tournament, but a plane is a plane and if you're not flying one, you're not a pilot—you're an *ex*-pilot—and neither of us were quite ready for that.

However, time marches on and, like it or not, nature makes you keep in step. The business was running smoothly so I retired from the Papago in 1996 and moved to Mesa. To keep busy and put to good use some of the lore I'd picked up over a lifetime in aviation, I volunteered for the Champlin Air Museum at Falcon Field, a few miles away. The place—the whole Valley of the Sun—had changed enormously since we flew there during WWII, so it was kind of reassuring to see these old war birds, many of which I'd flown myself, including the F-86, the P-51, the B-25, and more, parked on the ramp or in our hangar. After a year or so, I became Docent President and set about re-building their program. I cooked up some tangible rewards for our hard-working volunteers, knowing their enthusiasm was infectious and hoping that at least some of their love for these old birds would rub off on visitors and leave kids and their parents (many of whom were younger than my own children) with a spark of affection and appreciation for these marvelous

Pete doing what he does best: at the controls of his aerobatic T-34 Mentor.

Bill's tenure as the last Director of Falcon Field's Champlin Air Museum saw a upswing in revenue and attendance. He organized the transfer of its aircraft to the Seattle Museum of Flight, where tens of thousands of aviation enthusiasts enjoy the collection each year.

machines and the role they played in our nation's history.

In 2000, Doug Champlin sold his collection to the Museum of Flight in Seattle. Doug was a great guy, but he couldn't foot the bill for a costly museum forever. He wanted to keep his collection together and maintained by a group that would display it properly. The Seattle Flight Museum gave the collection a good home, but it needed some remodeling; they just didn't have the space on hand to absorb our little air force. So until their expansion was complete, our board needed an experienced manager who understood airplanes, docents, and special events to run the Falcon museum. They offered me the job, and despite my initial reluctance (it took me about two-and-a-half seconds to decide this time), I accepted and became the museum's last Director. My mandate was to keep the turnstile open until the last minute, then preside over an orderly transfer of displays and equipment.

Well, I did the best I could, which turned out to be better than most of us hoped. In my first year as Director, I doubled our gross and attendance was up, but not enough to prevent losing at least some of our birds to Seattle. We established a fund-raising drive; all we needed was a million dollars to keep our major exhibits in place, but that's a lot of money to get by passing the hat. We hired a professional fund-raiser, but she turned out to be a disappointment. We then re-calibrated our sights. If our propeller planes went to Seattle, we figured we might be able to operate as an all-jet museum, a unique attraction that didn't need as much space. We ran the idea by the City of Mesa but they had other plans for taxpayer cash. (I suspect they also had other plans for our space, such as leasing it to new tenants at a much higher rate.) So our effort became a race between local fund-raising and the expansion in Seattle. In the end, the ticking clock won.

Health problems began to drag me more frequently from my desk and despite our turnaround in attendance, it was clear that turning Falcon into a true visitor's mecca would be a pretty steep row to hoe. A handful of aviation veterans and enthusiasts, including Pete, formed an exploratory committee to take Seattle's jets, add them to ours, and start a new fighter museum either in an upgraded facility at Falcon or at the Scottsdale Municipal Airport, which was a bit more accessible to tourists. But, despite our best efforts, we just couldn't grab that brass ring to get commitments for the minimum funds needed to move the birds or improve the facility—so the idea died on the vine. That was doubly disappointing, since the museum's docent organization had petitioned the board in 2004 to restore a recently acquired, Korean-War vintage F-80 in my old, yellow-tailed Headhunters colors, painting "Little Dottie" on the nose. But it was not to be. By 2005, we'd run out of resources and ideas and I reluctantly turned the keys to our facility over to Mesa officials. This time, I vowed, my retirement would be for real.

PJW: I thought it was great that Bill once again came through when I needed him. Mary Lou and I were spending a lot of time putting out brush fires at the Papago and other properties, mostly because of personnel problems, and we needed a General Manager that we could trust and, just as importantly, our employees would respect and respond to. Bill was a real life saver in all departments; and although we knew we couldn't keep him at that GM's desk forever, we at least improved the view by giving him a couple of corporate airplanes to fly whenever the need and desire arose. It wasn't exactly the same as skipping along the Everglades in floatplanes or skip-bombing bad guys in F-80s, but it was the best we could do at this stage of life so we made the most of it.

One of our most enjoyable projects was sponsoring a reunion of the 8th Fighter-Bomber Wing in Scottsdale. The group had been getting together periodically for many years, and we always got invitations, but for one reason or another Bill and I never went, mainly because of conflicting schedules, but also, I suspect, from our secret aversion to seeing all the guys we remembered as young warriors turned into bald-headed, pot-bellied old men. Of course, we'd kept track of other old friends in aviation: Bill through his membership in the Society of Experimental Test Pilots (SETP), Helmet and Goggles, and the many North American retirees who lived around the area; and I saw many of the old gang from the 197th at various Guard functions over the years though the roll call got shorter as time went by. One year, however, the 8th got together in Colorado Springs and since the agenda included a tour of the Air Force Academy, we found it too hard to resist. Despite our "shock and awe" at all the white hair and pot bellies, we had a good time. At the final banquet, the organizers, as they always did, asked for volunteers to honcho the next reunion.

Three "hot sticks" from the 36th Fighter Squadron at an 8th FBW reunion. Pete (right) and Paul Wine (left) in formation with Jim Kiser, whose F-80 was downed by a MiG-15 beginning an odyssey of escape-and-evasion, and eventual capture, in North Korea.

Bill and I looked at each other, wondering who'd be dumb enough to volunteer for a job like that, when Mary Lou raised her hand and said, "Scottsdale would be a perfect place for the next reunion, so Pete Wurts and Bill Yoakley volunteer to be the sponsors."

Well, orders are orders and we just got ours. Along with Bob Schwartz, another veteran from the 8th, we set up a reunion for the fall of 1998. To tell you the truth, I was not all that anxious to spend three or four days reliving the past, let alone acting as co-host, where you can't exactly duck-out if things get boring. Like high school or college reunions, once or twice is fun—it's nice to catch up with old friends and recall prior adventures, but life takes people in different directions and after three or four decades, most attendees don't have that much in common. Bill and I decided that our event, at least, would involve something more than an afternoon of golf for the guys, shopping for the gals, and an evening of boozy reminiscing. *Our* reunion—like the one in Colorado Springs—would celebrate flying as well as the flyers.

Long story short: by all accounts, the reunion was one of the best the 8th ever had, if we do say so ourselves. We arranged a tour of the USAF F-16 training facility in Tucson, Arizona, and outings to Lake Powell and Verde Valley, both "only in Arizona" natural wonders. We even had two celebrity speakers, veteran test pilot and aerobatic legend, Bob Hoover, and retired Air Force General Richard Secord of Iran-Conta fame (who had collaborated on a book in the early 1990s with my son, Jay, who'd gone into publishing). Hoover had enough hair-raising flying stories to write a book, which he subsequently did; and Secord (still a consultant to the USAF on special ops), brought us up to speed on the many changes occurring in the modern Air Force, a truly remarkable organization that few of us old timers would recognize. The banquet room was decorated like a war-time air base, complete with camouflage nets, and everybody had a great time. It presented a tough act for any new organizer to follow, so tough, in fact, that (besides the natural attrition among flyboys our age) there hasn't been another reunion since; although old wingmen always find ways to rejoin, even without an engraved invitation.

About this time, Mary Lou and I decided we wanted to spend more time traveling and at our house in the mountains (first in Sedona, then in Prescott,

Arizona) and began a systematic plan to simplify our lives, though that was harder than it sounds. Flying the Crusader and the Mentor had been fun, but there's not much point having a fully instrumented twin when those navigation charts start looking fuzzy even *with* your glasses on, or wearing a parachute to do aerobatics when those old bones *really* don't want to bail out. Wisely, I think, we sold the airplanes and decided to leave the driving to younger pros.

To do something useful between business trips and cruises, I joined the Volunteers In Protection (VIP, of course) program with the Yavapai County Sheriff's Office, putting some of that old Phoenix PD training to good use. We volunteer deputies were sworn law men, armed and dangerous, though our duties were usually confined to chores like transporting prisoners and responding to highway accidents so that the full-time officers could answer the really hairy calls, though we, too, had our share of those. In police work, you never really know what to expect until you're on the scene, so even the part-timers had to stay sharp.

In all, I was amazed at how much law enforcement had changed over the last 50 years—not just the technology and legal environment, which everyone knows has become more complex and sophisticated—but the social environment as well. In addition to more laws, and more complicated laws, there are far more constraints on police activity; even the most enthusiastic crime-stoppers really do things by the book; there is simply no other choice if you want to remain a cop. Oddly enough, although there has been a great increase in public awareness about individual rights, citizens in the '40s were much quicker to challenge a peace officer on some technicality, such as an officer's right to enter a premises, take someone into custody, and so forth, than they are today. These days, such things are usually left to lawyers, who sort them out after the fact. It's nice to think that citizens today simply trust peace officers more, or that bad guys know resistance is futile, but I don't think that's the case. We've cultivated a system where suspects are not only presumed to be innocent, they're assumed to be "victims" of police discrimination, poverty, you name it, and honest citizens have been conditioned to be very passive about their own well-being. That may make things easier for some politicians, and may even have saved the lives of some officers, but I'm not sure it's created a better, safer society.

Pete served several years as a volunteer Deputy Sheriff for Yavapai County, Arizona: the capstone to sixty years of service in and out of the cockpit.

Drugs, and a deeply embedded drug culture, were another surprise. Even though drugs have become pervasive in our society and are at the root of much property and violent crime, they were much more stigmatized in the old days and viewed more seriously by courts, police, and citizens. Today, as drug-related crimes clog the courts, jails, and prisons, we seem to take them for granted, and drug abuse by citizens—young and old alike—as something that's inevitable. For some people, I guess it is; but like so many things, if it isn't stopped by parents at home, it sure isn't going to be stopped by police officers in the street. It may be part of that pattern I mentioned of surrendering more and more of our personal choices to some "higher authority," whether that power is a law or a politician or a bureaucrat. But when that power is a drug, the user has no choices at all.

One thing that hasn't changed is the influence of alcohol on people—most of it bad. It's hard to think of a serious traffic accident or incident of domestic violence—even a drug-related crime—where alcohol didn't play at least a supporting role. I'm the last guy who wants to bring back prohibition, but more people need to remember that their right to take that drink ends at the other guy's bumper, or their spouse's nose.

After awhile, commuting to Phoenix and Scottsdale on a regular basis, whether to troubleshoot problems at Papago, work with the fighter museum committee, or just visit the dentist, simply became too much work. If Bill could retire—and mean it—so could I. We sold the Papago in 2004 to an investor from New York, although we still retained ownership of (and use as a convenient place to hang our hat locally) the two-bedroom Scottsdale house where Bill and subsequent GM's lived when they ran the motel. The Papago is still going strong, a home-away-from-home to a legion of loyal guests who've been coming to Scottsdale for a couple of generations for everything from baseball's spring training and football's Fiesta Bowl to family visits and business meetings, although the greater Phoenix metropolitan area now looks more like the LA basin than the old Valley of the Sun. The more some things change, the more others stay the same—and that includes our memories. When you think about, that's the way it ought to be.

✪ ✪ ✪

*D*ottie passed away in 2004, a year after Maxine, and both of us have donated big chunks of our pension checks to various doctors, hospitals, and pharmacies to keep our "props turning," though at reduced RPMs, like a couple of old Stearmans. Bill now lives in Florida, in Green Cove Springs, in a beautiful little house, complete with workshop, near Don and his family. Pete and Mary Lou spend most of their time in Prescott, where they are allowed by their dogs, Skye and King, to share a home amid the mountains that Pete's Dad, that champion of far horizons, so admired. Most of our flying now is confined to airliners or flights of the imagination—as when we tell our friends and family tall tales about our aeronautical exploits, most of which are true, though we'll never say which ones. We also plead guilty to the occasional, wistful glance at the faded pictures of "old timey" airplanes (as our great grandchildren call them) like the F-80, F-86, F-100, and F-104 that grace our walls and albums. Many of the fine pilots we once knew have "raised the gear" for that last flight into undiscovered country: great flyers like Bill Kemp, Ted Crane, and "Big Stu" from Korea; though a few are still with us. These men were masters of their machines and of the mission, great guys to have not only on your wing, but in the lead. We appreciate them more with each passing year, especially when the two of us raise a glass to salute them, along with that guy "across the table" though the other end of that table now is a continent away. We feel privileged to have enjoyed a friendship that lasted longer than the lives of many of these great pilots. Knowing them—and each other—has been the rarest of gifts.

EPILOGUE

*I*n 2005, on a trip to California, Pete happened onto a bookstore whose aviation shelf contained a thin, paper-bound picture book about F-80s in Korea. On the cover was a yellow-tailed fighter clearly from the 80th Squadron–the Headhunters–Bill's old combat unit. Even more coincidental, the plane had a yellow cloud painted on its nose. In the cloud was a name: "Little Dottie."

Of course, Pete bought the book and gave it to Bill as soon as he returned to Arizona.

"Hey, look at this!" he said, proudly pointing to the picture. "Here's your old airplane–right on the cover!"

"Really? Well I'll be darned. Let me take a look," Bill adjusted his glasses and studied the picture. "Nope. That's not mine."

"But look–it says "Little Dottie" right there on the nose!" Pete was getting exasperated. "It's got a yellow background and everything. How many pilots in Korea could've named their aircraft Little Dottie?"

"Well I don't know, but that's not my plane. My bird got washed out by the next pilot just before I rotated home. And its tail number was 677. Look–this guy's tail number is completely different. And the yellow background around the name–that's different, too. Still, it's a real pretty bird."

Well, this puzzled us both. Unless this was some kind of ghost ship, the odds against another pilot in the Headhunter squadron painting the same name in the same way on the same type of aircraft at more or less the same time in Korea was astronomical. Then after we thought about some stories we'd heard from other combat pilots, the mystery cleared up.

Some ground crews, it seems, are very superstitious. They may not fly over enemy territory and risk getting killed or captured, but they care a lot about the guys who do. When a combat plane is given a name which proves lucky for one pilot, they often give the same name to the ship replacing it, hoping some of that good luck rubs off. Turns out, it's a very old tradition, going back to WWII. Since "Little Dottie" had been lucky for Bill, they apparently painted it on another plane after we'd rotated home. Even in war—especially in war—life goes on. Things change, people come and go, but continuity counts. In fact, passing that torch, keeping each other in the fight, and doing whatever we can to help the other guy—even if it's only keeping our fingers crossed, is what flying is all about. That's what wingmen are for.

APPENDIX

In February, 1951, Lt. Peter J. Wurts was leading a flight of eight F-80s on a pre-dawn armed reconnaissance mission into North Korea. Before daylight, they spotted the reddish glow from the fire of a locomotive down in the darkness below. The train, traveling without lights, was a prime target. This particular action inspired the following poem.

Across the Skies

Across the skies
In swift ascent
The Free World knew
We were Heaven bent.

Then high above
Our world below,
We dropped our tanks
And prepared to go.

Few people knew
In the dark down there,
Of the job we did...
Or could hear our prayer.

But down we flashed
Towards the distant glow;
Down from the Heavens
To the depths below.

The following short poems were written by PJW over the course of his flying career.

Never Forgotten

When everything's still
In the dead of night
In the distance we hear
The old jet in flight.

And yet our souls yearn
To be up there again
High in the Heavens
Just us and our plane.

To roam the bright skies
In search of a fight
And to dive her again
For just one last flight.

High in the Sky

High in the sky
There's a flash of light
The sun reflect
From a plane in flight.

High in the sky
There's a human there
Not bound to this earth
But as free as the air.

High in the sky
Far, far away
His freedom is endless
Day after day.

High in the sky
In the heavens above
A man and his soul
Roams forever with love.

In Memorium

The eerie scream
And the mournful whine,
That used to come
From the "Seventy-nine,"
Is gone forever;
And in its place,
A monster came
To haunt this base.

Its smoke and oil
Have fouled the ramp,
And its evil spell
Is felt in Camp.
But off in the shade
'Neath the monstrous bore,
Some men still dream
Of the old "One-Oh-Four".

The Recall

In the blackness of space,
Eons ago,
A brilliant light flashed,
And our World was aglow.

Now that time has gone by
And our planet has cooled,
We've learned how to fly
But we haven't been fooled.

For now our souls yearn
To return to that void
One way or another
We cannot avoid.

In a rocket so swift
Or a great blinding flash,
One way or another
Into blackness we'll dash.

Suit of Blue

They tell me you are leaving,
Your papers in and signed;
You'll turn your back and walk away,
To leave it all behind.

But time will take you far—too far,
And you'll speak of where and when;
Memories fade and faces blur
As you turn from what has been.

Yet one day in your reverie,
A voice will whisper true
You were the best you've ever been
When you wore a suit of blue.

342013